HOME DESIGN

HOME DESIGN

Lorrie Mack and
José Manser

Orbis Publishing
London

First published in Great Britain by Orbis Publishing Limited, London 1982

Printed in Czechoslovakia

ISBN: 0-85613-420-1

Acknowledgements

Aerofoam, Aladdin Industries, And So to Bed, Armitage Shanks, Balterley Bathrooms, Barking Grohe, Bath Studio, Bathrooms & Shower Centre, Baxi Heating, M.H. Bedford, Berger Paints, Berglen, British Gas Corporation, Chloride Shires, Christies, Crown Paints, Designers Guild, Di Lusso Kitchens, Dimplex, Dorma, Doulton Sanitaryware, Elon Tiles, GEC-Xpelair, Grovewood Products, Habitat, Halric Designs, ICI, Ideal Standard, Incover, Jon Isherwood, Laura Ashley, Living Daylights, Magnet & Southern, Myson Group, Angela McKelvie Public Relations, Metlex Industries, Mothercare, Nair Press Office, National Magazine Company, W.H. Newson, Orbis GmbH, Pandpro, Pilkington's Tiles, Pland, Poggenpohl, Potterton International, Prowoda, Ratcliffe Bros, Reylon, Sanderson's, Schreiber, Slumberland, Solabro Fitments, Solid Fuel Advisory Service, Sommer Allibert, Stam Marketing, Sunhouse, Syndication International, Taylor Gardener Associates, Thorn Domestic Appliances, TI Creda, TI Parkray, Twyfords, Walker Crossweller, Elizabeth Whiting Agency, Wicanders, Winchmore Furnithre, Wonderland, Wrighton International Features, ZEFA Picture Agency.

Manufacturers List

Bathrooms

Magnum Mark 2 modular fitted bathroom
Metlex Industries
Sumner Road
Croydon Surrey
CR9 3BQ

Gard wallpaper sealer
Manders Paints Limited
P O Box 9
Mander House
Wolverhampton WV1 3NH

portable bidet
Transatlantic Plastics
Garden Estate
Ventnor
Isle of Wight

Celeste undulating seat WC
Taylor Gardner Associates
1 Russell Street
Royal Leamington Spa
Warks CV32 5QA

studded rubber flooring
Pirelli rubber floor tiles
Dunlop Semtex
Brynmawr
Gwent NP3 4XN

Bedrooms

mattress with pocketed springs
Sleepeezee Limited
Morden Road
Merton
London SW19

basket drawers
Elfa Systems Limited
Wingham Trading Estate
Wingham Canterbury
Kent

Living Rooms

Maya unit seating
Aerofoam Limited
30 Dalston Gardens
Honeypot Lane
Stanmore Middlesex

Bildasuite self assembly seating
Halric Designs
19 The Broadway
Southgate
London N14

skirting radiators
Myson Group Marketing Limited
Industrial Estate
Ongar Essex
CM5 9RE

Milium
Milium Promotions Centre
Wellington Street
Bury Lancs
BL8 SAY

Children's Rooms

plastic maxi bins
Dexion Limited
Dexion House
Empire Way
Wembley Middlesex
HA9 0SW

adjustable-height furniture
Pandpro Limited
51 Aldwych
London WC2B 4AZ

Contents

Introduction

HOME CAN MEAN MANY DIFFERENT THINGS. IT can be a one-room flat with everything packed into that room except perhaps a tiny separate bathroom. It can be a much more expensive affair with large rooms, a balcony and splendid views across the city. It can be a compact semi built any time during the past fifty years, or it can be a detached Victorian villa in the suburbs, of sturdy construction and spacious rooms, or an Edwardian terraced house such as those found in the centre of many big towns, with pretty stained-glass windows and dark passageways. Perhaps it's a mansion or a group of boxy rooms in a tower block, or a bungalow, or a shared bed sit, or a variation on any of these things. Whatever it is, it is home to you, a place where you spend a lot of time, certainly leisure time, and somewhere to be made the very best of whatever its limitations, since it is difficult to think of anything more creative and enjoyable than making a home. It is something you can do as and when you have the time; it can become a hobby for both young and old, one about which you can never learn too much, and in which techniques, materials and products are constantly changing and being improved. Some things you may do yourself, some you will want to have done for you, but the choice, the arrangement and the ideas will always be yours. The result should give you constant delight and make a relaxed and happy background for family and friends.

If you are very hard up, all this may sound like so much pie in the sky; something for others, but not for you. This it certainly is not. Many of the ideas in this book do cost a lot of money to execute. Many others depend more on imagination and hard work, since there are a great number of jobs around the home which, with the sort of expert guidance given here and some more specialist reading, you can do yourself for no more than the cost of the materials; jobs which – done by a skilled tradesman – would cost a considerable sum. And although new or antique furniture is expensive, somebody with ideas and determination can refurbish other people's cast-outs so they take on new and shining personalities of their own. I'm not talking merely about refurbishing valuable pieces of furniture which have fallen on hard times and ended up in junk shops (though that is always a possibility), but about such things as battered utility sideboards dating from the war years, cheap wooden chairs with the splay legs of the 1950's which no-one loves any more, or 1930's three piece suites which have degenerated into shabby hulks with burst upholstery. They can be revived and restored for relatively small sums to give character and style to a creative person's home. And in fact this is the time when the owner of the very small home – the bed-sit or one-room flat – scores over his more affluent neighbour, because the spaces and furnishings involved are more limited, and the results therefore quicker to achieve, but no less satisfactory for all that. Once you start thinking about home planning as a hobby and a creative activity, it is no longer a chore but something to absorb and fascinate you for the rest of your life.

Detailed and specific advice about various area of the home is given further on in this book, but there are several more general points worth considering – overall planning for example. Now if you live in a one-room flat this will concern you very little, but once you move on to something larger it is vitally important. It means thinking about every room – and every corridor or hallway – before you start planning. Because doors will open, one room will lead into another and there will be through views from say, hallway to living room, landing to bedroom. It follows then that each should complement the other. It would be horribly discordent to decorate the hall and staircase in pale yellow, with bright orange carpet, and then have a vivid pink bedroom through one door, complete with its deep pink carpet butting onto the orange one in the hall. Or to have a pale blue kitchen with blue and white floor tiles leading into a dining room where the walls are dark green and the carpet a green, white and pink pattern – however pretty each of these rooms might be individually. It is in fact quite a good idea to have one colour carpet throughout the house (certainly on each level), perhaps with differently coloured or patterned rugs for each room. This certainly makes an area look more spacious as well as giving a feeling of coherence. And it is better not to change the colour of the paintwork too often between rooms, or indeed to change the general colour schemes too sharply between rooms which run into each other. White or cream paint everywhere is always a safe (but not necessarily dull) way to start.

A suggested all-over scheme might comprise a pretty soft green carpet in most rooms, with a green, dark green and white patterned carpet in the hallways and on staircases which get a lot of wear, dark green walls in the dining room, pale honey-coloured cork tiles in the kitchen, maybe some sparky red touches in a teenage boys room – and so on. There are innumerable variations on this scheme. Try to start though with a background colour, which in this case is the green of the carpet. The background gives the home an overall unity, and other colours, patterns and styles fit into this framework.

It is a quite a good idea, incidentally, to plan out the whole home with the help of colour boards such as are used in professional designers' offices, one for each room, on which are mounted small samples of the paint colour to be used, wall covering, curtains, upholstery fabric, carpet etc. When they are completed, lay tham all out on a table and you will see if the overall concept is what you had hoped for or a patchy, jarring hotch-potch. Even if, like most of us, you are not tackling the whole house at one go but over a period of several years, you can still follow this formula, adding a new board to the existing ones as a new area of the house is drawn into the scheme.

This leads on to a second important point. Do not regard your home as something static, which you plan, work at, finish and then forget. For a start, it is unlikely you will be able to arrange everything as you want it now, or indeed that your life will remain exactly as it is for the next ten years or so. The beautiful kitchen you covet may have to be purchased in easy stages – some cupboards this year, some next, the dishwasher the year after that – but it can all be thought about and planned for now. Children will be born, or they will grow up and leave home. Plan for these eventualities so that there is a room set aside to transform into a nursery, or alternatively, one ear-marked to be turned into a study when its present occupant sets up on his own elsewhere. You may have only one bathroom now which is adequate for just the two of you; when you have children you will find life much more comfortable if there is a second bathroom (or at least a shower room), so any new plumbing which is being put in or any reorganisation of bedrooms should be carried out with that eventuality in mind.

Do aim though to get really basic jobs (the type which inevitably involve dirt and confusion in the household) done at the very beginning. The installation of central heating, the laying of new wood floors, the knocking down of walls, the making of new window openings and re-wiring of the electrical system are all jobs which will make the home an uncomfortable place while they are being carried out. So if you can possibly afford it, have them done at the beginning of your occupancy while the first wave of enthusiasm is still upon you, and while there is no new paintwork or fresh upholstery to get spoiled with the resulting dirt. Even if this means waiting a while for new furniture or carpets, pretty bed linen or kitchen cupboards, it is incomparably better done this way. Tackle things in the right order, and you will gradually but surely see your home coming together in the way you hoped and envisaged it would.

Quite apart from the major planning and changing of a room to different uses, there are all kinds of other changes you will want to make in the home from time to time if it is to remain as attractive and comfortable and full of character as you would like it to be. Don't just settle your furniture into place and leave it there for the next twenty years. Shift things around every so often – it is amazing how a room can be revitalised by the simple movement of one piece of furniture – or add something new. When the time comes for re-painting, don't just redecorate a room as it was before. Take a look at new wallpaper designs and paint colour, splash out on a luxurious rug which will pep up an ageing carpet. Have even one chair recovered, make some new cushions, dye the bedcover a strong rich colour, treat yourself to one huge houseplant for the entrance hall. Homemaking never ends and you want to be constantly rethinking your ideas about the details and trimmings. It is rather like the rest of life; easy, probably more comfortable, to settle into a comfortable rut which you planned years ago, and to let things jog along in this way, but infinitely more stimulating and rejuvenating to look again and make some changes in line with your current thinking.

Sometimes, of course, the time will come for an overall reassessment. If, for example, the whole of a large family has left home for good, or an elderly grandparent has come to live with you, a husband or wife has died or, more happily, you have just had twins. In all these cases a gentle reshuffle is invariably not the answer – you must think about extending the house, or dividing it into separate flats if it is too big for you, or joining together two rooms, or splitting one up into two small ones, or moving. But again, the message is clear: plan, think carefully about your new needs and put a lot of creative energy into making sure you achieve them.

In the chapters which follow every aspect of planning, decoration and choice of furniture and equipment has been covered for all the main rooms in a home. If you apply even some of the suggestions and information given to your own, it should help to make it a much more comfortable, good-looking, functional and perhaps happier place to be.

THE KITCHEN

FROM ONCE BEING THE LONELY DOMAIN OF THE COOK or the housewife, the kitchen has long since emerged as the true centre of the home; the place where every member of the family gathers. If space permits, it is certainly not restricted in its use to simply cooking and washing. Nowadays, the kitchen is a room where most families eat at least one meal of the day – if not all of them – where children often do their homework or watch television, where people telephone their friends, make wine, do the ironing and read the papers. In other words, it is a room which needs to be just as comfortable and inviting as any other in the house. Even if your kitchen is no more than a tiny corner in a bed-sitter, that small area needs to be treated with just as much care and interest as the rest of the room – perhaps even more so, as it is constantly on view.

Despite these multifarious family activities, the kitchen is quote probably a place where some pretty high-powered cooking goes on, since cooking these days has become a cult as well as a necessity and is just as often undertaken by the male as well as the female members of the family. In response to this, the kitchen will have to accommodate an ever-increasing range of highly sophisticated gadgets and pieces of equipment (many of them electronically operated) and also reflect the family taste in decoration, from the easy-going nostalgic charm of the traditional country kitchen, to the ultra slick and modern look.

The kitchen is often the most intimidating and difficult room in the house to plan. The number of possibilities available is overwhelming; the amount of money involved *can* be astronomic and the possibility of making wrong decisions is quite likely without very careful forethought. Many people regret the purchase of at least one expensive piece of kitchen equipment, or land themselves with absolutely the wrong lay-out to suit the family's lifestyle. It is hardly surprising then, if some amongst us choose to sink back in lethargy and make do with that we've got, however inadequate and unattractive that may be.

For these people, as well as for the less faint-hearted, the following chapter is a guide which will take them through the maze of planning and kitchen and selecting the equipment for it. All the mystery and confusion about how to choose fitted kitchen units from the many advertised in magazines is explained. The worries of selecting a sink and the taps to go with it, of deciding which of the available appliances you really need and then fitting them into your own rather limited space, are tackled and overcome, with suggestions for alternative kitchen layouts. The importance of good lighting is pointed out and the salient characteristics of the various types of kitchen floor and wall coverings are listed. In fact, there is absolutely no excuse at all for ending up with

When properly planned and designed with as much concern for comfort as for working efficiency, the kitchen can become the centre of home life and a room to be enjoyed by all the family.

a room which is not the very heart of the household and a magnet for all its occupants.

The kitchen is a place which should be very thoughtfully planned and gradually built up to an ideal room over a number of years – that is because few of us are rich enough to re-design, fit and furnish this most expensive of rooms completely in one fell swoop. Ultimately, if your basic planning is right in the first place, the kitchen will not only look good, it will function so smoothly that cooking will be a delight, with everyone willing to chip in with the menial chores. Best of all, as a warm and informal background for family life, it will be unsurpassable.

A small old-fashioned pantry at the side of a main kitchen area can be used for housing large domestic appliances as well as food and wine. A washing machine and a spin or tumble dryer take up quite a lot of floor space and can be usefully tucked away in a space like this. The pantry area can also house general cleaning equipment such as hoovers and carpet sweepers. Dangerous substances such as household bleach can be kept on a high shelf away from children and pets.

Planning the kitchen

To give a new look to the room in which the cook in the family may spend anything up to eight hours a day deserves more than a quick attempt to copy the neighbours or the latest kitchen brochure. It all comes down to a question of pre-planning rather than panic buying. There will always be discount offers and sales bargains in the kitchen field so don't rush into buying an ill-assorted collection of units and appliances.

There is no short cut to planning a successful room layout. When you think of the years of training needed to qualify as an architect or designer you will realize why you have to sit down with paper and pencil for a whole evening – or more – to do some serious calculations before achieving your own dream kitchen, however modest.

First you need some large sheets of squared paper – graph paper of ten small squares per 10mm (or 12 small squares per inch) is convenient for quick scale drawing. Select the scale, say 100mm (or 12in) per five (or six) small squares. If your room is 3 × 3.6m (10 × 12ft), your basic floor plan outline will only measure some 150 × 180mm (or 5 × 6in). But don't start off with too small a sheet of squared paper as you need to mark in a lot of useful data apart from the actual floor plan.

Measure your existing kitchen area at ground level and at about 900mm (or 36in) from the floor as you may find an unwelcome variation; then be sure to mark the smallest measurement on your plan. At windows and doorways it is best to include the frames, mouldings and trims within the window or door measurement. Don't forget some units can be cut away to allow for projecting skirting but it is preferable not to have to disfigure your units in this way. Check your opposite wall length measurements to see they match up; small inaccuracies soon mount up and complicate your planning when it comes to choosing equipment for a critically close fit. it is also worth doing spot check measurements across from wall to wall as frequently you will find the opposite ones are not parallel. This affects your flooring calculations and may result in an unfortunate gap (that will need filling in) between the wall and a long line of rigid, rectangular units or a curving away if you follow the line of the wall.

Settle on a simple code for the necessary details such as existing lighting and/or power points, water/waste outlets and gas supply.

If you are considering major alterations but are not sure if these will work out or if you can afford them, it is worth drawing out two basic ground plans – Plan A with anticipated alterations (the ideal) and Plan B without – as obviously your whole Plan A arrangement of equipment will be useless if you decide the alterations are not possible.

Then stick down another sheet of graph paper onto thin card and draw out the length and width (front to back) of every piece of existing equipment you intend to retain, including tables and chairs, and any new appliances you have already selected in advance. Where cupboard doors open out and fitments have drawers it is worth indicating this with an arrow or even drawing out the extra space needed and bending this area up as a flap. It will act as a reminder not to put doors at right-angles to each other so they interlock or open the wrong way at corners. Write in the length × width × height (always in that order so you know the height figure comes last) in each card outline and cut out the various pieces. You will then have a permanent record on card of all your kitchen equipment which you can move round on your graph plan like pieces of a jigsaw puzzle.

Floor plan code

⊗	light point
X	power point
W	water/waste outlet
G	gas supply
V	ventilation duct/airbrick
(door symbol)	right/left-hinged door
(wavy line)	window

Above Galley-type kitchen with wall-hung refrigerator, oven-grill unit, separate hob, sink and worktops (Grovewood wood veneer units). **Above right** Spacious 'L' shape allows for machines to be wall-hung or built under worktops (Schreiber slatted oak finish units) **Far right** Classic 'U' shape with refrigerator, sink, hob and work surfaces all within easy walking distance (Grovewood teak trim units) **Right** Specially designed island work station with hob and dishwasher

Choice of basic layout

The aim is to minimize the amount of movement required between the three major work centres: sink, cooker and food preparation/storage area. These centres should be positioned about 1200–1800mm (4–6ft) apart in the form of a triangle, with the work centres at the three angle points, enclosed by lines of worktop surfaces and storage cupboards **(see 1–4)**. If work centres are in one long line you will find yourself walking considerable distances to get from one to another. The total walking distance between sink, cooker and food preparation/storage areas should be no more than 6m (20ft). Try measuring out your existing layout and see how it matches up to this ideal.

Safety is a point often overlooked in favour of convenience. Your cooker should not be opposite your sink as the dangerous situation of carrying scalding liquids across the kitchen will arise several times a day. Cooker and sink should be along the same wall or at right-angles on adjacent ones.

Even if your kitchen is spacious, the arrangement of units is largely dictated by the shape of the room, the position of windows and doors and to a degree the plumbing and other service points. The more 'open plan' your scheme, the tighter your actual cooking area will need to be to allow plenty of space for eating, working or playing. There is nothing worse than a kitchen-living room that fulfils none of these purposes conveniently.

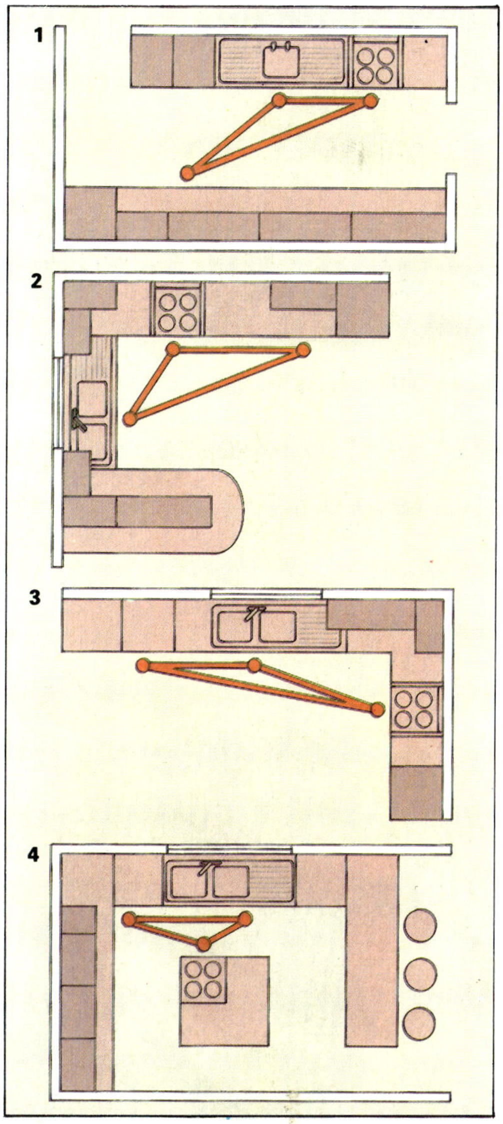

Galley or corridor type (1) In a long, narrow area with doors at each end you have little choice other than one line or two facing rows of appliances and storage units. And you should allow at least 1200mm (4ft) for a safe walk-through corridor between two rows. If it is possible to move one of the doors to a side wall, so much the better as you will then be disturbed less while cooking and have more planning scope through breaking up the parallel lines.

U-shaped arrangement (2) This compact formation is very convenient as all working areas are near to hand. It is often the only choice for small kitchens or ones where the eating and doorway areas are confined to the corners at one end of the room.

If you want to incorporate a breakfast bar here you can have a peninsular unit at one end of the 'U', but work out first that it does not divide you from a door leading to the garden or children's playroom, for example, or you will find yourself running round it many times a day.

L-shaped arrangement (3) For difficult room shapes with doors and windows in awkward places, this is often the best solution. With a large area to play with you can incorporate room divider/breakfast bars and laundry areas, leaving your 'heart of the home' dining-cum-work table to take pride of place in the centre of the room instead of being tucked into one corner.

Island work station (4) Usually thought of as a luxury kitchen idea, the island unit could well be the answer to many quite ordinary kitchen problems. If you are short of wall space or your walls are in very bad shape, sloping or include a lot of windows, doors, alcoves and projections, pipework, various forms of heating etc., it is worth considering putting some of your major appliances in the centre of the room. Should you wish to 'take it with you' when moving house, an island unit involves you in less of the statutory 'making good' for the incoming people than when you remove a mixed collection of fitted or free-standing items.

Major alterations
With these basic requirements for kitchen planning in mind, now is the time to consider your own situation. Is your existing layout practical and will it include all the items you have now and will need in the reasonably near future? It might even be worth building a home extension to house all, or part, of a new kitchen. Brick-built ones are ideal as they can be tailor-made to your requirements, but there are many prefabricated ones that are well insulated and without excessive window area, making them eminently suitable for use as kitchens.

On a more modest scale moving a door, or even rehanging it to open outwards, can make a big difference to a kitchen layout. Try changing an internal door for a space-saving folding concertina type, a fold-aside or sliding door. A semi-open plan can be achieved quite easily by introducing a pair of saloon bar swinging louvre doors between living/dining room and existing kitchen, although these are not suitable where small children are running around.

Above Use fold-aside (or bi-fold) doors where space is at a premium (W. H. Newson)
Above right With a pair of sliding louvre doors you can change your kitchen layout for easier access. Be sure to sink the track into the floor to avoid a change of level (Magnet & Southerns)
Right In open plan kitchens these swinging saloon-type doors in louvred pine are decorative and space-saving (W. H. Newson)

Although you do not want too many windows in a kitchen as it cuts down on storage space, you do need good light. It is often possible to enlarge a small window or make a new one facing a good view at the sink area to make washing-up more of a pleasure. Picture windows should have opening top lights or louvres while small, self-actuating plastic ventilators can easily be fitted to any windows.

Before making holes in walls for new windows, consider the problems of condensation and where extractor fans or hoods will be most needed.

The position of items like the sink, dishwasher and washing machine will be governed to a certain extent by the existing drainage systems and layout of water supply pipes. But plastic waste pipes and copper water pipes make it practical to have your plumbed-in items more or less anywhere on, or reasonably close to, an outside wall.

If you are doing away with an old-fashioned boiler system you should also remove all the old, unsightly pipes and start afresh so you can put your new appliances where you want them. But don't forget to allow for some type of back-up heating, either in the form of portable convectors, central heating radiators or underfloor heating.

Unless your kitchen is fairly modern you will have to install additional power points, so it is better to rewire now rather than be stuck with insufficient outlets in inconvenient places. The same goes for gas – it is far more important to have your gas-powered appliances where you want them, even if it involves having a new length of gas piping fitted. It is important to get your basic priorities right at the planning stage, even if you anticipate having to wait months – or even years – before acquiring all the desirable kitchen appliances.

Make a list of all powered equipment you hope to have – and might want to use at the same time:
cooker, separate oven, hobs, grill etc.
kettle, mixer/liquidizer, coffee grinder
toaster, can opener, knife sharpener
water/central heating, washing machine, dryer
dishwasher, iron, vacuum cleaner, polisher

Allow for all the socket outlets to be at the right height (and in the right area) for the various appliances. You will be surprised how many power points small labour-saving aids require.

Good light, apart from daylight, is essential in a kitchen and should not be thought of in terms of the finishing touch to your kitchen scheme. You may need to channel in wires in the ceiling and disrupt walls with new wiring, so this should be done before any redecorating. The choice of lighting may even dictate the siting of your major appliances.

Planning for kitchen appliances
The appliance priorities here are obviously a sink, cooker and refrigerator, with powered cooking aids, dishwasher, freezer and waste disposer close behind. Your kitchen may well have to accommodate a washing machine and dryer as well as ironing facilities. Even if many of these appliances are still dreams of the future, it makes sense to allow for the day they might become a reality.

Choosing kitchen units

One of the biggest headaches in the kitchen is finding enough room for everything. The solution is to choose the units – apart from style and quality – that cater for your individual requirements so there is a place for everything and everything has its place.

On the face of it you would think choosing kitchen units was the easiest part of equipping your kitchen – just a case of what design and colour and what size to go where. But there is much more to it than that, for the best ranges offer a wide selection of interior fittings and you might as well get the ones that cater for your particular storage needs.

The basic choice lies between the more costly ready-made (rigid) units, with their greater variety of style, colour and finish, and self-assembly (known as S/A) ones, which arrive packed flat for you to put together at home. The best advice, as always, is to pay the most you can afford within either range. Even the smallest kitchen can be made a pleasure to cook in if you take time to select units with the best combination of working facilities and storage.

Before deciding on a particular colour scheme or style for your kitchen you should visit as many showrooms as possible and look at whatever illustrated catalogues you can so you have an idea of the range available.

Working out priorities

The choice is so wide you have to sit down with paper and pencil and work out exactly what you want from your kitchen fitments. Make out a list of priorities and then see whether you can find – and afford – what you need in one range or prefer to build up from individually selected units.

Appliances Sink, cooker, refrigerator/freezer, dishwasher, washing machine, tumble/spin dryer etc. Are these to be built in (behind special housing units with or without door panels) or built under (necessitating a worktop or extra run of worktop surface joining neighbouring units)? If appliances are free-standing, objects can fall behind them or down the side and will be difficult to retrieve; also dirt will collect and you may not always be able to move them to clean round.

Working area Are you confining this to one wall or to particular areas? In either case you must make careful calculations to see what mix of standard unit lengths and widths (front to back) most conveniently cater for your requirements.

Storage space Are you expecting to house everything within your kitchen cabinets and units? If so, apart from base units you will need to cover as much wall space as possible with wall-hung units. These are available in two (and sometimes three) heights in the better ranges so you can fit them right up to ceiling height where desirable or add one unit on top of another for the desired height.

Warning Don't forget few ceilings and walls form true right-angles when it comes to fitting ceiling-high cupboards. You have to measure up carefully and make your base line allowing for the lowest ceiling height. The increasing gap above or towards one end of the row may not be visible or even unsightly, but it will attract dust. You can close it with filler or a strip of wood or plastic cut to size.

When calculating the all-important wall-hung unit area you must allow adequate working height between the worktop surface and the base of the wall unit. This should be about 450mm (or 18in) and the wall unit should measure less from front to back than the base unit below it otherwise you will be continually hitting your head.

Wider (from front to back) wall units which give more storage space must be hung at a greater height from the worktop surface to avoid this hazard. With these wider units, and the higher up you go, you will find it more convenient to have a choice of shelf widths – narrower at the top – or to use plastic-coated wire platforms at the back to give

Below Everything the busy cook needs is contained here in one long kitchen wall: combined oven-grill, single drainer sink, four-burner hob and refrigerator, with cupboards above and below. There is plenty of room for all your kitchen stores from fresh fruit and vegetables to cleaning equipment, pots and pans, tableware, cutlery and table linen – all near to hand (Magnet & Southerns storage units with lipped-edge Formica worktops. Tricity appliances)

1

2

3

1 Paint your walls in strong colours to set off plain-fronted units with curved-edge laminate worktops and full length handles (Grovewood Original Milk and Honey Self-Assembly units)
2 Make good use of space by curving round your corners with open end shelves large enough to take a mixer – and sewing machine – and a wall unit for books or ornaments (Grovewood S/A Impact)
3 Choose planked effect units in natural hardwood with top cupboards to give ceiling-high storage space or,
4 raised panel doors. In a choice of honey, cherry or nut brown finish, or white-wood to paint yourself.

4

extra space for storing smaller items. You must also take into consideration the correct height for lighting your worktop area if using strip lights behind pelmets fixed at the base of these wall units.

Worktops
Choose from reconstructed marble (terrazzo), ceramic tile, stainless steel or heat-resistant plastic laminate. The last comes plain or patterned and in several wood grain, marble, leather, slate or other textured effects. The more uneven the texture the more difficult it is to keep clean; but if your kitchen is open plan, forming part of your living or dining room, you may think it worthwhile to go for the exotic finishes and accept the extra maintenance.

Front edges can be square-cut or curved and backs heightened to form splashbacks or to make a neat join with the wall. Aluminium strips are available for waterproof joins at corners or with neighbouring units. If you want the real thing by way of solid wood or marble, you will have to order this specially or find old butcher's blocks and discarded marble washstand tops and cut them to size.

Most kitchen unit manufacturers will cut specified areas in their worktops to take standard sink bowls and hobplates or to your own dimensions at extra cost. Special water-resistant adhesive is recommended if covering a surface with plastic laminate where excessive splashing is expected; otherwise you should use stainless steel, ceramic tiles or marble. Where hobplates are concerned you will need nearby worktop space for putting down hot pans. For this you must either provide ample trivets or use stainless steel ridged parking plates or flat protector sheets with one right-angled rim to fit neatly over your worktop edge. These are available in several sizes.

Warning If your floor is very uneven – and many kitchens suffer from this defect – you will find it greatly to your advantage to buy from the ranges with screw-adjusted levellers for base units. Equally, it is wise to choose wall units with adjustable mounting brackets if your walls are out of true. Look out, too, for plinths that are set back so as to allow you to stand close up to worktops without stubbing your toes.

Carcases, doors and drawers
Although units without backs obviously cost less, they sometimes prove a false economy in that they are not so easily moved and cannot be used as dividers; and dirt collects behind them. The better ranges with fitted backs are melamine-faced inside for easy cleaning. Apart from solid wood frames, the choice in doors and fascia fronts lies between solid wood panels, plastic laminate, pigmented polyester and melamine-faced chipboard, or white-wood to paint yourself.

Details to watch out for are smooth-running drawers and easy-to-open (and close) doors whether by handle, magnetic catch or touch-and-push method. Hollow rim pull-type handles running the full length of the door panel are particularly good for the disabled as they give a wide area of pull.

The more you pay the more facilities you are offered, such as adjustable and full width (back to front) shelves, totally melamine-faced interiors, choice of three heights for wall units, removable plinths for easy cleaning underneath or drawer plinths for extra storage, peninsular units with doors both sides, matching fascia panels for ends of runs of units, extra long worktops for odd dimensions and narrow base units to fit these odd lengths for use as tray recesses or to take telescopic towel rails.

Standard dimensions

When ordering kitchen units check whether the range quotes exact dimensions in metric or Imperial. It is quite simple to fit matching filler units or infill strips, so it is better to underestimate your wall-to-wall lengths than find yourself having to cut down your newly acquired units by a few millimetres to fit existing space.

Most floor base units are 900mm (or 36in) high and 600mm (or 21in) wide, front to back, with an infinite choice of lengths and formations. Wall units are usually 600 or 900mm (or 21/36in) high and 300mm (or 12in) wide, lengths again to choice. Tall cabinets come as high as 2000mm (or 80in) according to style, some combining separate door-opening top units, others allowing for storage above or below housing space for specific appliances such as ovens and refrigerators. A minimum of 25mm (1in) must be left above such appliances for air circulation and the same between oven and refrigerator units if placed side by side.

If you already have some appliances that you wish to fit above floor level into wall housing units, be sure to find out if the range you select can take them, or you must treat them as built-under types.

Basic details

When ordering, remember to specify the correct side for door openings – right-hinged or left-hinged. Some corner base units have a revolving door that disappears inside as carousel shelves swing out, while corner wall units are available with fold-back hinged doors to allow for opening half the door at a time or the whole door in half the usual space. Some wall units have tip-up hinged flap fronts that stay put until you pull them down again. Sliding doors come in matching panels or clear or smoked glass to display your tableware. With open shelves bridging gaps between wall units you can fit special canisters or jar racks underneath to add to your general storage facilities.

Drawers can usually be ordered at the right or left of cupboard space in base units, singly or as

5

6

7

8

9

10

11

12

5 Swing-out carousel baskets give plenty of room for kitchen stores and make full use of corner cupboards
6 Pull-out can racks are just right for those awkward narrow spaces at the end of a run of cupboard units
7 Fold-back hinged doors on corner units allow for easy opening where space is at a premium
8 Alternative door style – tip-up hinged flap front that stays up until you pull it down again
9 Keep your preserves in wide floor units and add to your storage space with shallow racks on door backs
10 Keep your napkins, table cloths and tea towels in pull-out tray drawers behind cupboard doors
11 Combine household stores on narrow shelves with tall brooms and hang the iron on the door
12 This pull-out mini store with larder unit and optional bottle rack is ideal for generous party-givers

13

14

15

16
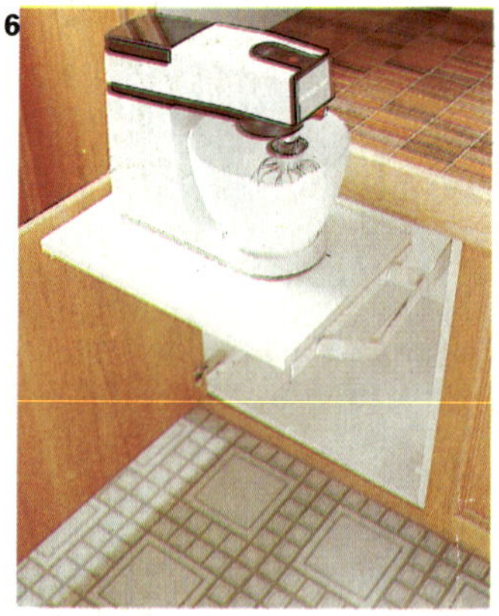

multiple drawer units. Some ranges fit shallow drawers behind doors, suitable for table linen which tends to get jumbled up in the usual depth drawers.

Cooker hood housing units or fascia panels are often available to match your choice of units, as well as end or infill panels and of course peninsular or breakfast bar tops to fit a variety of angles and spaces.

Accessories

If you really care about what goes into your units and how, then the choice of interior fittings is almost more important than their design, finish and colour. So look around before getting too involved with the outward appearance. The obvious choice in storage facilities (apart from conventional shelves) starts with wire baskets or trays for fresh vegetables and dry goods in units with air-vented back panels, or cans or bottles. These pull out from behind doors or fixed fascia panels. Door-back racks allow for lightweight, shallow storage.

Rigid plastic cutlery liners are made to fit most drawers. These give you far more storage space than with separate plastic cutlery trays and the whole drawer area is much easier to keep clean.

Many ranges offer waste-bins fitted to door backs, with an automatic lid-lifting device when the door is opened. Tall broom cupboards have shallow racks at one side for household cleaning items. Narrow base units (heated if desired) have telescopic rails for tea towels.

Pull-out table flaps are large enough to provide eating space for up to four people. Hinged ironing boards fit into standard-sized units. Special platforms swing out and up for powered mixers and their accessories. Chopping boards slide out from under convenient worktops to add to your work preparation surface.

Many units designed to take inset hobs have extra deep shelves for pots and pans where they are readily to hand while cooking and not exposed to dirt and grease as they would be in open saucepan stands or hung on the wall in country kitchen style.

Where draining space is at a premium try fitting a wire drainer above your sink at wall unit height and behind a matching fascia panel. Out-of-sight

17

crockery can then drip into the sink without taking up valuable worktop space.

If you use many powered appliances, a wireway panel at the back of your main preparation surface to house all electrical socket outlets is a neat arrangement. This can also incorporate an electric clock and timer devices. Some wall units include lighting pelmets at the front edge base for strip lights over your worktop area, but you can buy separate ones to fit as you need them. One manufacturer supplies special horizontal lighting panel fitments to tie in with the wall units in the form of a continuous strip.

The ultimate refinement is perhaps a trolley on castors disguised behind a matching fascia panel. You can surprise your guests by wheeling it out complete with electric hotplate to heat and serve your party dishes where you want.

13 Fit a door-back refuse bin, with automatic lid-opening device, under the sink ready to take all the kitchen waste

14 Hang a plate rack high above your sink (behind a matching fascia panel) and let the plates drain

15 Pull out a steady table flap from your floor unit at teatime or for informal family meals and snacks

16 If you have a large mixer, what better place to keep it than a glideaway shelf cabinet which rises up to counter height

17 Single, double or triple telescopic towel rails fit into spaces too narrow to take a standard kitchen unit – and there is room for trays here as well

Kitchen wall and floor coverings

Having considered carefully the appliances and fittings you need to make your kitchen efficient and easy to care for, you should now look at the choice of floor and wall coverings.

Walls and ceilings

Non-porous wall coverings are the best choice for kitchens, especially poorly ventilated ones, as they will not absorb grease and moisture.

Paint

If you want gloss paint, confine it to the woodwork as a shiny high gloss finish on walls tends to show up condensation runs. Instead, go for emulsion or satin finished paints which are easy to clean and durable, even on woodwork.

Wallpaper

This term now includes everything from plain, uncoated paper to expensively processed plastics. Choose a good quality, preferably smooth material as tiny particles of grease and dust can lodge in uneven surfaces, although some slightly textured papers are easy to wipe down.

Washable or spongeable papers have a slightly coated surface which can be wiped with a dampened cloth, but not scrubbed. Particularly suited to kitchens are vinyl wall coverings – PVC applied to ordinary wallpaper for extra toughness and washability.

Wood panelling

Although more expensive than most other wall coverings, wood cladding or panelling provides an attractive, hard-wearing surface which is less prone to condensation. It can be fixed vertically, horizontally or diagonally direct to existing walls or ceiling or, if these are very uneven, mounted on timber battens. Mounting the panels on battens gives the added advantage of hiding electrical wiring which would otherwise be unsightly. Walls must be completely sound and free from damp before applying wood panelling.

Ceramic tiles

Durable, easily cleaned and heatproof, ceramic tiles make an excellent covering for kitchen walls (and work surfaces). They come in various shapes and sizes and in a wide range of colours and patterns. On smooth, sound walls they can be fixed direct, but if the surface is uneven they should be

Above Dark paint makes a dramatic contrast to natural wood units, cork flooring and a plain tile splashback spanning the entire wall (Salarbo kitchen design)

Previous page Designer's scheme for a luxury kitchen combining a bold geometric design on the wall with a traditional chequer-board floor made of durable vinyl tiles

Left Sophisticated scheme mixes plain black units and floor-to-ceiling Venetian blind with warm-looking wood floorboards

mounted on plywood or chipboard screwed to a timber batten framework.

Splashbacks

The wall around sinks, cookers and working surfaces is exposed to constant splashing and should be given extra protection.

Tiles Two rows of ceramic or plastic tiles fixed to the wall at problem areas will make washing down easier; use a coloured grout to fix the ceramic tiles as this will not show the dirt. If you incorporate the 'soap-dish' shape tiles sold with bathroom fittings you will not need an extra container for your soap and scouring pads.

Clear PVC sheeting In small, isolated areas it is not always practical to fix tiles for protection. In this case use transparent self-adhesive PVC sheeting which is very easy to clean. (This is also useful round light switches and sockets to protect the wall from wet or dirty fingers.)

Far left Pine cladding to picture rail height helps to define the kitchen/dining area of a large one-room flat

Left Design for a small kitchen based around brick-shaped quarry tiles – on the floor, up the walls and over the work surface

Above In this tiled kitchen the single colour theme is carried right through even to the striped Venetian blind (Pilkington kitchen design and ceramic tiles; Faber blind)

Right An effective combination of natural colours and materials – pine units, cork flooring and provencale-shaped ceramic tiles between the wall and base units (Wicanders kitchen design and cork floor)

On the floor

Kitchen floors get a lot of very hard wear so the covering you choose should be tough as well as non-slip, but above all easy to clean.

Before putting down any flooring, make sure the surface is sound and flat. Uneven solid floors will have to be covered with a concrete levelling compound. You can do this yourself, but it is tricky and many manufacturers of the compound sell it only through contractors who come in and do the job for you. The compound is mixed with water and applied with a special trowel; as it dries it levels itself out and provides a smooth, even surface. This substance can only be used on solid floors since it will only adhere to cement or concrete.

Cork

Available in sheet or tile form, cork is warm, non-slip and quiet underfoot. Choose a water-resistant type or you will have to apply a polyurethane sealer after the cork has been laid to protect it from grease and water stains.

Wood

Although not the most practical choice for the kitchen, wood flooring is warm and wears well as long as it is properly maintained. Existing floorboards in good condition can be sanded and sealed to improve resistance to grease and water.

Hardwood blocks These come individually or in small panels arranged in basketweave, brick or herringbone pattern. They can be laid on concrete or on a plywood or chipboard base. This flooring improves with age, again provided it is properly cared for by regular polishing or efficient sealing.

Clay and concrete tiles

Ceramic, clay, brick and concrete tiles are all hard-wearing and easy to clean, but they are cold, hard and rather noisy to walk on. Also, any crockery dropped on them will certainly break. Clay, concrete and brick should be laid only on solid floors as they are very heavy; ceramic tiles can be laid on suspended timber floors covered with plywood. Concrete is porous, so always seal the surface to make it waterproof and grease-resistant.

Stone

All stone floors are cold, hard and noisy, but they are very tough and particularly suitable with under-floor heating since neither their appearance nor their durability is affected by constant changes of temperature.

Quartzite A matt crystalline rock with a slightly sparkling finish.

Slate Non-porous stone available with either a polished or non-slip surface.

Sandstone, limestone and granite All hard-wearing, but limestone stains fairly easily and should be sealed or varnished.

Thermoplastic tiles or sheeting

Flexible plastic flooring, usually vinyl, is one of the least expensive ways of covering your kitchen floor. Plain or textured finishes are available in a variety of widths to reduce the amount of joining required. Go for a reverse-printed, rather than a surface-embossed, finish as this produces a more rounded outline which does not hold dirt and prevents slipping if the floor is wet.

Most tiles are self-adhesive, but ones with a honeycomb-like backing can be loose-laid as this grips the floor and holds the tile in place. Those without adhesive on the back should be fixed continuously with special vinyl flooring adhesive. If the floorboards are uneven, lay the covering on a base of tempered hardboard or plywood.

Vinyl asbestos tiles More rigid than ordinary thermoplastic flooring, these tiles will wear longer, insulate the floor and provide extra fire resistance. They should be laid only on a solid floor; if laid on timber they will crack as the wood expands and contracts with the temperature.

Rush matting

Even though it looks extremely warm and attractive, don't be tempted to close-cover your kitchen floor with rush or coconut matting. It will harbour spilt food and dirt and you will have to lift the whole lot to clean under it. Use a more practical overall flooring and put a single rush mat on top but away from the cooking area to get a similar effect without the cleaning chore.

At the window

Choose an easy-to-clean window covering in a material which will not absorb cooking smells. If you decide on curtains, always use a light washable fabric make sure they are easy to take down and hang up again and site them clear of the cooker.

Roller or Venetian blinds are ideal but avoid paper, wood or cane ones which could be stained by the greasy dirt that collects in the kitchen.

Above When using a striking pattern on the floor, keep the rest of your kitchen decoration plain and pick out the main colours (Nairn kitchen scheme and vinyl sheet flooring)

Choosing sinks

Washing-up is never the most enjoyable of kitchen tasks so it's particularly important you have all the facilities you need to hand. You'll be surprised at the extensive range of sinks now available; they come in all shapes, sizes and colours, which means you can have just the one to suit your needs.

As the style of the sink bowl or unit you select will influence the layout of your kitchen even more than your cooker, we illustrate the possibilities of this essential piece of kitchen equipment before all others. You should be able to stand at the sink in a good natural light during the day, ideally overlooking a pleasant view. With artificial lighting you must be able to use the sink without being in your own light or hampered by undesirable shadows. But whatever your location options, you need to consider the following important – but often neglected – requirements of your sink.

For washing up dishes, pots and pans For this you need one medium size bowl and preferably a second one (that can be shallower) for rinsing.

For household washing (and fabric dyeing) A large bowl is essential and if you are without a spin or tumble dryer you need a second, not too shallow, one for rinsing.

To cater for non plumbed-in machines In this case you will need to feed hot (or cold) water to the machine and receive the waste flow at the sink. Some machines plumbed-in for water intake still need to empty their waste into a sink, which means you do really want a second bowl or you may find dirty water discharging unexpectedly into your washing or while you are preparing vegetables.

To cater for extensive food preparation If you cook more than one main meal a day and go in for fresh vegetables in a big way, you will spend considerable time in food preparation at the sink. So you would do well to consider whether you need to improve on your present facilities.

The right combination
The basic choice lies between single or double bowls, with draining space on either or both sides. Your choice can be in the form of a self-contained, free-standing sink unit complete with base cabinet, or inset sinks to put onto an existing base matching your other kitchen units.

Alternatively you can buy individual bowls and drop them into specially cut holes in your chosen worktop surface of plastic laminate, wood, slate, ceramic tile or marble. If you do this yourself the difficulty lies not so much in cutting the correct size

Stainless steel sinks come in a variety of settings – from simple, circular bowls to drop into your worktop, with tap control anywhere you want, to the combination double sink/double drainer making up a long line of action. Here we show you a few alternatives to help you make your choice

Right Wash up looking at an attractive view if possible, surrounded by smooth, easy-to-clean ceramic tiling. Single bowl with large drainers at either side (Wrighton sink unit, Pilkington tiles)

Far right Single drop-in bowl fitted with a waste disposer hole (top) and twin bowl inset, one deep and one shallow for draining or rinsing, with handy refuse tidy between (Berglen)

Below A double sink and double drainer unit for the larger family with one bowl a narrow oval for easy rinsing (Pland)

aperture as in ensuring a leakproof seal between the flat flange (or curved lip) rim and the worktop.

Once you start thinking in terms of more than one bowl the choice widens as to size, shape and arrangement. An ideal form is one deep bowl for normal washing-up and one shallow 'drainer' bowl for rinsing and vegetable preparation fitted with a 90mm (or $3\frac{1}{2}$in) hole for a waste-disposer, with a small refuse 'tidy' recess between the two.

If you use a dishwasher you do not need so much draining space. Many of the new sink bowls set into a long worktop have specially fitted plastic-coated wire drainer baskets and cover-up chopping boards. When not in use the basket remains in the bowl while the wood (or marble) chopping board fits on top to give extra work preparation surface. When washing up you remove the board, take out the basket and place it alongside the sink bowl ready for draining the wet dishes. Dirty crockery can also be left stacked in the basket while it is in the bowl until you are ready to wash up. With this arrangement you do not need a draining board.

Bowl shapes are rectangular or square (with rounded corners), oval, narrow oval or circular. You can choose between chip-proof stainless steel, enamelled pressed steel, enamelled cast iron and

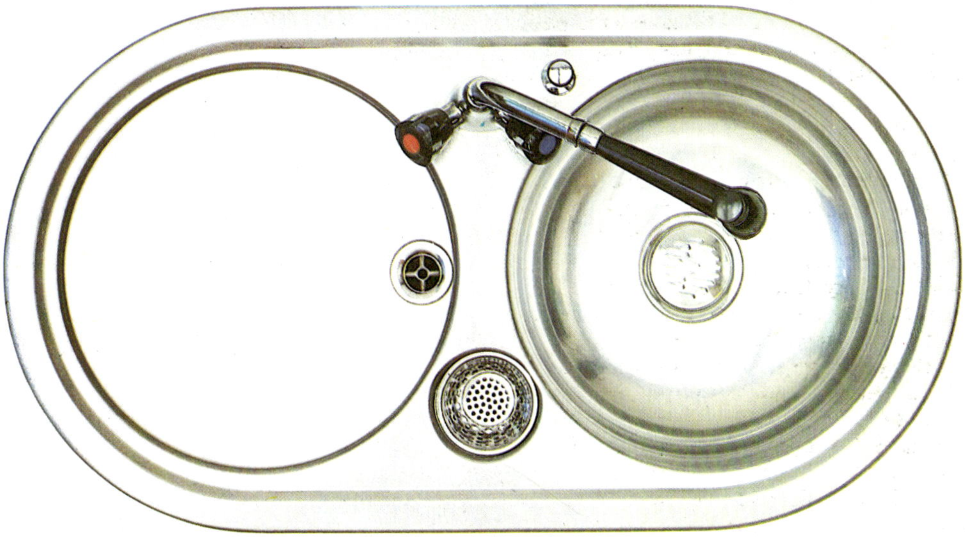

Developments in design include aids to draining, rinsing and food preparation at the sink and a good choice of colours for vitreous enamel bowls

Right With this perforated drainer and plastic waste bowl with outlet your fruit and vegetable preparation is made easy (Therma inset sink in Poggenpohl unit)

Below For colour conscious cooks there are many bright combinations of single and double, shallow and deep vitreous enamel sinks. Some have pull-out rinse sprays on a flexible hose to clean up your vegetables, others come with wooden chopping boards to fit over the shallow drainer and wire baskets to set in the deeper bowl (Berglen)

lightweight acrylic or glass fibre. Some vitreous enamel models come in strong colours including tomato red, orange, green, khaki and chestnut.

The height of some sink units is 900mm (or 36in) as opposed to 850mm (or 34in) for food preparation worktops. This is a point to remember if you want a long line of worktop surface incorporating hobplates and sink bowls since, unless you are making up the whole unit to suit yourself, you will have to opt for the standard height of base cabinets. This means your sink bowls could end up some 50mm (2in) lower than usual. If you do not require a deep bowl you can compensate for this to a degree by installing a shallower one.

The under-sink area will probably need to house your waste-disposer and a collection of buckets and larger washing/cleaning items, but not dangerous caustic products that would be in easy reach of small children. Some of the newer sink units allow for a built-in dishwasher or front-loading washing machine under the shallow bowl.

Where a sink gets considerable use, steam from the hot water makes an overhead extractor desirable. If your sink is not against an outer wall, this may be ducted to your main extractor unit/cooker hood or to a nearby window or outer wall.

Right Double stainless steel inset unit with wire drainer over shallow bowl, pop-up waste for deep one and refuse tidy between (Franke sink at Masterplanners Kitchen Centre)

Above right Single vitreous enamel bowls in strong colours form a key point in your kitchen scheme. Taps can be set into worktop or as here with a mixer set and pop-up waste (Franke sink in Lynley unit)

Below Combining good facilities in a small space this unit of large and small bowl with single drainer is set into a long worktop

What type of tap?

The old-fashioned sink had bib taps projecting from the wall behind the sink and set very high to allow for filling deep buckets and tall water pitchers. Today most sink units and bowls include a back ledge with hole or holes ready to take your selected tap(s). The sink is therefore held down by the plumbing so you cannot move it out for spring cleaning or take it with you so easily when you move house. It is quite simple to have your taps plumbed direct into a ledge, or through the wall, behind the sink unit itself so you need only detach the unit from the waste pipe to move it without interfering with the rest of the plumbing installation. In this case you must be sure the tap is set high enough and the mixer arm is long enough to reach over the sink. You can then order your sink without tap-holes or have existing ones blocked up.

As to the taps themselves, a single mixer arm that swivels for use with double bowls is convenient. This may have hot and cold control heads at either side or both to one side. A spray (sometimes fitted with a brush attachment) on a flexible hose is a useful extra for washing delicate plates or cleaning your peeled vegetables.

Where garden hoses or washing machines need to be fed from the sink it is obviously better to have an additional cold water tap for this purpose.

For sink areas with very little working space from front to back it pays to have your taps installed to one side rather than centrally. This allows more working room in the bowl itself and lessens the chance of cracking glasses or crockery against a projecting tap spout.

The flow of the water into the sink is important as if it hits the wrong place at the wrong angle you will be continually splashing yourself when turning the tap full on. Use only a type of tap recommended for the sink you are installing.

Fitting in your kitchen appliances

Power appliances in the kitchen form a valuable part of any home's domestic armoury. But you will only get the best value out of them if they are placed where they can give the most practical use. Space and budget will dictate your choice, so plan carefully for what you want.

The basic function of a working kitchen is to provide the framework for a collection of essential cooking equipment and desirable household aids. To establish some reasonable order in your kitchen for these miscellaneous items you must plan with what you have now, allowing for what you hope to get in the future. This does not mean you should restrict yourself to serried rows of uniform kitchen floor (or wall) units, each one designed to house a kitchen appliance of some kind or other. But you should take the main sources of power into consideration when replanning the existing layout.

With the development of split-level cooking equipment the whole concept of everything having to be centred on the cooker is changed. So your first consideration should be what type of cooker to choose or what additional piece of cooking equipment to add to your present one if desirable.

Cooking equipment

Separate ovens and hobs are more convenient (but more costly) than the traditional all-in-one cooker for which you can shop around for cash discounts. Not only can you site split-level units on different walls and worktops, but you can store pots and pans in open shelves or closed cupboards underneath them, where they are easily to hand without becoming greasy dust traps (as they are when hung from the ceiling or stacked on open stands).

Ovens These come singly or in double, two-tier form (with grill in the lower oven) for the prolific bakers. Single combined oven/grill units, although space-saving, mean that if you are cooking dishes to a precise temperature in the oven section you cannot open the shared door to do some quick grilling at the same time.

When hanging an oven on the wall you must check that the shelves will not be too high for lifting food in and out. If it is to be built in, make sure the housing unit can be fitted where you want it.

If you use much deep-frozen food you may find it worth investing in a quick defreezing microwave oven, for which wall or worktop space must be allowed in addition to an ordinary baking oven.

Grills Foldaway, spit-roasting grills can be hung on a wall or used on a worktop and are especially useful as extra cooking facilities if you are keeping a small, free-standing cooker in your kitchen plan rather than splashing out on new oven/grill and hob units. But you should place these separate grills with a view to effective ventilation if they are some distance from your extractor area.

Hobs Versatility is the keynote of the new hob designs. You can start with single, circular gas or electric hobs set individually into your worktop or go for double or multiple units. If you install a double electric hobplate next to a double gas one you have the best of both worlds. You can extend your hob area to include a matching, set-in deep fryer, a solid cooking plate or a barbecue unit with a permanent bed of volcanic rock in place of charcoal. Some hobplates come with eye-level grill and backplate attached or you can fix a self-contained wall grill above your hobplate at a convenient height.

The all-over ceramic hob unit has several advantages. The continuous sheet of ceramic glass makes cleaning very easy and the marked areas heat up separately (turning yellow or glowing red according to the colour of the glass), leaving the surrounding areas cool enough to touch or use for dishing up if all cooking areas are not being used at once.

Whichever type you choose you must site the cooking equipment near your main food preparation area, with sufficient work surfaces for mixing and serving up on either side. It is not a good idea to place the hob too near a corner or at the end of a row of units. If you prefer an oven in the traditional place under the hob you can still achieve a streamlined look with a separate built-under oven.

Solid fuel cookers Installation of this type will be a major item to plan for in your layout, especially if you want to incorporate water heating facilities, so consult a heating engineer.

Powered kitchen aids

It is easy to forget that mixers, liquidizers and grinders are often more trouble than they are worth if not conveniently placed, so space must be allowed for them to be permanently on suitable work preparation surfaces or stowed away near a power point.

Other kitchen appliances

Obviously the more items you can hang on the wall the more floor space you will have for other equipment or storage cupboards. The following items are not all geared to cooking, but if you have

Opposite A foldaway spit-roasting grill can be placed on your worktop or hung on the wall, but be sure to hang it so the gas jets are not at eye level.
Grill measures 546×422 (open)×425mm high/ $21\frac{1}{2}\times16\frac{1}{2}\times17$in (Flavel Snackmaster)

Below This luxury kitchen has a wall-hung refrigerator and double oven built into matching housing units. The double gas and double electric hob units, and deep fryer, are set into a spacious tiled worktop (Neff appliances, Wrighton Cotswold solid pine units)

the space it makes sense to house them in the kitchen or ideally in a nearby 'utility' room.

Refrigerators/freezers Low level, free-standing models with worktops add to your preparation surface area. With built-in models you can fit matching worktop panels to join your line of cupboard units. A wall-hung refrigerator or fridge-freezer is better at the end of a run of units, unless you want to make a definite break in surface heights.

You can place a refrigerator adjacent to your cooker if you allow about 25mm (1in) ventilation space between, but obviously the hotter the surrounding atmosphere the harder your cooling unit will have to work, thereby increasing the running cost. With large freezers you will probably have little choice of position. If you are lucky enough to have a larder or pantry for less perishable foods and stores, you will not need such a large capacity refrigerator. Vents and airbricks at the back of kitchen units set against outside walls will help with this fresh food storage problem, but there is really no substitute for the old-fashioned cool pantry.

Dishwashers For quick clearing-up, your machine needs to be as close as possible to your sink, whether it is built-in or free-standing. Models without pumps may require the drain-off to be above sink waste outlet level, which may mean placing the machine on your second draining board. But as you can house so much of the dirty crockery in the machine before starting the washing programme it is no great hardship to forgo this second drainer provided you still have enough stacking space nearby.

As regards capacity, for two-person households it is more convenient to buy a medium sized one and run it twice when the load is heavy than be stuck with a large one which takes days to fill with your dirty dishes and necessitates a large supply of everyday crockery for use between washes.

If your kitchen plan allows for either a top or front-opening model, try loading and unloading both types to see which you find most convenient.

Above Versatile combination of inset hob units: two-burner gas hob, black ceramic electric plate and new-style barbecue grill with nuggets of volcanic rock so you avoid having to lay in stocks of charcoal. With this barbecue you need to fit a small surface ventilator nearby on the hob (Gaggenau at Masterplanners Kitchen Centre)

Below Ceramic glass hob with touch controls. Surrounding areas remain cool and so give additional dishing-up space (Moffat)

Above Cover up your solid electric hobs while they are still hot – for safety and to provide extra dishing-up space. With chrome feet attached, these patterned or plain enamelled steel covers double as trivets for your serving dishes (Prowoda)

Left For extra fast cooking of fresh or deep-frozen food, a microwave oven is the answer. The oven remains cool while the food cooks and the dishes are warmed by heat transference from the food being cooked (Moffat)
Below left Dishwasher fits conveniently under the drainer side of the sink and behind a matching 'decor panel' (Neff built-under dishwasher, Alno units, at Masterplanners Kitchen Centre)
Below Gas-fired central heating boiler can be wall-hung or set neatly behind louvre doors (as shown here) to match other kitchen units (Baxi)

bearing in mind at what height it will be fixed. You can go through the actions of loading while selecting in a shop or you may be able to experiment on a friend's machine.

It is advisable to choose a model that contains its own built-in heater so as not to affect your existing hot water supply. But it is not necessary to have separate plumbing facilities for the waste as this can empty through a flexible pipe into the sink.

Central heating boilers/water heaters If you are short of floor space these can be hung on the wall, but you must consult a heating engineer over the correct placing. Some models are conveniently small and can be stowed away in cupboard units if they do not fit into your kitchen design scheme or be placed elsewhere in your home.

Washing machines and tumble/spin dryers Try to place these machines adjacent to each other and close to the sink if not plumbed in. If they are set on castors you can wheel them to the sink and store them elsewhere. Tumble dryers need to be near an outside wall for venting and this may affect their placing.

The ideal layout

These factors all bear on your choice of position for the various labour-saving appliances designed to make cooking and household work more of a pleasure. A separate utility room for laundry and freezer equipment is the ideal solution but not everyone has the floor area for this arrangement. If you are really short on space think hard which machine you need most (and enjoy using) before investing in too many items for too small a kitchen.

Ventilating your kitchen

In its most basic form ventilation can be provided by opening a window – unless you have permanently fixed double-glazing, of course. Open-window ventilation is seldom if ever very effective and in bad weather just not practical; in winter you could also pay a fortune in lost heat. What you need is a mechanical method of ventilation.

The simplest mechanical ventilator is called a 'self-actuating' fan. This is designed for mounting in a window pane and literally runs on air, the fan blades turning in either direction according to the difference in pressure between the inside and outside air. For kitchen use, however, this type of fan is rarely suitable because you cannot always extract fumes and steam when you want to; if the pressure is higher outside than inside the fan will draw in fresh air and may, in fact, push the fumes, smells and steam further round the house.

A good kitchen ventilation system must provide you with positive control over fume, steam and smell extraction, which means installing a system that incorporates an electrically-powered fan. There are two basic types: extractor fans and fan-operated cooker hoods. No kitchen, whatever its size, should be without one or the other.

Extractor fans

The majority of extractor fans are available for window or external wall mounting, although there are ceiling-mounted fans which can be used, for example, in single-storey kitchen extensions. Most leading fan manufacturers have a comprehensive range of leaflets on their products and you would be advised to obtain a selection to help you make your choice.

Window-mounted extractor fans are generally the cheapest to buy and to install. They do, however, tend to be rather noticeable, especially if you have only a small window area in your kitchen. They also restrict your choice of position, which will affect the ventilation efficiency. Most are circular in shape, but rectangular models are available if you want one in keeping with the rectangular shape of your window. Mounting in the wall, although involving more work, does make the fan less obtrusive and also gives you greater flexibility in siting.

Although many of the smaller kitchen fans are single speed and controlled by a cord-operated switch, other models can be operated from a conveniently placed switch and have two or more speeds for more precise control over the extraction rate. Some models have a reverse control to draw in fresh air when required, although they do cost considerably more than the basic single speed types. Most models have draught-proof shutters which open or close automatically when the fan is switched on or off.

Above The ceiling-hung ventilation unit over the island work station is boxed in to match the general scheme. Its frame provides a ledge for plants and spare china, while the raised hob cooking area allows for ample eating space around three sides (Poggenpohl kitchen design)

Left Ducted extractor hood is fitted between matching pine wall units in this country kitchen (Solarbo solid pine kitchen units, Scholtes hood)

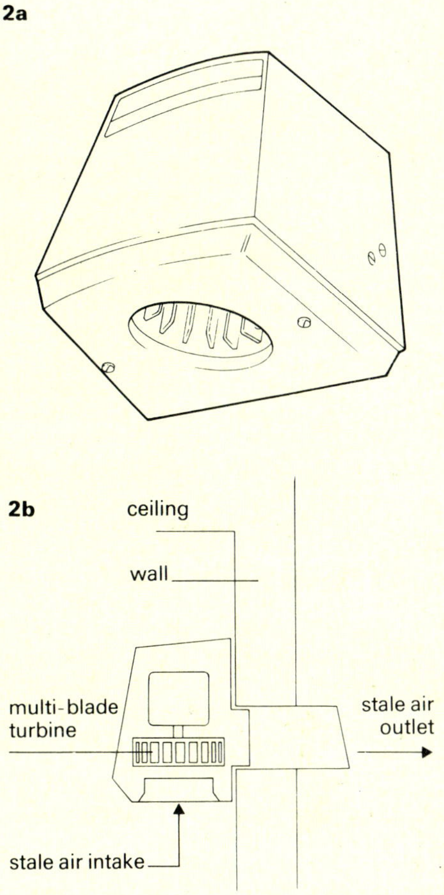

Canopy type extractor for vertical or horizontal fitting to wall or ceiling, direct or ducted. Speed regulator switch available. 300cu m/hr (10,500cm ft/hr) capacity 60 watts (Thermor Extractair canopy ventilator)

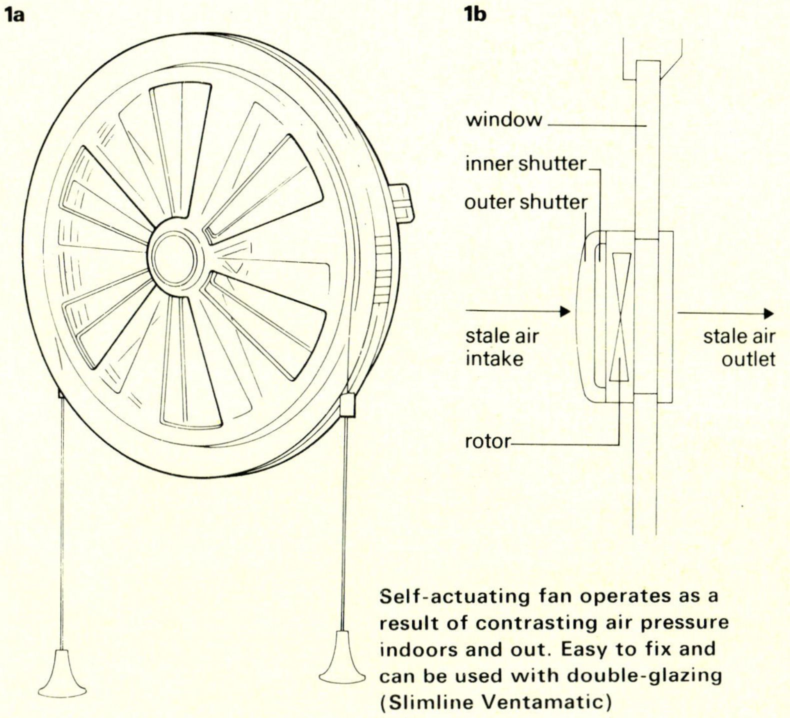

Self-actuating fan operates as a result of contrasting air pressure indoors and out. Easy to fix and can be used with double-glazing (Slimline Ventamatic)

A wall-mounted centrifugal fan is available; its multi-blade turbine considerably increases the suction efficiency and is not affected by considerable back pressure from strong wind.

The correct size of fan is of vital importance for effective ventilation. The size is related to the number of air changes per hour recommended and the amount of air to be moved. In kitchens, approximately 15 air changes per hour are required to cope adequately with fumes, steam and smells. To work out the size of fan required first calculate the volume of your kitchen (length × width × height) in cubic metres (or cubic feet). Multiply by 15 to obtain the total air movement required per hour. Then look through manufacturers' leaflets to find a fan capable of handling that amount of air.

Siting the fan is also very important. It should be as high up as possible in the wall or window, because the fumes, steam and odours will be carried in hot air which rises to the top of the kitchen. It should also be sited close to the cooker, if possible, for it is there that most of the fumes originate. Don't place the fan too near an air intake point such as a door or an airbrick, since this will affect the extractor's efficiency by diverting the flow of fumes away from the fan. Bear in mind you may have to reach a compromise between these various siting considerations to arrive at a suitable position.

In certain situations, such as a basement kitchen

or a long, narrow kitchen in a terraced house where the cooker is well away from the window, a window extractor or a fan mounted on an external wall may not be practical. Here you will either have to install a combination of extractor fan and ducting to take fumes and steam away from the cooker or fit a suitable cooker hood. If you decide on a ducted extract system contact the fan manufacturer or a heating and ventilating engineer for advice on suitable ductwork/fan combinations as the length and diameter of the ducting must be related to the power of the fan.

There are two further points that are important when designing a kitchen ventilation layout. If you have a gas or oil-fired boiler in the kitchen there must be provision for air to enter the kitchen when the extractor fan is working and the kitchen door is closed or the boiler will not operate efficiently. Also remember when you extract fumes, smells and steam you also extract heat. This is obviously worthwhile in summer, but can be expensive in winter as you will be paying to put the heat there in the first place. You can, of course, cut this loss by using the fan sparingly but this may mean having to sacrifice some of your ventilation system's effectiveness. There is, however, a special ventilator available for wall or window mounting which is designed to recover some of the warmth from stale extracted air and return it, mixed with fresh air, into the room space.

Another way of cutting heat loss is to provide a small air inlet in addition to the extractor fan. Air is drawn in from outside as the extractor fan operates; it passes over the cooker, picks up the fumes and goes out through the fan. The air inlet could be an airbrick or a special small window-mounted vent – both are available with shutters which can be closed when the extractor fan is not in use.

Cooker hoods

In most kitchens a cooker hood is an alternative – and generally a more expensive one – to an extractor fan, although in very large kitchens both can be used to good effect. The cooker hood has the advantage that it picks up most of the fumes, smells and steam at source, which is more effective. It will not, however, deal with the steam from your kitchen sink unless it is close by.

There are basically two types of cooker hood: recirculating hoods simply clean the air and return it to the room, while ducted types extract the air to the outside (in fact, most ducted types can be adjusted either to recirculate or extract). Included in the ducted types are models specially designed for use with island hobs.

The majority of hoods available are of the recirculating type. Though not as effective as the ducted ones they are simple to fit and as no extraction is involved they save heat too. They usually contain two filters: a metal one to catch grease from fumes and a charcoal one to adsorb smells.

If you wish you can have the canopy to surround the basic hood mechanism made to order. This may be circular, three-sided or rectangular and in brass, copper, stainless steel or other metal. (A local firm of panel beaters will probably make up the canopy for you, but consult manufacturers on the size of fan needed for the size of canopy.)

Also available are telescopic cooker hoods to fit between (or under) wall units, with matching fascia panels. The hood is operated simply by pulling out the fascia 'drawer'. When not in use the hood is

3a

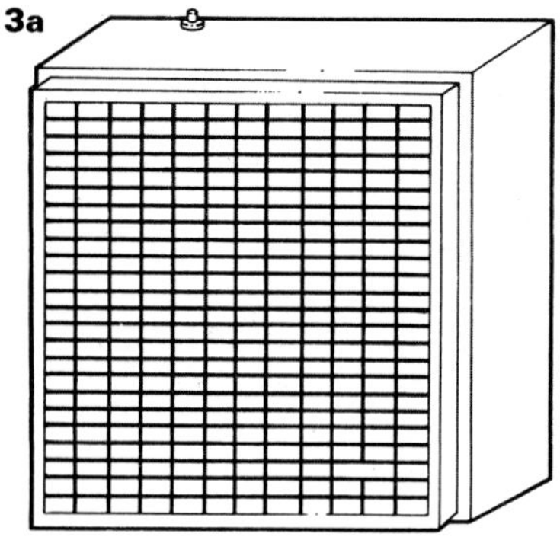

3b

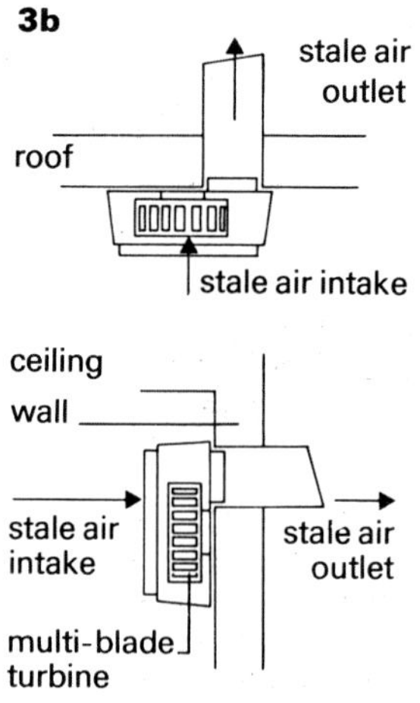

Multi-blade turbine centrifugal fan for wall/ceiling fitting, direct or ducted. 280cu m/hr (10,000cu ft/hr) capacity, 100 watts (Thermor Turbinex)

4a

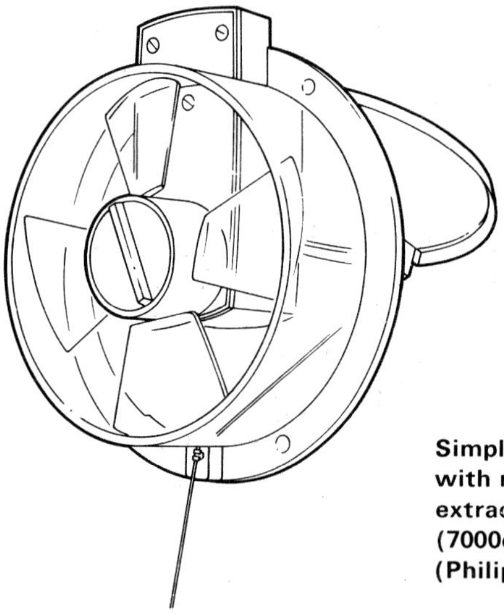

4b

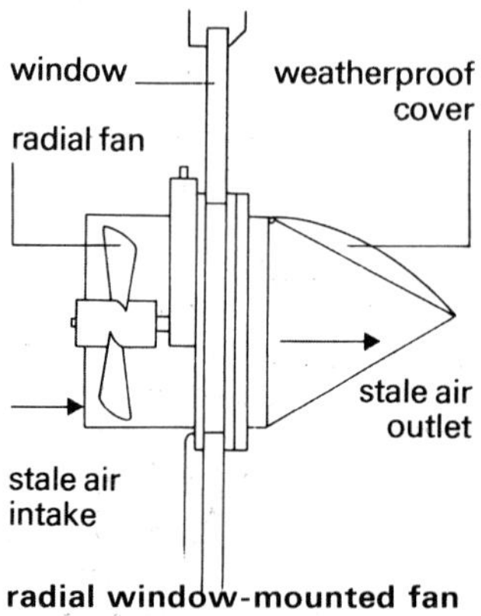

Simple, radial window-mounted fan with reversible motor for intake or extract. Single speed, 200cu m/hr (7000cu ft/hr) capacity, 15 watts (Philips HR 3404)

5a

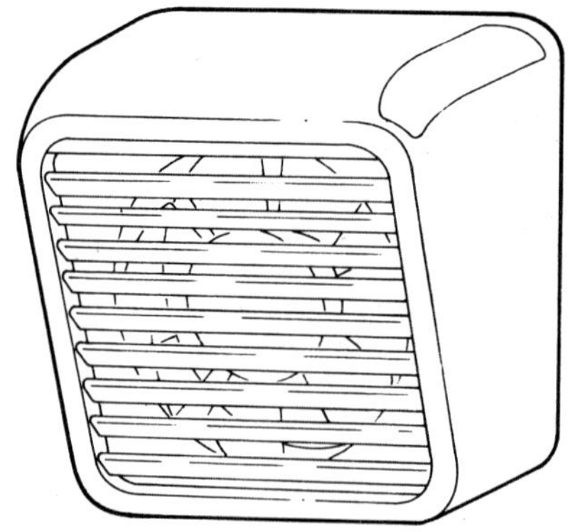

5b

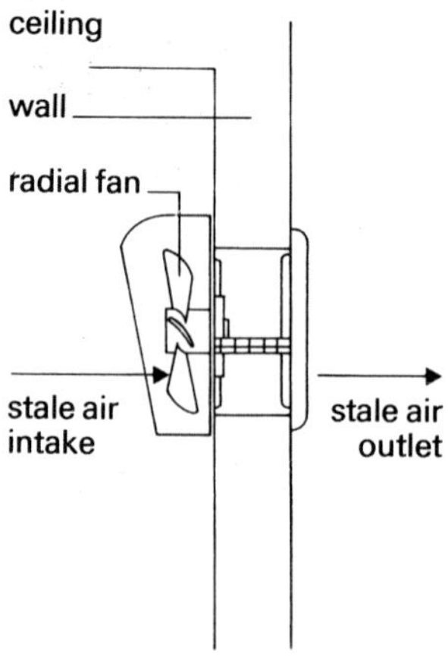

Window or wall-mounted fan with flat-faced shutters for easy cleaning. Single speed, 300cu m/hr (10,000cu ft/hr) capacity, 30 watts (GEC-Xpelair GXC6)

6a

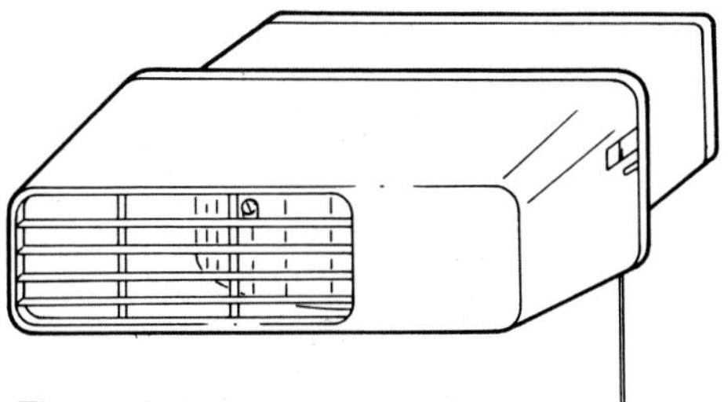

Thermal ring in this centrifugal fan type holds warmth from stale air to warm air brought in from outside. 254cu m/hr (9000cu ft/hr), 55 watts (Dimplex Room Ventilator)

6b

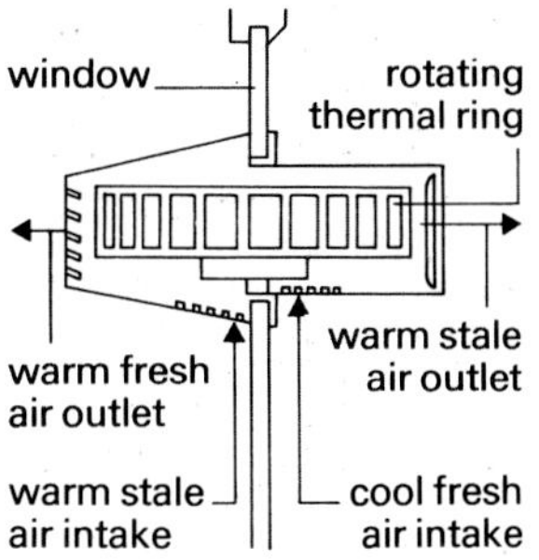

7

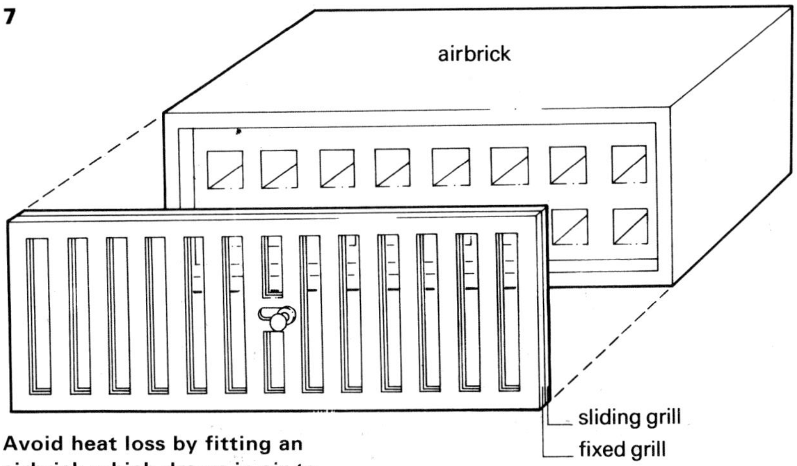

Avoid heat loss by fitting an airbrick which draws in air to pass over cooker, pick up fumes and be extracted through fan

8a

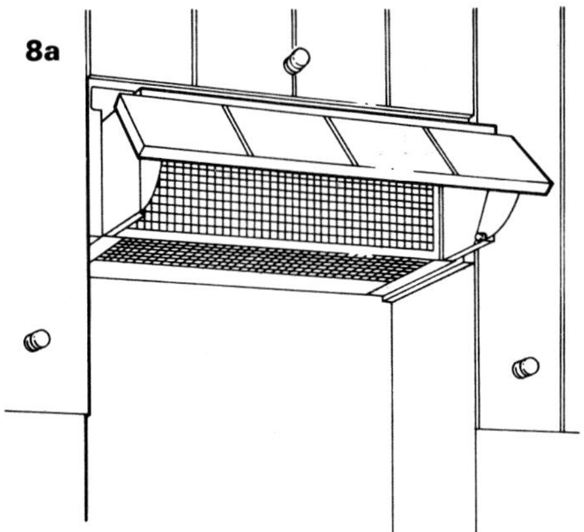

8b

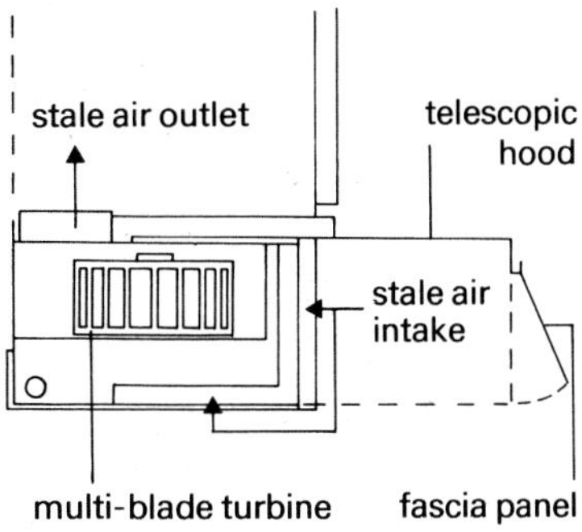

Telescopic hood behind matching fascia panel pulls out to operate centrifugal turbine fan and lights. Recirculating or ducted. 350cu m/hr (12,400cu ft/hr), 330 watts (Prowoda)

pushed back into place to form a neat line with the kitchen wall units.

Siting a cooker hood at the correct height is important. Check with the instruction leaflet for the manufacturer's recommendations, but as a general rule a cooker hood should be between 560 and 770mm (22 and 30in) above the cooker hob. On cookers with an eye-level grill there should be not less than 300mm (12in) and not more than 450mm (18in) between the hood and the grill. For eye-level grills most manufacturers provide a bracket to extend the canopy an extra 125mm (5in) or so from the wall for maximum efficiency. If a bracket is not supplied you can mount the hood on a suitable wood block screwed and plugged to the wall.

Warning Some types of hood are not suitable for use with eye-level grills, so check with the manufacturer to ensure you buy the right type.

Installation and maintenance

The easiest ventilators to install are window fans and recirculating cooker hoods, but even ducted hood systems should be well within the scope of a competent DIY enthusiast. Manufacturers supply detailed installation information and this should be carefully studied before you start work. The following points will give you an idea of what is involved.

Window-mounted extractor fans require an accurately cut hole in the glass pane and connection to the electricity supply. The electric cable will have to be buried beneath the wall surface.

Wall-mounted extractor fans need an accurately cut hole through the brickwork plus the electrical connection and some making good around the hole.

Recirculating cooker hoods just need screwing to the wall plus electrical connection.

Ducted cooker hoods and ducted extract fan systems need holes through outside walls, electrical connection and support for the ducting.

Maintenance of the above systems is minimal. Extractor fans need occasional cleaning to remove dirt and grease – many are designed for quick dismantling to make this easy (make sure the electricity supply to the fan is turned off before you start cleaning). The metal grease filter in cooker hoods needs occasional cleaning with washing-up liquid and the charcoal filter needs to be changed about once a year to ensure it operates at maximum efficiency in the kitchen.

Operating hints and running costs

Provided you have sited your ventilation system correctly, it should work efficiently from the moment you switch on. Remember it is important to avoid 'short circuiting' an extract fan system, so if the fan is near or in a window, keep the windows closed when you want to remove fumes in a hurry. It probably will not make a great deal of difference to the ventilation efficiency whether you have the door from the kitchen to the rest of the house open or closed – try it and see. And don't wait until your kitchen fills with steam and cooking smells to switch on the fan or cooker hood. Switch it on the moment you start cooking to make sure the air stays clean and fresh.

Running costs of electric ventilation systems are very low. Many extractor fans and ductless cooker hoods are rated at less than 100 watts and so will give more than ten hours continuous operation for only one unit of electricity.

Lighting your kitchen

As your kitchen probably fulfils many functions – apart from the actual cooking of meals – you need to consider your choice of lights and fittings very carefully: bright for working in, normal for everyday use and dimmed for mealtimes.

Good lighting is vital in the kitchen which is the 'workshop' of the home where most of the potentially dangerous tasks are carried out, such as working with sharp knives, jagged cans, saucepans of boiling water and overheated frying pans. And it is worth remembering kitchen lighting is not just for use after dark but is often essential to supplement inadequate daylight.

The days of the lone overhead 60 watt lamp bulb should be numbered. Efficient lighting can be created in a variety of ways: look through the

Good illumination in this kitchen comes from special light boxes fixed to the ceiling, and fluorescent tubes mounted under wall cupboards (Di Lusso Roma Self-Assembly units and boxes in hessian effect laminate, H. & R. Johnson wall tiles, Armstrong Cork vinyl flooring)

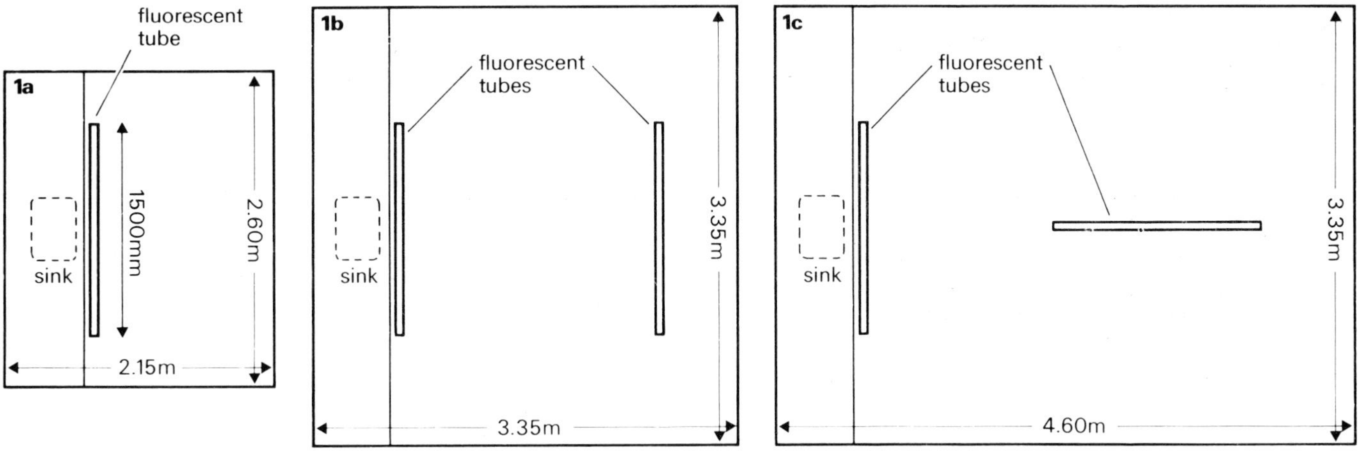

1a A single fluorescent tube is sufficient for a small kitchen if placed as shown in relation to the sink
1b and 1c Two tubes are needed for larger kitchens either parallel to each other or at right-angles according to the position of the sink and the proportion of the room

manufacturers' catalogues and visit retail showrooms to get a good idea of the wide range of lamps and fittings suitable for the kitchen. Good results can be achieved at a moderate cost since the real secret is in the way the lamps are positioned.

The main requirement is functional lighting that enables you to work safely under the most favourable conditions. That does not mean your lighting cannot be attractive as well, but always make sure the fittings and lamps are really suitable for use in the kitchen.

It is important to choose your lighting when you plan the rest of your kitchen and not when everything else is installed and the room is decorated. If you plan as an afterthought, you may find you have to spoil new decorations and take down cupboards to install the system you want.

Ideally you should provide both good general illumination and local lighting for worktops and other key areas, except in tiny kitchens when just overall lighting may be sufficient. Glare and excessive shadow are the main faults to avoid.

Fluorescent lamps

These are ideal for general illumination and some local lighting because they give an even spread over a wide area and produce about four times as much light as the equivalent wattage filament lamp (commonly called a bulb); they also last considerably longer. Do not be put off by the harsh effect you may have seen created by bare fluorescent tubes, because appropriate diffusers – either prismatic or opal – improve their looks and give much better distribution.

For tiny kitchens one fluorescent tube will give adequate light for areas of up to 5.5sq m (60sq ft) and should be positioned above and parallel to the front edge of the sink so you do not work in your own shadow (**see 1a**). At least two fluorescent tubes will be needed in larger kitchens, one over the sink and the other sited to give light over the remaining area (**see 1b and 1c**).

Create a built-in look by recessing the fittings into the ceiling (if space permits) and covering the aperture with a suitable diffuser mounted flush with the ceiling. This treatment can be extended to the whole ceiling, but if you want the diffusers to be illuminated evenly you will probably end up with too much light.

Low wattage miniature fluorescent tubes mounted under cupboards give good local lighting above worktops, but should be concealed behind a suitable pelmet to avoid glare (**see 2**). Many kitchen unit ranges are supplied with these pelmets. The 900mm (36in) 30 watt, 525mm (21in) 13 watt and 300mm (12in) 8 watt fluorescent tubes are ideal for under-cupboard mounting and you can even obtain ones as small as 150mm (6in) for very restricted spaces.

Fluorescent lighting is available in a variety of colours (not of the tube itself but the light it gives out) and choosing the right one is important. Those known as 'better colour rendering' tubes give the best results. These include Deluxe warm white (a British Standard colour), available under such brand names as Softone 32 and Homelite; it gives a warm appearance and blends well with filament lamps. Mixing colours of tubes, however, will not produce a particularly pleasing effect.

Tungsten filament striplights are not recommended for use in kitchens as they are not suited to the damp conditions that normally prevail.

Filament lamps

When put into downlighter fittings, tungsten filament lamps concentrate beams of light down from the ceiling and are available in various beam widths, from wide for general illumination to narrow for concentrated local light. You can position them over the main areas of activity, such as the cooker or sink, or use them on their own or in conjunction with fluorescent lamps. Fittings are available for recessing completely into the ceiling, partially recessing or mounting on the ceiling, depending on how much space there is between the ceiling and the floor above (**see 3**).

Some downlighters are designed for use with special internally silvered filament (ISL) lamps and do not contain reflectors; those with reflectors are intended for use with standard general service (GLS) lamps. If you choose these, check with the manufacturer whether a clear pearl or silica-coated lamp should be used and that the fitting is suitable for general kitchen conditions.

Spot lamps Concentrated lighting, such as for illuminating a cooker hob, sink or work surface, can be provided by spot lamps. Easily adjustable to give light exactly where you want it, they are even

2

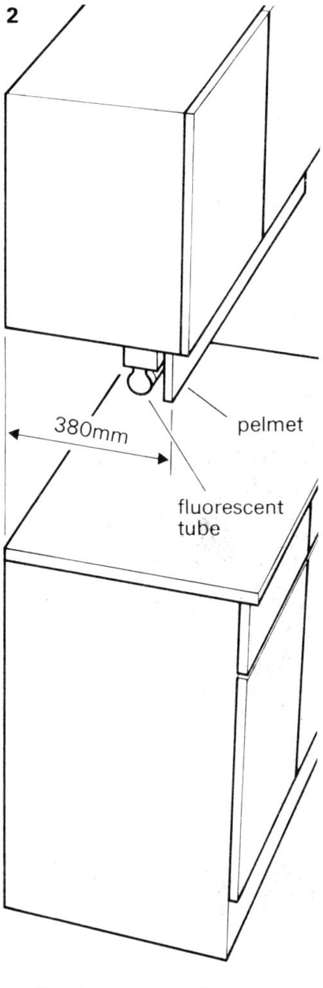

2 The best form of worktop lighting is low wattage fluorescent tubes mounted under wall cupboards and behind a pelmet to avoid glare. With this method you avoid any chance of working in your own shadow from overhead lighting or spot lamps. Tubes are available in lengths 150–900mm (6–36in), 4–30 watts

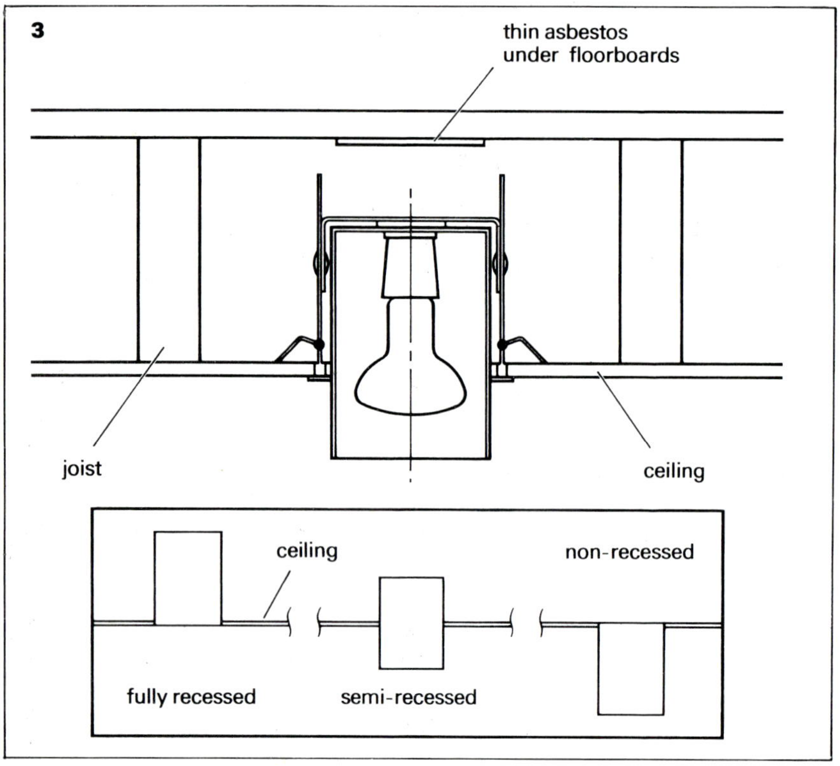

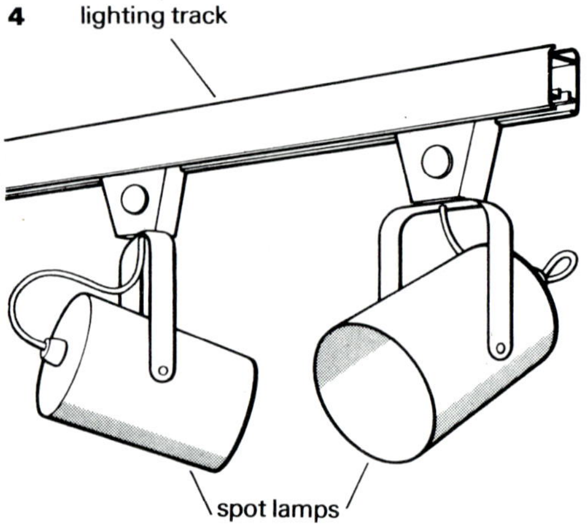

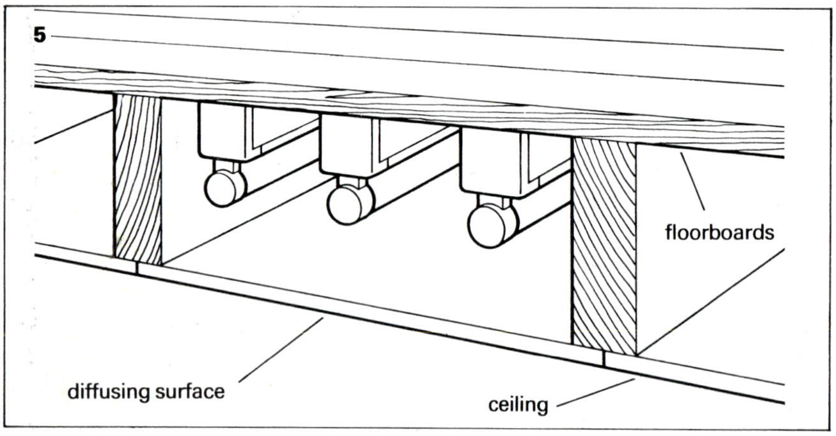

3 Downlighter fittings used with tungsten filament lamps concentrate a good beam of light from the ceiling to your work area, cooker, sink or table. This type can be fully or semi-recessed, or surface-mounted, according to your ceiling facility.
4 With one or two lengths of track (1 or 2m/3 or 6ft) and one or more spot lamps angled as you want them, you can achieve a good mix of light
5 For overall ceiling light you need to work out the number of fluorescent tubes required (in watts per sq m/sq ft) and their spacing in relation to each other and the diffusing surface if you are boxing them in

more flexible if mounted on lighting track (**see 4**). As one length of track will take a number of different fittings and you can change the position – and angle – of each spot, you could create your complete lighting system on tracks.

Kitchen/diner If your kitchen is also used for eating in, one or more downlighter fittings over a breakfast bar will enhance it as a focal point, while a pendant light sited low over a dining table will help create an intimate atmosphere. If this is used with a rise-and-fall fitting you will be able to raise the lamp for general illumination when the table is not in use.

Quantity of light

The amount of light provided is vitally important. Too little and you will obviously not be able to see to do all your jobs properly; too much and you will have problems with glare.

With better colour rendering fluorescent lamps you need to allow at least 15 watts per square metre of floor area ($1\frac{1}{2}$ watts per square foot) when using a diffusing fitting and 10 watts per square metre ($\frac{1}{2}$ watt per square foot) if you decide to have bare tubes (only acceptable in smaller kitchens). These estimates are for kitchens with light-coloured decorations. If you go in for dark colours increase the quantity of light by about one third. These levels will give quite acceptable results, but if you want a really bright kitchen double the figures.

Fluorescent tube lengths The following table shows the lengths of tube available. If you cannot find a suitable length buy several shorter tube fittings to make up the required wattage. If space is really tight, circular tubes are available. These give quite a pleasant effect when mounted in an opal diffuser, but they do not distribute light as effectively as a straight tube.

Length	Wattage
1200mm (4ft)	40
1500mm (5ft)	65 or 80
1800mm (6ft)	75 or 85
2400mm (8ft)	85, 100 or 125

Problems can arise if you want to illuminate your kitchen entirely from the ceiling with fluorescents, particularly in providing the correct amount of light without creating a patchy effect. The distance between the tubes must not be more than one and a half times the distance from the tubes to the diffusing surface (**see 5**). This often means more lamps than are needed have to be provided to ensure an even effect.

Filament lamps With these lamps you must allow more watts per square metre than with fluorescent tubes because they produce less light per watt. For kitchens with light-coloured decorations 40 watts per square metre (4 watts per square foot) is sufficient; increase this by one third for dark colours.

Controls

The more switches you have for your lighting system the more variety and flexibility you will gain from it. The main light switches should be sited by the door leading to the rest of the home; if you have a second door, a two-way switch arrangement will be useful. Separate switches for local lighting at the point of use are also worthwhile, especially in larger kitchens as they will save you a lot of unnecessary walking.

Dimmer switches are effective if you have a kitchen/diner because they enable you to reduce the main lighting and concentrate attention on the eating area. Dimmers are available for both filament and fluorescent lamps, but the latter require special circuits and control gear and are not easily added at a later date. So decide at the planning stage if you want to use them.

The Kitchen: Top Designers' Tips

1. If you have **good-looking saucepans and dishes**, don't hide them away. Hang them on wire wall racks (chromed or coloured) on butchers' hooks, or stack them on open shelves to **make decorative and colourful patterns** of their own and avoid the need for expensive units.

2. If you have only a tiny space for eating, **choose folding chairs** which can hang upon large wall hooks when they aren't being used, or even a **hinged table** which folds down from the wall.

3. Consider **deep drawers for storage** rather than low-level cupboards. They are easier to see into, to use, and to keep tidy, and they can accommodate all manner of things from saucepans to bottles.

4. Fit the backs of cupboard doors (and the one on the larder) with **lipped shelves or racks** for extra storage.

5. Stay cool and **set a slab of marble** (bought from a dealer or in a junk shop) into the work surface for successful pastry making.

6. Line larder and cupboard shelves with **bright laminated plastic** for a beautiful, easy-to-clean surface.

7. Got money to burn? Splash out on a **colour co-ordinated kitchen** with sink, taps, cooker doors, hob, refrigerator and dishwasher in, say, bright red.

8. A stainless steel surface needs frequent buffing to stay **gleaming bright**, but it makes an excellent work surface near the hob and oven because it is impervious to heat.

9. Shut your front-loading washing machine or dish washer away in a cupboard, with **louvred doors for ventilation**.

10. Where space is tight, consider setting **the sink and the hobs** in a central island unit, or a projecting peninsula.

11. Ordinary wooden boards, cleaned and treated with several coats of matt or gloss lacquer, make surprisingly satisfactory kitchen floors, if the room will not get very heavy use.

12. Everyday plates can be stored permanently in **wooden draining racks** set above the sink or draining board.

13. Fix as many things as possible (cutlery box, tin opener, telephone) to the wall to leave a **clear working surface**.

THE BATHROOM

YOU MAY OR MAY NOT BE OLD ENOUGH TO remember the days when taking a bath was a rarity and something of an endurance test, when the amount of hot water available was limited by what a geyser could produce, when the temperature out of the water was much too low for comfort, and when the walls (often covered with cracked white tiles) consequently streamed with condensation which inevitably penetrated the towels making them into dank instruments of torture.

Things are entirely different now – or they should be! A bathroom can be a place of sybaritic comfort and visual delight – perhaps the only room in the home where you can be alone to relax, meditate and recover from the daily grind. A large bathroom is a luxury indeed, but there is absolutely no reason why even the smallest slot of a room – the sort generally found in modern speculatively built houses – should not be equally soothing and pleasant to use. Even a minute shower room, if that is all you have room for, can form such a haven.

It's all a question of getting your priorities right, then selecting the things to go into your room with great care. The modern bathroom must be warm (certainly if you are to avoid any danger of condensation), and there must be an ample supply of hot water, so make sure of these first. Then select the washbasin, WC, bath, shower and bidet (or whichever of these items you are going to have) which will suit your particular requirements. They come in an infinite variety of shape and colour and, up to a point, performance (as described in this chapter), so it is important to understand these differences and to ensure that what you get is what you really want. Buy the best quality you can afford because sanitaryware – unlike more transient and free-standing pieces of equipment – is not something to be lightly cast aside and replaced, so it must give years of service. Think carefully before selecting such things in colour, since you tire of them you will have to go to much expense and inconvenience in replacement, and they certainly will inhibit a change of colour scheme. The range of colours, however, is vast and we have tried to illustrate the main ones in this chapter.

Since the area involved is likely to be small, you can really go to town with decorations, indulging yourself in fluffy fitted carpet, exotic wallpaper, a dado of hand-made ceramic tiles and enormous, thick bath sheets – not all at once maybe, but as and when you can afford them.

A bathroom is a place you use mainly when you are at your weakest and most sleepy – early in the morning and late at night. Don't just skip in and out as quickly as possible – make sure you plan a room in which you will delight to linger.

To be beautifully functional is the key concept in bathroom design. This supremely elegant interior shows that it is possible to be totally streamlined without looking severely clinical.

In terms of structural planning, the bathroom tends to be given less consideration than other parts of the home. In older and converted houses awkward and ugly shaped corners are often partitioned off to make a bathroom and the usual jumble of exposed plumbing detracts even further from the appearance of the room.

The owner of this bathroom faced exactly these problems, but overcame them by using various methods of disguise. To effect a transformation like this, first box in all visible pipes; the plumbing under the basin can be enclosed in a cupboard which will also be useful for cleaning equipment and extra towels. Any pipes near the ceiling can be hidden by suitably positioned panels, which also allow for concealed lighting since they provide an ideal place to fit a tungsten or fluorescent tube. An all-over patterned wall covering is the best choice for uneven or awkwardly angled walls. As a change from standard wallpaper, paste up a collection of photographs and attractive labels – even newspaper or wrapping paper would work well. You must, however, treat any covering of this sort with a spray-on sealant to protect it from dirt and moisture.

If you use this kind of striking treatment, keep the fixtures plain and add a mirror and a bit of greenery to give the final touches to a completely individual room.

Planning the bathroom

The bathroom should be a place in which you enjoy spending time. If the one in your home is drab and unwelcoming because of poorly designed fittings, inadequate heating and lighting and uninspired decorations, there is a lot you can do to improve it without involving yourself in too much expense. This new series will give you ideas on how to plan from scratch or alter or extend your existing facilities, from the major fittings to the smallest accessories, bearing in mind the space you have available – and what your budget will allow.

All too often the bathroom is the coldest and bleakest room in the home. With a little thought and a minimal cash outlay, you can transform it into the comfortable and efficient place it should be. You may qualify for a local authority grant to bring your facilities up to modern standards but this grant is awarded at the council's discretion and usually covers essential work only. Before planning too far, check that any major plumbing or structural alterations comply with current building regulations.

First consider the number of people who will be using the room, their ages and their needs. If you have space for only one bathroom, try to stretch its capacity by adding a separate shower or an extra wash-basin to ease the morning rush when everyone wants to use the facilities at the same time. Remember that basic fixtures are costly so it is worth investing a lot of time and thought in finding the most suitable ones for your way of life. Visit bathroom showrooms and study manufacturers' catalogues. It could be, for instance, that by using a corner bath instead of a long one, you have room for something extra like a bidet.

Plain fittings give you plenty of scope to introduce a new colour scheme – or to change the existing one without much extra expense. Here the decoration has been kept simple, highlighting the lush greenery in the foreground

Drawing a plan

As described earlier in our kitchen planning section, draw a scale plan of the room so you see clearly where any new appliances can be fitted in. Mark in waste and water pipes and allow for doors, windows or cupboards which open into the room. Use pieces of card to represent each existing piece of equipment as well as any you intend to buy, and move them around until you find a workable layout. You could make more space by rehanging the door so it opens outwards or slides. Remember that careful planning is just as important for a large bathroom as it is for a small one; you do not want to end up wasting space unnecessarily by placing fittings too far apart.

Position of fittings

When planning a new bathroom from scratch, you will have to consider whether to include the WC in the main area or install it separately next door or elsewhere. There are points in favour of each arrangement and you should consider which is best suited to your needs. A separate WC is a considerable advantage if you have a large household but if only one or two people are to use it, you can save a good deal of space by putting all the fittings together in one room.

When you are working within a tight budget, keep your fittings close to the cold and hot water supply and to the existing waste outlet so they will connect to the drainage system without long runs of pipes. If, however, you can afford the expense involved in concealing additional pipework, you will have fewer restrictions on the position of the fittings as you can cover unsightly plumbing with a false wall, wood panels or cladding to give easy access for maintenance and repairs. If you decide to do this, try setting odd accessories like the medicine cabinet, soap-dish and toilet paper holder into the wall to give your bathroom a neat, uncluttered look.

Bear in mind that each fitting must have enough surrounding space for it to be used comfortably and easily. Allow 1100 × 700mm (43 × 28in) alongside baths and 2200mm (86in) headroom. Basins should have 200mm (8in) on either side and 700mm (28in) in front. WCs and bidets need 200mm (8in) either side and 600mm (24in) in front. For showers enclosed on three sides allow 900 × 700mm (35 × 28in) alongside and for unenclosed showers 900 × 400mm (35 × 16in).

It may seem as if you need an enormous amount of space to accommodate these appliances, but as only one or two of them are likely to be used at the same time, the activity areas can – and should – overlap.

Large or awkward fittings Before contemplating any new purchases, check you will have enough room to manoeuvre large or awkwardly shaped items into place. For instance, an extra long bath may fit perfectly into the upstairs bathroom, but will it go up the stairs and through the door? The same applies to rigid plastic shower cabinets.

Making space

If your bathroom is not big enough to take any more fittings no matter how carefully you arrange them, you may think it worthwhile to sacrifice a small bedroom or partition off a large one to create a completely new bathroom. A large cupboard could even become an extra WC. Adding a shower cubicle or even a wash-basin in one or more of the

Above These compact modular units are fitted to make the most of the existing space. The WC, bidet and plumbing connections are concealed under a clear run of laminate seating.

Below This carefully planned bathroom layout allows the minimum amount of space around each of the major fittings; no space is wasted because the activity areas have been arranged to overlap

Bathroom layout allowing optimum space around fittings

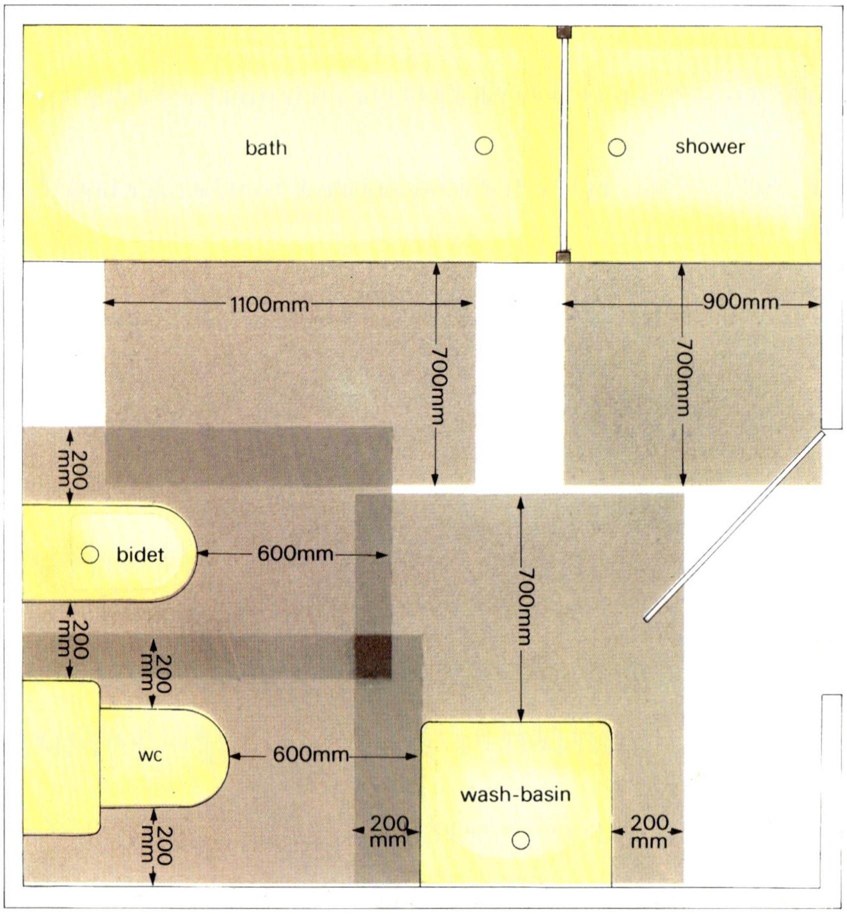

bedrooms would relieve a great deal of pressure on a single, communal bathroom.

Rules and regulations

Check with your local council about current rules and regulations regarding bathrooms and WCs. In Britain, for instance, a window is not required in a bathroom or separate WC as long as there is an extractor fan and duct connected to the outside, so you may be able to find room for a shower or WC on a landing or under the stairs. A bathroom containing a WC, or a WC in a room of its own, can lead off a room used only as a bedroom or dressing room, but it must not open directly into a kitchen, living or dining room. If the only bathroom leads off a bedroom, it must have another entrance not through the bedroom.

Colour and design

You will find a large range of fittings to choose from but think twice before selecting exotic colours or exaggerated shapes; you could tire of them in a very short time. With simple, less costly white fixtures you can introduce a bold colour scheme with paint, wallpaper and fabric to make your bathroom distinctive. You can afford to be adventurous in decorating it as you do not spend that much time there and can use a colour scheme which might be overpowering if you had to look at it all day.

One or two rolls of wallpaper are usually enough to decorate the room even if you decide to do the ceiling as well on the grounds that so much time is spent looking up at it. If the wallpaper is not a vinyl or wipe-clean one, treat it with special sealer to make it water-resistant. Hang pictures on the wall and keep indoor plants on shelves as many of them thrive in a steamy atmosphere.

Mirrors or mirror tiles make a small bathroom look bigger. Use an all-over pattern or the same colour for walls, ceiling, flooring and curtaining to integrate the room. Extend the floor covering up the side of a boxed-in bath to make the total area seem much larger or repeat the vinyl or wallpaper on the bath panel, protecting it with transparent self-adhesive PVC sheeting.

Don't assume that everything in the bathroom has to be basic and clinical; if you have enough space, add an interesting piece of wood or cane furniture, or a small upholstered chair. With a bit of ingenuity and style you can turn a utilitarian room into something quite special and stamped with your own taste.

Remove that clinical feeling from your bathroom by using natural materials such as wood or rush; and choose curtains and wallpaper which incorporate the colour scheme of your fittings

WCs and bidets

Although there are different basic types of WC and bidet to choose from, most people give these important pieces of bathroom equipment very little consideration – apart from making sure they match the rest of the sanitary fittings. And despite the fact that local authorities give grants for improving sanitation in the home, some families still have to use outside WCs.

The WC

This fitting, as with wash-basins, is usually made from vitreous china, although fireclay, glazed earthenware or plastic is used for the cistern.

Design of the WC

Old-fashioned WCs have a very high cistern supported on brackets and connected to the pan with a long, unsightly pipe and operated by a pull-handle and chain. Most modern WCs, however, have the cistern and pan close together and one style of fitting, called close-coupled, has them joined neatly together in one unit with the cistern slightly lower than that of the standard low-level WC. This type costs a little more, but is worth installing if you want to place the WC under a window.

The size of the cistern used to be dictated by the vast quantity of flushing water insisted on by local authorities. Since the regulations have been eased, smaller slimline plastic cisterns are available with a very narrow projection, the smallest one measuring only 114mm (4½in) from front to back. This type is essential for very restricted areas as the recommended space around WCs is 200mm (8in) on either side and 600mm (24in) minimum in front. If the WC is near the door, make sure there is room for the door to swing well clear of it. The slimline cistern is also useful because it can be substituted for the old high-level one without the lavatory pan having to be moved forward, which would be necessary with a more projecting cistern.

If you want to use the cistern as an extra storage shelf, choose a model with a flat top; otherwise you risk your toiletries dropping into the pan when the lid is open. (For the same reason it is inadvisable to hang a wall cabinet immediately above the WC.)

Apart from the type of cistern – and the close-coupled all-in-one suite – you can choose from floor-standing WC pans, wall-hung ones cantilevered out from the wall or back-to-wall models which contain all the service connections on one easy-to-clean unit. The wall-hung ones leave the floor clear for easy cleaning and make the room look larger. But before choosing this type, make sure you have a really strong supporting wall behind it and be prepared to accept a slightly more complicated plumbing system (more prone to blockage) than would be necessary for a free-standing (floor) unit.

Where you wish to conceal the cistern behind a false wall, you must allow for access panels so repairs can easily be made. If the cistern is concealed in an internal partition wall, between the bathroom/WC and corridor for example, it may be convenient to place access panels on the corridor side of the wall.

WC pans are now being made lower with the seat angled gently backwards; this is to encourage a

Above Choose a close-coupled WC and matching bidet for a neat co-ordinated look in your bathroom
Right Two types of waste outlet – the 'S' and 'P' trap

slightly squatting position which is now believed by medical authorities to be healthier and more natural. Unfortunately this style is not ideal for the old or handicapped, but special grip frames or aids are available to put around the fitting.

Seats and lids The disappearance of the old wood lavatory seat – especially the old-fashioned throne type WC chair with pull-up handle to one side – is mourned by many people. But it was not very hygienic or particularly easy to keep clean. Seats and lids can be bought separately from the pan, so you can choose exactly the type you want. If you need to stand on the lid (to make adjustments to a high-level cistern for example), make sure you buy a strong model. Plastic or nylon ones are available in a wide choice of colours; more expensive wood ones can be made to order. For the really self-indulgent there are heated seats which operate when the lid is lifted.

The latest designs include specially shaped, undulating lids to make a comfortable seat if you use the WC as a stool at children's bathtime. When open, the lid will also fit your back well while you are sitting on the seat, which is again designed to fit the contours of your body. This style is also suitable for small children, who sometimes end up slipping into the pan when using the standard shaped seat.

Mechanism of the WC

There are two basic types of flushing action – wash-down and siphonic. Wash-down types are less costly than siphonic ones but are much noisier and not always efficient, since they rely on the force and volume of water flowing into the bowl to clear it. You can fit a silencer in your cistern to lessen the noise of the refilling but check first with your local

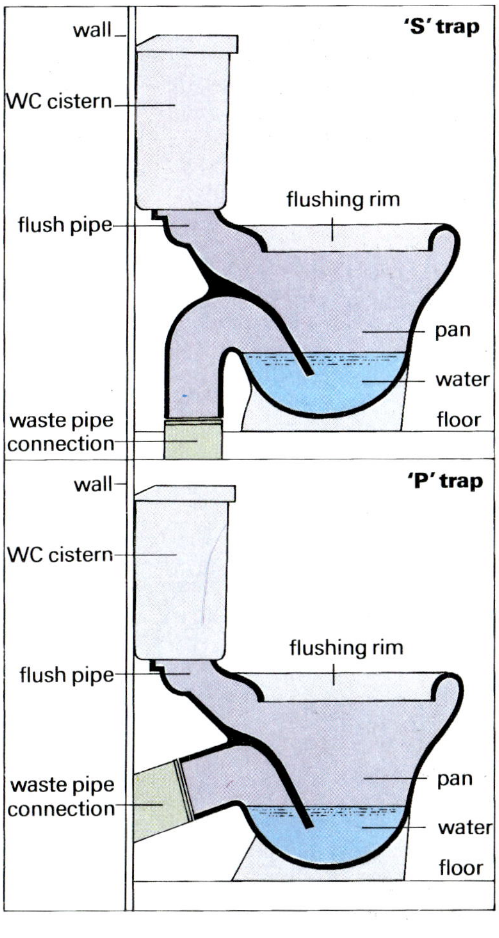

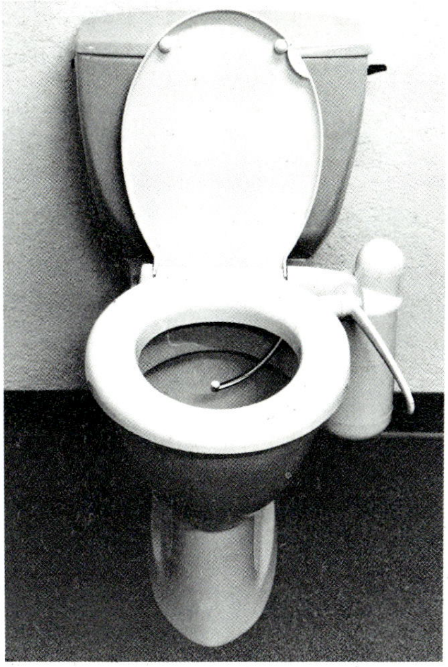

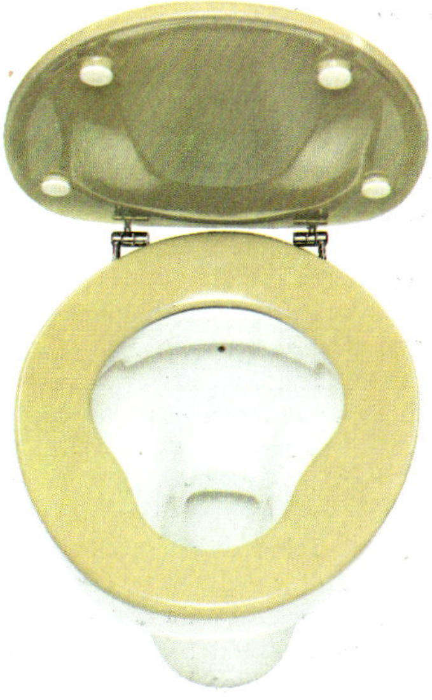

Left Low-level cistern with short unobtrusive pipe to pan
Below left Solid, back-to-wall WC to remove that awkward cleaning area
Below Luxury bidet with central ascending spray
Bottom left Bidet spray attachment to fit the WC
Bottom Specially moulded WC seat to give extra support and comfort

water board that they permit this. With the single trap siphonic type the contents of the pan are sucked into the drain as well as being rinsed away by a flow of water from jets under the rim. This is less noisy than the wash-down type, but the improved double trap siphonic one is the most efficient and quiet model.

There is also a choice when you come to consider the flush mechanism. The old-fashioned pull chain was simple, but often relied on a particular kind of action known only to those who used it regularly. Newer 'door handle' types are also liable to be temperamental. The push-pull button is popular, but if situated at the top of the cistern (as opposed to the side or front positioning of lever types) is not always within reach of small children. Some versions are poorly designed in that they pinch your hand when operated. If possible, try out the various mechanisms if they are fitted to suites in showrooms or builder's merchants. The most hygienic type of mechanism is the floor pedal, where there is no contact between the hand and flush control. But this may not be practical to fit since the mechanism has to be fixed into the floor.

Top Wall-hung WCs and bidets keep the floor area clear and make cleaning much easier

Above This new range of concealed bathroom fittings includes an unusual bidet which you sit on facing into the room rather than straddle facing the wall

Waste outlet The soil pipe waste outlet has a trap or 'U' bend to prevent waste returning through the pipe into the pan. The outlet is either vertical, running into the floor and known as an 'S' trap, or horizontal, running into the wall and known as a 'P' trap. The latter can be angled either right or left to help installation or save space.

The Bidet

Until quite recently the bidet was just an object of curiosity for people staying in continental hotels. Originally designed for intimate hygiene, its popularity is growing as more people realize what a useful fitting it is. The elderly or handicapped, who may have difficulty getting in and out of a bath or are unwilling to use a shower cabinet with its sometimes complicated water controls, would find bidets easy to use. They could be ideal for mothers bathing their babies, since they are halfway in height between a wash-basin and a tub. And, of course, they are very economical in the amount of hot water used. Useful for washing feet, they can also be handy for rinsing small articles of clothing.

Most modern bathroom ranges include a bidet, so you should have little trouble finding one to match or blend with your existing equipment if you are planning to add a bidet to your present bathroom facilities. They are available in the same materials as WCs – vitreous china, fireclay, glazed earthenware or plastic.

Design and mechanism

You must allow the same area for a bidet as the WC and, as with the WC, it can stand on the floor or hang from the wall supported by brackets. The plumbing arrangements are quite straightforward, since the bidet needs only a hot and cold water supply and a waste outlet similar to that for a wash-basin.

In its simplest form a bidet is really a very low basin, slightly altered in shape. It has hot and cold (or mixer) taps to fill the bowl – known as 'over-rim' supply – and a waste plug and chain. More sophisticated models have heated water warming the bowl as it fills and rinsing it afterwards; this type often includes a 'pop-up' waste controlled from between the taps. The luxury models have an ascending spray selector so water comes up from the middle of the bowl like a small fountain. These are more costly, however, and pose extra installation problems since most authorities insist bidets have their own supply pipes direct from the cold water storage cistern, which must be at least 2750mm (or 9ft) above the bidet. This is to prevent any dirty water siphoning back through the spray into the supply pipes.

If you do not have enough room to install a bidet in your bathroom, you can buy a portable plastic unit that fits on top of the WC. You fill it with warm water from the basin or bath and empty it by pulling out a plug, just as you would with a basin. This inexpensive unit is ideal as a baby bath, particularly when travelling.

A lever-operated fitting, which is mounted on an existing WC and includes a water heater and sprinkler, is also available. This device is costly, but if you do not have the floor space and you want the next best thing to a bidet, you may consider it a worthwhile investment.

Baths and Showers

Acrylic baths are lighter than metal ones and come in a variety of shapes. This generous oval fitting has a good size surround for storage and allows for end or corner tap fittings

Whether you decide to install either a bath or a shower, or you want to fit a shower over a bath or have both in the bathroom but placed separately, it is well worth checking on the many variations of design and shape and the different materials and finishes used.

The bath

Cast iron is the traditional material used for bath tubs; although heavy and expensive, baths made of this are very solid and hard-wearing. The surface is finished in porcelain to make it smooth, resistant to abrasion and easy to clean. If you move into a house or flat which has a cast iron bath, think twice before getting rid of it. Provided it is in reasonable condition, you will get a lot of wear out of it, apart from which you may have problems trying to disconnect the plumbing if you do decide to dispose of the bath.

Steel Most baths are now made from pressed steel sheet, cut and heat-formed into shape and coated with a vitreous enamel surface of fused-on ground glass. This provides a high gloss finish which is scratch-resistant and durable. Steel baths are generally the least expensive, although their cost varies according to the thickness of the steel. They are also lighter than cast iron baths, but the range of colours and shapes is more limited.

Plastic Baths made from acrylic and glass reinforced plastic are extremely malleable and can be formed into a variety of shapes. Because they are not rigid, plastic baths are supplied with a firm steel cradle and sometimes have a chipboard panel underneath to give them support. They tend to shift slightly when you get in and out – which can make them a potential hazard if you should stand up to use an overhead shower.

Plastic bath surfaces are smooth and warm to the touch, but you must not use an abrasive cleaner or you may remove the finish and make the tub difficult to clean. Some scratches and chips can be made good with metal polish. You must also remember not to smoke in or near this type of bath because a burn will damage the surface.

Sizes and styles

The standard bath is approximately 1700mm long, 710mm wide and 560mm deep (or 66 × 28 × 22in). If you have a small bathroom, you can buy rectangular tubs as short as 1500mm (or 60in). Even if you have enough space for a standard bath, you may decide on a small one if you like sitting up and reading in the bath without slipping. You may decide you want space for a tiled area at the non-tap end of the bath to keep shampoo, sponges, soap, loofahs and other washing equipment. And a bath pillow resting against this sort of ledge will provide a more comfortable position than against a bath rim and an end wall.

If you have enough space, plenty of hot water available and a tendency to stretch out, you can get tubs as long as 1850mm (73in). If space is a problem, consider moving the other fittings to accommodate a larger bath or choose a small corner model which is shorter than the shortest rectangular bath but still provides a regular-size oval tub.

Elbow room If you want a shower fitted with your bath, choose a tub wider than standard to provide enough elbow room. This is particularly important if you fit a rigid glass or plastic panel instead of a flexible shower curtain. Make sure the bottom of the bath is flat and safe enough to stand on, especially if the tub is to be used by the elderly, the handicapped or the very young. Grip handles at each side are an added advantage here – as is a moulded non-slip base, although this can become uncomfortable if you like a long soak. One slightly dropped side also makes it easier to get in and out of the tub. There may be advantages in having taps at the side or at a corner instead of at the front or toe end. There are models without tap holes (acrylic baths are often made this way) so you can plumb directly into the wall, leaving the bath rim clear.

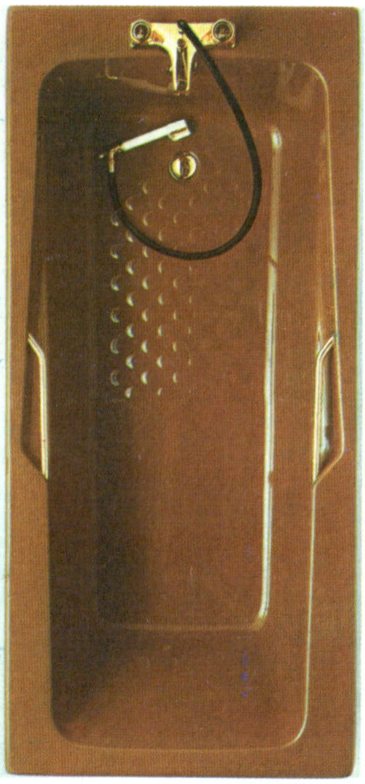

Above A moulded non-slip base and firm handles add safety to the bath
Below This luxury tub with a useful seat and large soap shelf can be installed above the floor or recessed into it
Below centre Large enough for two, this elliptical bath can also be recessed or installed above floor level
Below right This oriental style tub takes up little floor space but is deep enough so you can soak your shoulders. It may be recessed, semi-recessed or fitted above floor level

Left An ingenious corner model with a full size tub, even though it is shorter than a conventional rectangular fitting
Below If your cold water cistern is too low to give enough pressure for a normal shower fitting, install a special 'booster' unit

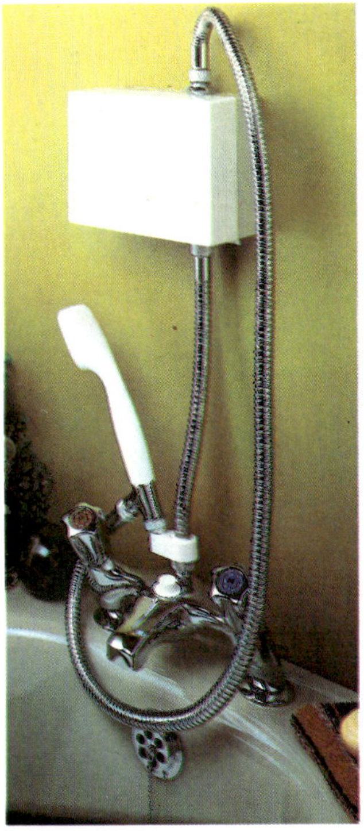

Bath panels

Modern baths are designed to be built-in and some come supplied with matching panels. Standard panels are available from builders' merchants or you can make your own from hardboard or plywood and cover them with tiles, cork, wallpaper or carpet to blend in with the rest of the room.

Luxury tubs

For sheer luxury you can choose from circular, triangular, square, high-backed, kidney-shaped and sunken tubs in unusual dark colours or with gold borders and painted flowers. One unusual model worth mentioning is a deep, sunken fitting which takes up little more floor space than a large shower. It has a built-in seat and a hand shower so you can soap and rinse yourself clean before filling the tub with hot water up to your shoulders for a relaxing soak.

The shower

If you have to choose between a bath and a shower remember showers save space, hot water and time. They are also considered to be more hygienic because you are not sitting in a tub full of dirty water.

Whether you are installing a shower fitting over a bath or in a separate cubicle, your first consideration must be the amount of pressure or head provided. There must be at least 1000mm (39in) between the draw-off point on the cold water cistern and the shower, although some mixer tap units need at least a 1500mm (or 60in) head to work properly.

Make sure the shower head is movable, that it can be adjusted to a height suitable for anyone to use and that it leaves both hands free.

The walls around the bath must be waterproof and you can fix either a flexible plastic curtain on a rail or a rigid glass or plastic panel to keep the rest of the bathroom dry.

If you want a separate shower in another part of the bathroom, you can either have fitted a base

Above Thermostatic controls are a safety feature especially valuable with children or the elderly
Top centre A flexible shower hose can be fitted into wall brackets at varying heights to suit every member of the family
Top right This neat prefabricated cubicle is ideal when you want to install an extra shower unit outside the bathroom.
Above right A fixed shower head with all the necessary plumbing concealed behind a tiled wall
Far right This extra deep shower tray doubles as a sit-down tub – and an ideal bath for children

tray and door panels (or curtains) or buy a prefabricated cubicle.

Shower trays are available in vitreous china, vitreous-enamelled pressed steel, glazed clay, acrylic or glass reinforced plastic. Prefabricated units come complete – including a seat in some cases – but they are often bulky and difficult to integrate in an existing bathroom. Their most useful purpose is to provide extra showering facilities elsewhere in the home – in a bedroom, for example, or a downstairs cloakroom.

Shower taps

There are several bath/shower taps on the market. These include ones that automatically return to the bath setting, to avoid a soaking when you next run a bath because you had forgotten to switch the tap back after your last shower. A thermostatically controlled mixer valve is the ideal arrangement, especially where there are invalids or young children in the family who could otherwise scald themselves. There are single-control hand-operated mixers which adjust the water temperature and dual-control hand-operated ones for independent temperature and pressure control to give you the flow of water you want.

If your hot water system is unsuitable for a normal shower fitting, the instantaneous electric heater type is a reasonable alternative. You will have to accept that the maximum flow of hot water is only just over half that of a mixer shower because the water is heated as you use it. This system costs more but it is still cheaper than taking a bath since you use much less water.

Wash-basins

Wash-basins are very much part of the basic equipment in any bathroom. The variations in design give plenty of scope for you to use your imagination to choose the one that looks well and fits where you want it – on the floor, on the wall or in a corner. Plumbing is another important consideration, so don't be carried away with a design that is not practical.

A basin in a busy family bathroom has to serve more people and purposes than one in a bedroom or in an additional WC/cloakroom. So when it comes to buying a new basin it is worth spending some time considering not only how many people will be using it, but also all the different uses to which it will be put.

Apart from size, shape and fixing, you must decide what material you prefer. Most basins are of smooth, hard vitreous china, although glazed earthenware, glazed fireclay, plastic, stainless steel and enamelled pressed steel are also used. Acrylic plastic, or glass-reinforced plastic (grp) basins are light and often come in unusual shapes, but are susceptible to cigarette burns and other stains.

If you have enough space you should consider whether it would be worth your while to have two basins in the bathroom. The installation cost of an extra basin will not necessarily be that much more and with several people using a single bathroom – particularly if the bedrooms do not have their own basins – you will be surprised what a difference two basins make in a busy bathroom. You can buy a ceramic fitment combining two bowls, or two individual ones, or set twin bowls into the same countertop. One could be strictly for the adults and the other for the children or, if you prefer, you can keep to a 'his' and 'hers' arrangement with cupboard or shelves for shaving kit and male toiletries close to one basin and for cosmetics and perfumery near the other.

Ideally you should allow a minimum space of 200mm (8in) either side and 700mm (28in) in front of your basin, to avoid hitting your head on the wall in front of you when washing your face or bumping against the wall behind you when you step back. The average height for the top surface of a basin is 800mm (31in), but this will be determined by the height and preference of the users.

Basins are usually fixed in one of three ways: with a pedestal base, directly onto the wall or built into a surrounding countertop.

Pedestal style

Originally designed to hide the ugly U-bend waste trap, the pedestal is not intended to support the basin (which must be attached to the wall with brackets) and has the added disadvantage of dictating at what height your basin is fixed. With a family or household of differing heights you may find that not only is the standard pedestal height inconvenient but that it clutters up the floor and does not, in fact, hide all your pipework.

Wall hung or cantilevered

Be sure you have a solid supporting wall before buying this type and follow the manufacturer's instructions exactly; almost all the problems with these models are due to faulty installation.

Apart from being able to place your hanging brackets at any height, an added advantage here is that the floor is left clear of pipes or pedestal, making it easier to clean as well as giving an impression of space. To conceal the plumbing you must either box it in or install it behind a false wall or projection. If you like the idea of exposed pipes, then it is best to choose the neat stainless steel bottle trap type. All pipework must be accessible for repairs, so your boxing-in must have easy-to-remove inspection panels to allow for this.

Countertop units

These take up more room than the conventional pedestal or wall hung basin but they conceal the plumbing and provide useful storage space around and underneath the basin. You can buy ready-made 'vanity' units (sometimes called Vanitory units).

If you cannot find the size you need, you can make one up or have a top cut to fit your specifications. The manufacturers usually insist on providing the basin for this or cutting the top to fit your actual basin since it is essential that there are no gaps for the water to seep down between the basin and its surround. Ceramic basins, for example, are not uniform in shape, so it is no good specifying the model number; it is the individual basin that has to be fitted.

Some vanity units come with an integral splash-back to avoid leaky joints; otherwise you must be sure to seal the angle between countertop and wall. If you decide on a countertop unit there are several types of basin style and fixings.

Raised lip The basin is set into the surround (usually with a decorative laminate, ceramic tile, slate or marble surface) and the size of the aperture is not critical as the basin settles into it; however any spilt water cannot be mopped up straight into the basin. Depending on shape and size, the whole basin can be set into the surround, or just the two sides and back, leaving the front rim exposed. This last method is useful where the front-to-back space is limited.

Metal trim Some models are set in almost flush with the countertop, with a stainless steel trim covering the join between basin and top. This looks neat, but if the metal trim is not correctly sealed you can have trouble with leaking water.

Built-under With this type the basin is set in under the countertop surface and requires careful installation to ensure a snug fit. The end result is very neat and the basin is less conspicuous than with other countertop types since it appears to be slightly recessed, leaving a totally flat top without projecting surfaces.

All-in-one If the standard widths available suit your layout, a one-piece fireclay or enamelled steel countertop basin including a spacious surround to fit over a cupboard or shelves (or be supported on wall brackets) may be as economical as investing in a more elaborate unit. Some models are available with contrasting coloured surrounds to the basins, which may help to emphasize your chosen colour scheme or add variety.

Top This wall-hung basin is neatly fitted to show the minimum amount of plumbing

Above left A metal flange can be fitted around vanity basins to waterproof the join between edge and countertop

Above Although they do not fit as snugly as other vanity basins, raised lip ones are easy to install

Left If you are recessing a basin into the countertop, make sure it fits accurately to avoid leaks

Top right This all-in-one basin and countertop fitting ensures a continuous leakproof surface

Right With taps set to one side, the risk of bumping your head on the fitments when washing your hair is minimized.

Previous page The column under the pedestal basin is meant to hide the plumbing, not to support the bowl, so wall brackets are vital

Size and style

There is more to choosing a basin than just considering the style and type of fixing: size is all important. Is it for general use only, that is hand and face washing by several people possibly including children who are not too fussy about splashing the water around? Or will someone want to soak, wash or even dye clothes in it, or wash precious china and ornaments? If in a bed-sitter, it will be used for washing dirty dishes as well. Hair-washing presents a whole new requirement – not just that you should clean out the trap regularly to prevent loose hair blocking it, but that it should be of a convenient shape and size. Asymmetrical bowl shapes with the taps at one side are the best for this purpose and a pop-up waste device, or a plug and chain that will not pull out too easily or get entangled with long hair. A pull-out shampoo spray tap fitting on a flexible hose is ideal, but if the basin is sited near the bath shower tap you should be able to use the same fitment.

If your bathroom (or bedroom) space is very constricted, you might need a basin that is narrow from front to back, usually an oval in shape. Alternatively the limited area you have available might call for a squarer, less wide model.

There are several designs for really small spaces such as WC/cloakrooms or tiny bedrooms. The most space-saving design is a corner fitting model (the actual basin being more of an oval shape set across the corner) or a longer, but narrower oval,

Above This semi-recessed upright basin is ideal in a separate WC where space is at a premium

Below Part of a complete range of bathroom fittings, this basin features a delicate floral design

Below right Available in a large range of colours, this small shell-shaped basin is suitable for a bedroom or downstairs cloakroom

Opposite Vanity basin plumbed into an old cupboard for a pretty effect

or a new style rectangular fitting that has to be recessed into a false wall. It is not unlike a large wall-fitted soap tray but with taps set into the wall at one side.

If you choose one of the highly decorative miniature basins, make sure it takes standard taps otherwise you could find yourself spending a great deal of money for special fittings, since these models are designed for the luxury market where budgets are unlimited.

As for style and shape (apart from size), there are models to suit every taste. Some have deep recesses for soap, defined areas for tooth mugs and plenty of surface for bathroom toiletries; others sacrifice utility for a streamlined look and you may find your soap slithering back into the basin for lack of a deep enough recess, or nowhere to stand a tumbler or a shampoo bottle. The curve of the bowl itself is significant, the flatter the bottom the more water it holds – and needs – for a full basin for washing.

The waste outlet is sometimes unsightly, and you may prefer the models that hide this aperture at the inside front of the bowl instead of the usual, visible placing at the inside back.

The final considerations are colour, outline and surface pattern. Although some models come complete with taps (especially in the case of a ready-made vanity unit), on the whole you are able to choose the type of tap you want. The choice for basins is described below.

Dark colours are decidedly dramatic but you will probably want to order a whole new matching suite – to include bath, basin and WC, and bidet if you want one. Shell-shaped basins are very pretty; and if you like marble effects or flower or fish designs, there are several patterns from which to choose. But remember, with luck basins should last a lifetime; if you buy a colour, shape or pattern you find you do not like after a few months, you will be stuck with it for a long time.

Taps and fittings

Before deciding on a basin it is as well to look at the choice in taps, since not all basins have the tap holes in the right place or can accommodate some of the more elaborate fittings. Most people find the screw turn tap more convenient than the press-down type, as with the latter you have to keep pressure on the tap for the water to run. On the other hand, this press-down type is economical in the use of hot water – an advantage to be considered where children are concerned.

If you want wall-mounted taps, be sure they have sufficient reach to flow conveniently into the basin without undue splashing. Some basins come without any tap holes (specifically for use with wall-mounted taps), or you can stop up any existing apertures with special ceramic or metal plates.

Some mixer fittings incorporate a pop-up waste control which eliminates the conventional plug and chain, allowing the basin to be emptied by pressing a knob between the two tap heads. These, however, are not suitable for wall mounting.

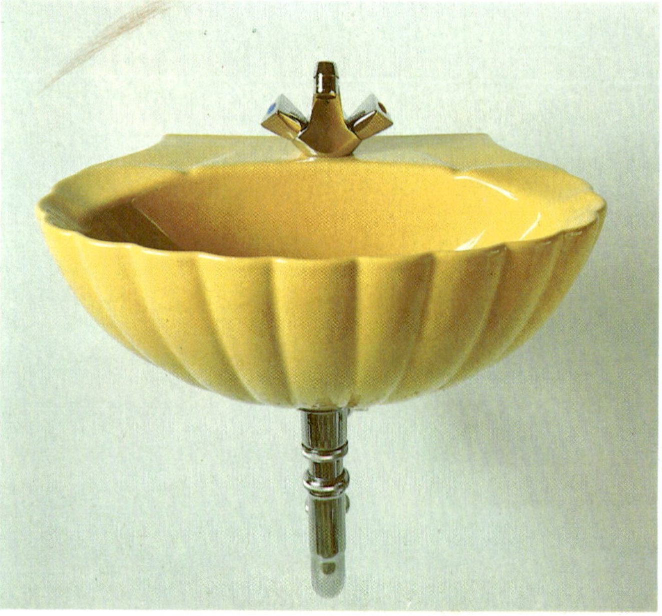

Choosing taps and accessories

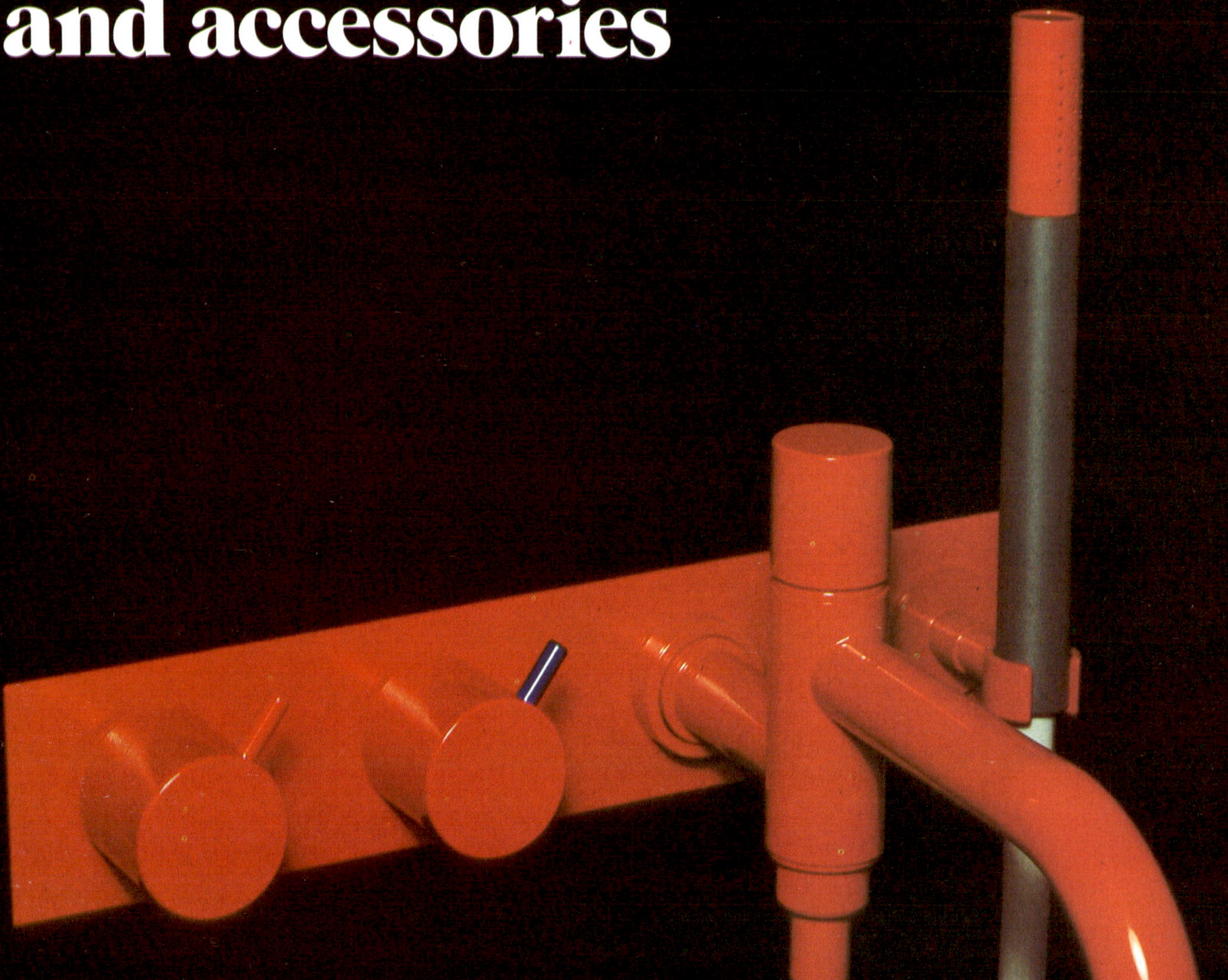

There are many small but often vital pieces of equipment which are not only functional but can help complement the overall appearance of your bathroom. These include a whole range of taps and other accessories, so before choosing make sure they are easy to operate and do the job you want – and that they blend in with the other fitments or decorations in the room.

Types of tap

Most manufacturers of bathroom fittings produce their own range of taps and it is often easier and less costly to choose these from the same range as your other fittings.

The first consideration is whether you want individual or mixer taps; individual ones are less expensive, but you might find it worthwhile paying a little extra for a mixer unit which means you can wash your hands or hair with exactly the temperature of water you want. Many bath mixers incorporate a shower head on a flexible hose which you can hang on a wall and stand underneath – or hold in your hand.

Though most baths, basins and bidets are made with holes for tap fittings, you can buy designs without, which enable you to fix bib taps straight from the wall to give you a clear washing area. There is also a one piece (monobloc) mixer which takes up far less space than the conventional three-piece design. One model has, under the spout, a single central handle which adjusts the temperature and controls the flow of water. Another has its control on the spout; this is called a Supatap.

Where there are young people in the home, choose thermostatically controlled taps to prevent scalding and those designed with an extra inner ring to minimize splashing.

Hospital-type handles which have an elbow-operated lever action are simple to work, but may not be installed on domestic taps without special permission from the local water authority. This is usually only given in the case of elderly or handicapped people, who would have difficulty gripping conventional controls.

The finish of the tap is also important. Most have a chrome finish over a brass base, but gold-plated ones are widely available if you are prepared to pay extra, and a hand-painted ceramic set is now being made to match a specific range of ceramic tiles. The head of the tap is usually made from the same material as the body, although you can buy taps with plastic tops. Try out the tap handle first, either by using a friend's tap or checking in the showroom, to make sure it is comfortable to hold and easy to turn – even when your hands are wet and soapy.

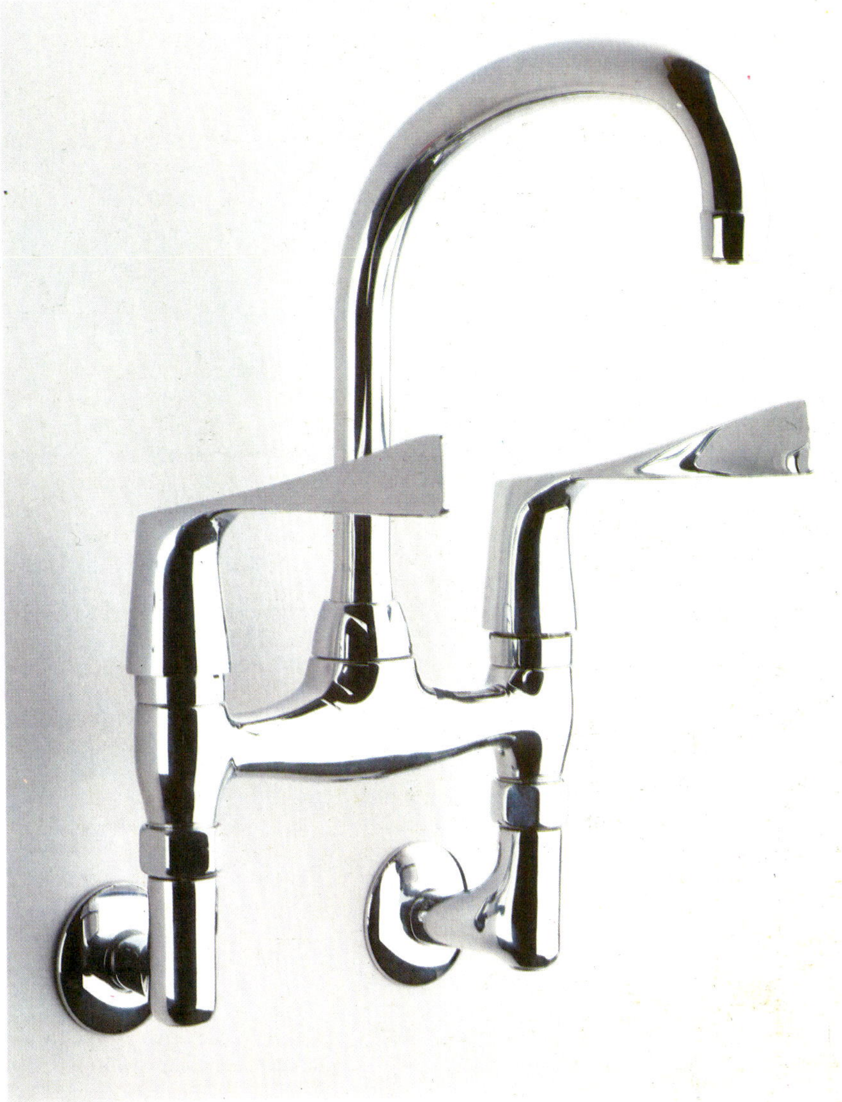

Left This striking bath/shower mixer is made from brass and has a stoved epoxy finish, available in a wide range of colours to complement any bathroom (Bath Studio)
Far left A space-saving, single-control tap which not only adjusts the temperature but also regulates the flow for economic use of water (Barking-Grohe)
Above Lever-operated taps are easy to control, but check with your local water authority whether you can fit them for normal domestic use (Barking-Grohe)
Right The raised nozzles on this set of separate taps make cleaning the basin – and the taps – easier (Barking-Grohe)

Plugs and waste units

To save you fishing around in dirty water to pull out the plug, some mixers have pop-up waste units operated from a knob between the taps or a weighted chain which retracts automatically when you pull it towards you. To facilitate rinsing the basin after use, a mixer with a spout that swivels is available.

Most plugs are still made of rubber, although plastic ones are becoming more common. Measure your waste outlet and choose a plug made to fit. The large flat variety which covers all sizes of waste outlets is rarely effective.

Range of accessories

Many different items are constantly in use in the bathroom – including soap, flannels, towels, toothbrushes, shampoo, shaving equipment, mugs, toilet paper, combs and hairbrushes, cosmetics and medicines. If you can store these things neatly, you will avoid cluttering up the room and also prevent items that should be kept dry getting splashed, or bottles being knocked over. It is always a good idea to list all the things you expect to keep in the bathroom and decide where you are going to put them. Have you, for example, got a separate linen cupboard or will your spare towels be kept in the bathroom? If you do not have an airing cupboard, you can pile your towels on an open shelf so their colours brighten the room. Do you want to keep dirty laundry in the bathroom? If you do, you will need a linen basket or you can double up with a stool and linen container combined.

Your fittings will have to be cleaned regularly, so have you got somewhere to keep the cleaning cloths, detergents etc? If you have a counter-top basin, build in a cupboard underneath – or provide a separate unit somewhere else in the room. This space could also be used to keep spare toilet rolls and packs of soap – and your washing powder, if you wash small clothes in the bathroom.

Basic fitments such as soap dishes, toothbrush and mug holders, towel rings, hooks and toilet roll holders will all have to be positioned, if you decide you need them. It is important they are fixed in the most accessible places, near to where they are being used. For example, you will want to reach the toilet paper from a sitting position without rupturing your back and you will not want to walk across to the other side of the room to fetch your toothbrush.

Most of these basic fitments are made of stainless steel, anodized aluminium or sometimes vitreous china – often to match the main fittings. Some are designed to be recessed into a wall and there are manufacturers of ceramics who make them in the same modular units as tiles to be fixed at the same time and in the same way. Anodized aluminium is popular because it will not corrode and is easy to keep clean.

Some of the newest fittings are made from moulded plastic, which allows a great variety of colours and shapes; mirrors, bathracks, shelves – even nail brushes and tissue holders – are designed as part of complete ranges of fittings.

Above left Mixer taps allow you to choose exactly the water temperature you want (Barking-Grohe)
Above centre Ceramic taps are now made to co-ordinate with wall tiles (Elon Tiles)
Above A monobloc mixer leaves the basin surround clear (Barking-Grohe)
Below left This standard wall cabinet has all the important features – lock, mirror and adjustable shelves (Allibert)
Below Some luxury wall cabinets include a striplight and shaver socket (Allibert)
Above right These neat plastic fittings are tough and take your bathroom clutter (Habitat Designs Ltd)
Right A simple range of accessories will keep your bathroom tidy (Habitat Designs Ltd)

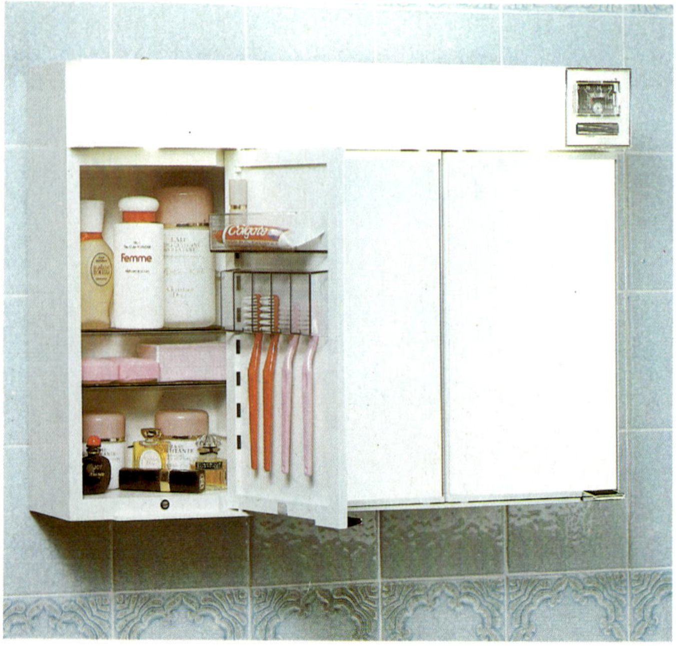

Wall cabinets These are available in several sizes, so you can house all your toiletries, cosmetics and medicines. Laminated units are probably the most practical since they are easy to clean and are not affected by the damp, steamy conditions that often exist in the bathroom. For the same reason glass is sometimes used for shelves. It will not suffer from deterioration and can be wiped easily, but it will show fingermarks, dust and deposits of talcum powder very clearly. Check the unit you buy has shelves of various heights to take all those awkward-shaped bottles and containers. Models are available with racks inside the door and some luxury ones include striplights, shaver sockets and thermometers.

One important feature of the bathroom cabinet is that it either locks or cannot be opened easily, especially if there are young children about. If it is fitted with a lock, you can keep your medicines safely out of reach; at any rate, try to fit it high enough so it is not a temptation.

Mirrors It is a good idea to choose a cabinet with a mirror on the front. Placed above the basin or next to it, it can be used when shaving or putting on cosmetics. Otherwise make sure a mirror is positioned or fixed somewhere accessible. You should always have a mirror long enough for every member of the family to use – so check on the optimum height necessary before fixing. Small portable mirrors with goose necks can be bent to any height and direction you want and you can fix extendible models to the wall. These are fully retractable when not in use.

Mirrors are not only important for the many jobs performed in the bathroom; they can also alter the whole appearance of the room. If you fix a wide mirror along a wall, it can give the effect of doubling the size of the room, which is particularly valuable if your bathroom is very small.

Make sure, when buying a mirror for the bathroom, that it is made out of suitable material; some cheaper ones may contain silvering that is affected by moisture; acrylic mirrors, however, should stand up to a fair amount of steam.

Towel rails Try to allow as much rail space as possible so all the family towels can dry without being bunched up together. Towel rings are attractive, but the towels will not dry so efficiently and it is never easy to get them in and out.

The ideal situation is to have a heated towel rail, but you can fit rails over an existing radiator; this is cheaper and does the same job. Always remember when fitting any towel rail or holder not to put it too near a shower spray or the bath to save dry towels getting splashed.

Hooks These are always handy in the bathroom to hang up your clothes if you are undressing there and not in the bedroom. You may have bathrobes that you also want to keep in the room. Double or multiple hooks are most practical and can be fixed either onto the back of the door or in a convenient position on one of the walls. Again make sure they are out of reach of any splashing.

Electrical fittings

There are several electrical fittings you may decide would be useful – and add to the comfort of your bathroom. There are, however, restrictions on what can be used and the ways in which they may be fitted. These extras include wall and ceiling heaters and shaver sockets, which will be covered later.

Bathroom floor and wall coverings

There is no reason why you should not introduce the same decorating flair to your bathroom as you may do to the rest of the house. Everything you use, however, must be resistant to damp and moisture; since many modern materials incorporate this quality, you will have a wide choice.

On the walls and ceilings

Before you start decorating make sure all your bathroom walls and ceiling are free from damp penetration, otherwise you may ruin your new coverings – even though you may cover the damp for a while. If you choose to paint most of this area, be sure you use a good quality vinyl matt or silk emulsion. Gloss paint is impervious to moisture but shows up every bead of condensation, an important consideration in a room that is subject to considerable changes in temperature.

Ceramic or vinyl tiles Areas around the basin, bath and shower need extra protection and ceramic or vinyl tiles here are ideal. They are waterproof, easy to clean, hard-wearing and come in an enormous range of styles, quality, sizes and price. If you can afford it, and your walls are strong enough, tile the whole room – except for the ceiling, since this can

provide a potential hazard if these heavy tiles ever fall off. Plain tiles are cheaper and also give you more freedom to change your scheme than other more sophisticated patterns. You can make them look less clinical by choosing different shapes than the usual square, such as rectangles or tiny mosaics.

If you do not want to cover the paint or wallpaper with tiles in the 'splash' areas (such as round basins or baths), protect these parts with a glass or perspex panel. If you do, remember to round off the edges to avoid the possibility of getting cut. Small metal tiles, often with their own self-adhesive backing, are available and do the same job as ceramic ones.

Warning Before fixing any tiles, make sure your wall is clean and dry and free from flaking paint or plaster; old tiles make an excellent base as long as they are sound and securely fixed.

Wallpaper Many modern wallpapers are suitable for the bathroom, but always choose one with a vinyl or washable coating. If you are uncertain about the paper you have bought – and if the room is particularly small and steamy – give the paper a protective coat of a special sealer or varnish to make it moisture-resistant and easy to clean. Hang it with a heavy-duty waterproof adhesive containing a fungicidal ingredient to prevent mould forming underneath.

One range of wallpaper has a raised design which looks like ceramic tiling but costs much less. You can scrub it and, because it is soft and warm to the touch, it is less subject to condensation than ceramic tiles. One big advantage is you can fix this material over existing tiles, even in heavy-wear areas such as showers.

Wood panels Wood cladding or panelling is expensive but very warm looking. It is suitable for bathrooms if you seal it with several coats of polyurethane lacquer to keep out moisture. This type of covering is fixed either directly to the wall or on timber battens and has the added advantage of enabling you to hide unsightly pipes and plumbing. You can 'lower' a high ceiling by fixing tongued and grooved cladding horizontally.

Mirror glass Huge pieces of mirror glass will give a luxury look to any bathroom and visually increase the size of the smallest room. But make sure the edges are sealed to prevent moisture damaging the silvering and giving a mottled effect.

Cork tiles These are a good insulator in a chilly bathroom and are pleasantly warm to touch although fairly expensive. They come in a variety of shades and textures and must be sealed.

Laminated panels If your walls are in poor condition you can install specially made moulded panels faced with laminate which give a smooth, hardwearing continuous surface. Before committing yourself to this type of covering, check whether there is enough room to manoeuvre the panels through the door.

Opposite page Contrasting treatments to bring out the best in bathrooms and the WC

Left Cork flooring is not that expensive for small areas and is attractive and warm underfoot

Below left Use a dramatic colour scheme in a small, separate WC

Below right Wood cladding can be used in any shape of bathroom, but make sure your walls are free from damp before putting up the material or it will rot

Below left In this bold scheme, the waterproof tartan paper complements the simple look of plain ceramic floor tiles

Bottom left The tiled effect in this bathroom is achieved with easy-to-clean wallpaper

Below Quarry tiles on the bathroom floor work best in warm climates or where there is underfloor heating

On the floor

Your floor must be smooth, dry, firm and clean before you lay any floor covering. It should also be resistant to damp, since nothing you lay down will be unaffected; even with ceramic tiles damp will seep through the grouting. The join between the floor covering and the wall is particularly vulnerable; if your family do a lot of splashing, it is advisable to fix narrow skirting there.

Plastic flooring Flexible plastic materials such as vinyl are very practical, especially if there are young children about. Vinyl is waterproof and easy to clean, but rather cold underfoot and slippery when wet. This is available in sheet or tile form; water seepage is less likely with vinyl sheet, but tiles are easier to work with and give you more scope with design. For safety and comfort you should use a rubber-backed bath mat with vinyl floor coverings although cushioned vinyl sheeting has a raised design which helps to reduce accidents. Again, plastic floor coverings must be laid on a sound, even surface and stuck down securely especially at the edges, where the smallest amount of water leaking underneath could loosen the material.

Carpet A fitted carpet is a good choice if the floor is not going to be subject to constant soaking. It is cosy and soft and provides a safe non-slip surface, which is particularly suitable for elderly or handicapped people to stand on. Also bottles and jars are much less likely to break when dropped on carpet. Synthetic pile with synthetic backing is preferable to a natural wool carpet because it absorbs less moisture, but the use of a thick bath mat should prevent either getting too wet and being seriously damaged.

Carpet tiles are suitable for bathrooms because they are easier to cut around awkward fittings and you can lift them out to dry if they do get soaked. Because the room is comparatively small, it need not be expensive to carpet. You may even be able to do it with offcuts from other rooms.

Tiles Cork is one of the best choices in terms of looks, warmth and practicality. You can buy easy-to-lay tiles sealed with vinyl – or seal them after they have been laid. It is wise to renew the seal every year or two to keep it waterproof.

Other tiles such as ceramic, quarry or slate are durable and impervious to water; but they are also very hard, chilly to walk on with bare feet and dangerously slippery. They also need a strong solid floor to support them and are only totally satisfactory when combined with an underfloor heating system. A thick bath mat with rubber backing provides an extra precaution against slipping or sliding on a damp floor.

Studded rubber This is becoming increasingly used because it is tough, quiet, safe, easy to clean and totally water-resistant. It is not cheap, but the total cost for a small area will not be that much. It is often used on areas surrounding swimming pools and is available in several gauges and six bright colours, plus black. The thinnest and cheapest gauge rubber will be quite suitable for domestic use and you should have little difficulty finding a colour to blend in with your existing colour scheme. This rubber flooring is sold in metre squares (39in sq) and should be stuck down with an epoxy resin adhesive.

Below Vinyl flooring comes in a wide range of colours and patterns to blend with any scheme

At the window

Ideally all bathroom windows should have a pleasant view and not be overlooked. Unfortunately more often than not they face a brick wall with another window in it. If you want all the light you can get without your neighbours looking in, make sure you have frosted glass in the window.

Blinds These are a good choice because they take up very little space and are easy to operate and maintain. Cotton covered with PVC (polyvinyl chloride) is ideal for a roller blind because it cannot be affected by splashing and is available in a wide range of bright colours and patterns. Venetian and pleated paper blinds can be used, but pinoleum (slatted) or cane blinds are not suitable since you can sometimes see through them.

Curtains Always choose a firm, closely woven fabric that will not shrink in very damp conditions. Hang curtains on an aluminium or plastic track that is not subject to rust.

Warning Remember to decide first whether you want your blinds or curtains to hang within the window recess or outside it. This will partially depend on whether you are using your window sill to store your working equipment, cosmetics and other bathroom accessories, where the blind or curtain would get in the way and possibly knock things over if hung in the recess.

Top left Fitted carpet in the bathroom provides a warm and safe surface
Centre left Studded rubber flooring is costly, but ideal in bathrooms since it is completely waterproof
Bottom left Blinds can be used instead of curtains and have the advantage of being easy to maintain
Below Make sure any material you choose for curtains has a firm weave which will not shrink

Lighting, heating and ventilating your bathroom

Even if you plan your bathroom carefully and choose the ideal fittings, you can still end up with a dark, cold, damp and unpleasant room if you do not pay enough attention to the lighting, heating and ventilation. But if you decide to buy new equipment, remember people are much more vulnerable to serious electric shocks in this room than in any other; so every electrical item must be correctly connected.

Lighting

Because the bathroom is a relatively small area in which a restricted number of activities are undertaken, the lighting arrangements can be fairly simple, but at the same time totally effective, making the room efficient and safe to use. Basically you need general light of some kind, plus a strong working light near the mirror so you can see to put on make up or have a shave. In general diffused lighting is better than any direct source.

Whether your general light comes from a tungsten lamp, fluorescent tube or an adjustable track system, be sure it is totally enclosed with a shield or cowl so it is impossible for anyone with wet hands to touch the metal part of the lamp itself. If your ceiling is low, choose a flat or recessed fitting which will not get in the way. The costliest and most luxurious general light source is an illuminated ceiling, made by concealing striplights behind panels of frosted glass.

Ideally, the working light should come from either side of the mirror; if that is not feasible, a strip across the top is the next best thing. The traditional theatre dressing room arrangement of bulbs all round the mirror is certainly effective,

Below left Choose a mirror with a diffused light surround for the most efficient illumination

Bottom left A strong striplight above the mirror should be bright enough for most needs

Below This dramatic arrangement gives an intense light, although some might find it excessive

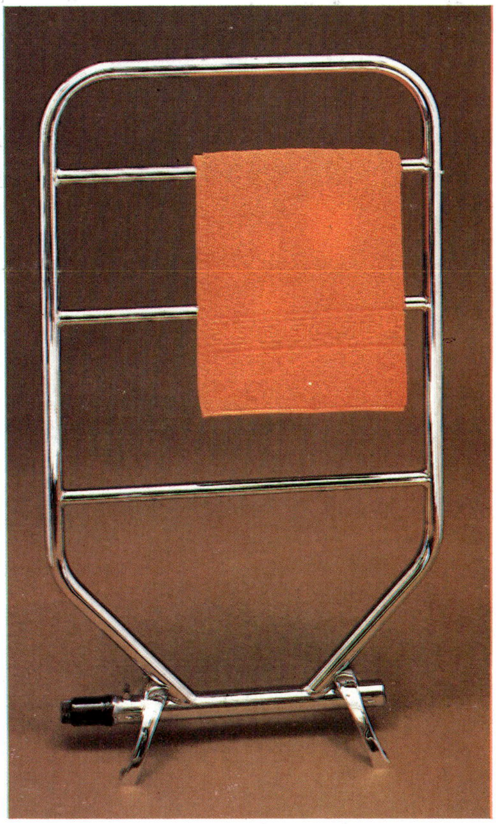

Above Striplights along both sides of the mirror give a balanced source of light
Above right If you have room for it, a large heated rail will provide a constant supply of warm, dry towels
Below Combined light/heater units are adequate in small bathrooms or WCs
Below right This wall-mounted light/fan heater with thermostatic control will keep your bathroom at a constant temperature

but you may find so much illumination shows up more than you really want to see. Many bathroom cabinets come complete with striplights – along the top, down each side, or both. The important thing is that the light is directed at the person in front of the mirror rather than at the mirror itself. If you cannot look directly at the fitting, or if you see an after-image when you look away, there is too much glare; use a diffusing bulb or panel, or bounce the light off a wall.

If you are in the habit of reading in the bath, you may need an additional fixture here, but always make sure it is completely out of reach of wet hands.

The most suitable bathroom light fitments are made of plastic, glass or aluminium, since some types of metal corrode in a constantly damp and steamy atmosphere. All switches should be controlled with a pull cord or from a switch located outside the room.

Heating

There still seems to be a puritan prejudice against warming the bathroom properly, even though it is not expensive to fit an effective heater; most have a fairly low running cost since they heat such a small area. Constant, general warmth in this room not only makes it more pleasant to use, but also keeps the fittings at a comfortable temperature and helps to prevent damp and condensation.

The ideal set-up is a central heating radiator, warm air grille or underfloor heating system. If

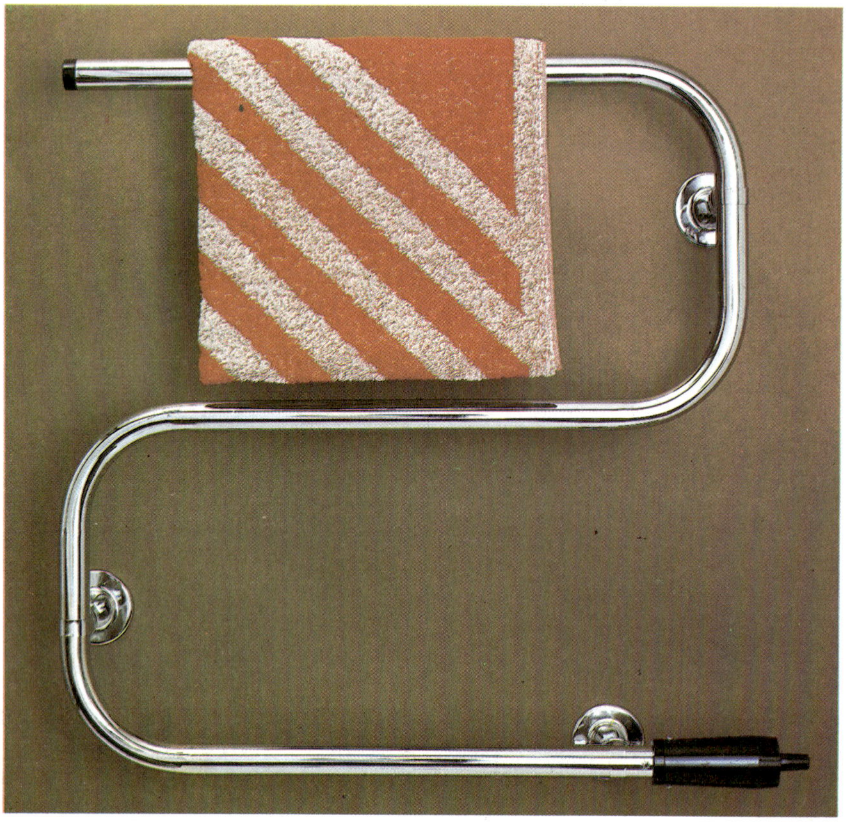

Above Heated towel rails which can be fixed on the wall are ideal in restricted areas
Below The simplest way to ventilate a bathroom is with a window-mounted self-actuating fan
Below right A ventilator mounted on the wall is particularly efficient since it can be fixed in exactly the right position

your bathroom is small, you might get away with an efficient heated towel rail on its own, but in this case it would be wise to use the traditional method of connecting it to the hot water system rather than the central heating so it can operate all year round. This type can, of course, be turned off when you do not need it. If you want an independently operated electric towel rail, you can choose one which is mounted on the wall or have a floor standing one. Oil-filled radiators with thermostatic controls are costly to buy, but fairly economical to run because of the size of the room involved.

Infra-red radiant heaters will heat only a small area effectively; if you are installing this type, make sure it is fitted high on the wall and well away from curtains and towels, but that the pull cord hangs down far enough for the shortest family member to reach. Some models fit onto the ceiling, particularly those that combine a heater and lighting; these will help to warm a small room, but you may find you need another heat source to make it really comfortable.

For safety reasons, make sure all gas appliances have a balanced flue and do not, under any circumstances, take a portable electric fire into the bathroom – or, for that matter, any portable electrical appliance other than a shaver, which can be operated if you have an isolated shaver socket specially for use in bathrooms.

Ventilation

In a lot of old houses that have not been modernized there is little need to supply any kind of ventilation artificially – badly fitting doors and windows and sometimes chimney flues do this job ably. Newer and modernized homes are usually better heated and insulated, keeping warm air inside; at the same time stale air will hang about and this means using artificial methods to get rid of it.

Moisture and odour are two very good reasons for efficient ventilation in the bathroom. Constant dampness can seriously damage electrical fittings, wallpaper, mirrors and curtains; this happens most frequently when there is no permanent source of heat in the room. Condensation problems increase with the amount a bathroom is used; if you have a large family, you will need more air changes per hour than a smaller family – a minimum of 15 to 20. A shower increases humidity, so if you have one make doubly sure your ventilation facilities are adequate.

Most people let fresh air into the bathroom by opening a window, but this method is rarely satisfactory since cold draughts make the room uncomfortable to use and actually increase condensation because of the contrast of cold and warm air. The simplest mechanical ventilator is a plastic self-actuating fan fixed in a window pane, a job that does not involve any wiring.

The most efficient, though more expensive to buy, is an electric extractor fan which is operated by its own switch or connected to a door-operated switch or to the light switch so it comes on when you enter the room or turn on the light. If you have an internal bathroom (with no window) building regulations not only insist you fix this type of ventilation, but also stipulate the size of fan you must have and the type of duct to the outside. You may get away with a smaller model than you think since internal rooms are naturally warmer and therefore less subject to condensation than those on an outside wall. You can install an extractor of this type in a non-opening window, but a wall-fitted model is better because it allows you to position the fitting for maximum efficiency – high on the wall and away from doors and open windows.

This kind of mechanical ventilation can be very noisy, but the problem can be reduced if you position the fan as far away from the vertical part of the duct as possible and install an anti-vibration mounting.

The Bathroom: Top Designers' Tips

1. If you have some natural daylight in your bathroom, **plants add instant luxury and glamour**. Some species of fern positively flourish in the slightly steamy atmosphere. Consult your local nurseryman to discover other suitable specimens.

2. Few of us can afford the Roman luxury of a sunken bath. If the floor space in your bathroom permits it, **create the effect of a sunken bath** by building a two-step plinth around the existing one and carpet it to match the rest of the floor.

3. If you are tired of plain white coloured modern tiles in the bathroom, **buy a run of decorative Victorian tiles** from a second-hand shop and make them into a dado above the modern ones.

4. Don't despair if you have only a tiny bathroom area but would prefer a bath to a shower. Remember that a **sitz bath** (a two-level bath in which you sit upright) is only about 1m (3ft 3in) long and should fit the most cramped space.

5. Make the most of a really **tiny bathroom space**. If you line the walls and floor with tiles, you don't need a space-consuming shower cabinet and curtains: just a floor recess with a drainage hole and a shower set into the wall above.

6. Still stuck with acres of clinical plain white tiles? Sharpen the whole scheme with a new application of **coloured grouting**: bright red, green or royal blue look dazzling and show dirt less quickly.

7. A clutter of damp towels is not glamorous. For a **capacious towel rail**, run a wooden pole or chrome tube the whole length of one wall in a small bathroom.

8. Mirror is still the best way to lighten, brighten and enlarge a small, dreary space. **Make a huge mirror cheaply** by buying an old picture frame in a junk shop and fitting in a piece of cheap, lightweight mirror. If you have no wall space for such a large item, fit mirror into the panels of the bathroom door using special adhesive pads made for the purpose.

9. Is your bathroom grey, depressing and north-facing? **Create a rosy Deco effect** by sticking a pink mirror-glass mosaic on the bath panel, and in a stepped Deco effect over the vanity basin. Add shell wall lights on either side for additional subdued glow.

10. Thinking of buying a new bath? For sheer drama, forget pastel shades and **buy black**; it can be the most versatile colour of all.

11. Open out one wall of a small bathroom with **a lively mural**. If you can't afford to employ an artist, have a go yourself at a bright and breezy sea-side scene. Keep it fresh and simple with a wide expanse of sky, fluffy clouds, frothy waves and tiny coloured bobbing boats. Remember that the sea gets lighter in colour at the horizon.

12. **A cork-tiled floor** is very welcoming to bare feet, but make sure it is sealed to protect it from damp. For a stream-lined effect, use cork tiles on the walls, on the bath panel and as a surface for a dressing shelf. Cork comes in different colours; use a deep brown for most surfaces with a decorative inset stripe in a pale golden colour.

13. Combine **Victorian charm with mod cons** by plumbing a modern wash basin into an old-fashioned wash-stand. Complete the effect with good quality reproduction taps in brass with porcelain insets.

THE BEDROOM

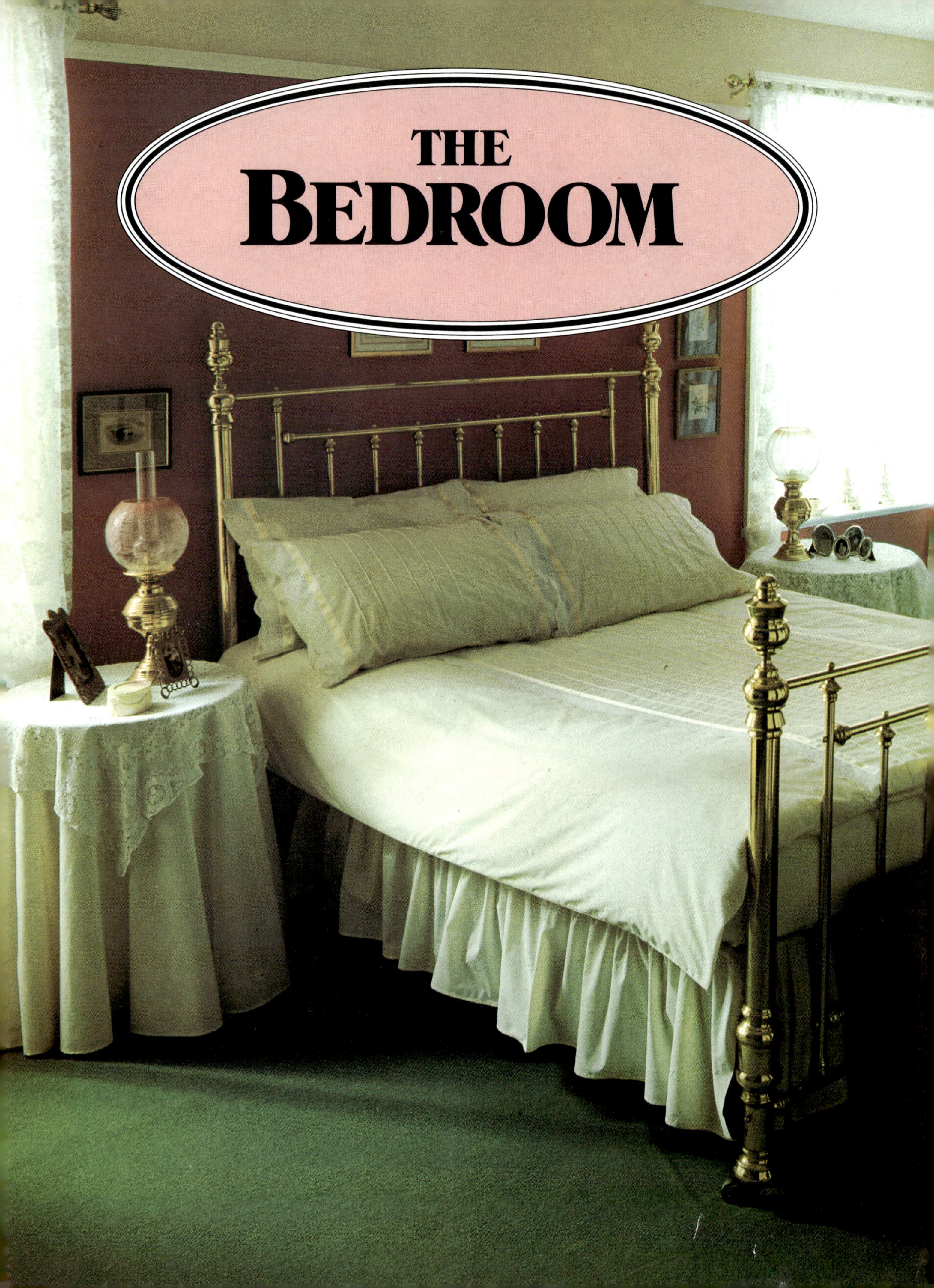

A BEDROOM IS A FASCINATING ROOM TO PLAN AND arrange and decorate, since it is so personal. Whether it is for a child, a teenager or an adult, it will not be used by all and sundry, but by one or two people only, and consequently their tastes and habits can be indulged to the utmost.

It is also a room in which we spend at least a third of the day (albeit asleep most of the time), so as much as any other room in the house it deserves planning with care and attention to detail. Assuming then that you have dealt with the all-important matters of a comfortable bed and adequate storage, this personal room is the one where mood should be carefully considered. What sort of person (or people) are you who will enter and close the door on the outside world each night? Brisk, bright and sporty? The room can be that way too with tailored bed covers, smooth carpet and neatly patterned wallpaper. Glamorous and languorous? Obviously you are going to want long-haired carpet, pastel-coloured silk lined walls and thick, luxurious bed covers. If you are the sultry type, go for deeply coloured painted walls, gilt furniture and oriental rugs. Are you an establishment-style bachelor? Mahogany furniture, maybe some panelling and almost certainly traditionally patterned wallpaper would be your choice. You may be another type altogether, or perhaps a married couple with several small children. Whatever your status or way of life there is a type of room which will suit it well, and in this the most personal room of all, why not have some fun and aim for it.

A bedroom, because it gets very light use, is the one room where it is permissible to economize on things like floor coverings and even furniture. You *can* have an inexpensive quality of carpet here, as it won't be very much walked on, and even a chair could be upholstered in a cheap but attractive curtain material for instance, since its use will be light. *Don't*, need it be said, economize on the bed and take full notice of all the information given about this important item of furniture in the following chapter.

If the bedroom is to be used for other purposes, such as studying, sewing or watching television (as is perfectly possible in a centrally heated home), be sure this secondary activity is comfortably catered for and not imposed upon the room as an afterthought as you have to co-ordinate the necessary furniture with the furniture and decoration in the rest of the room.

All the details which need watching if you are to make a success of this very individual and intimate room are discussed in the pages which follow.

Feel free to indulge your most romantic or extravagant design whims in your bedroom – the most personal room in the house. As bedrooms receive comparatively light wear, an abundance of lace, pretty cottons and other delicate fabrics can be given prominence here.

Planning the bedroom

If space and privacy in the bedroom are problems, you may consider providing extra rooms, although this can be costly. The obvious ways of doing this are by adding a single or two-storey extension or by converting the attic into a living area. Attic conversions involve such things as putting down suitable flooring, sometimes fitting a staircase and generally making sure you meet the necessary health and safety requirements, all of which should be investigated.

However it is possible to maximize existing facilities by a much simpler and cheaper method. In larger, older houses it has been traditional for parents to use the biggest (or master) bedroom, leaving the smaller rooms for the rest of the family. But it might be more convenient for the parents to take one of the smaller rooms so the largest bedroom can be used as a sleep/play area or be partitioned off for two or three children.

The cheapest way of doing this is with stud partitioning, but back-to-back rows of floor-to-ceiling storage units offer a more flexible arrangement. If you decide to knock down walls and reshape some of the rooms, you will find it less difficult on an upper floor where walls are not usually load-bearing: but any major alteration must have local authority approval.

Think hard before removing an attractive old fireplace, since the space gained may not be worth the loss of such a feature. If you decide to keep it, do not leave it boarded up – either open it up properly or block up the flue inside the chimney, restore the surround and the grate and use it as a display area for plants and accessories. In older houses a previous occupant may have installed cupboards in the chimney-breast alcoves. A structure of this sort can detract from the feeling of the room, especially if it was made badly or covers up an attractive cornice or moulding, in which case you can pull it out and possibly use the space for an antique or junk wardrobe – properly restored – in keeping with the period of the house.

Minimum space requirements

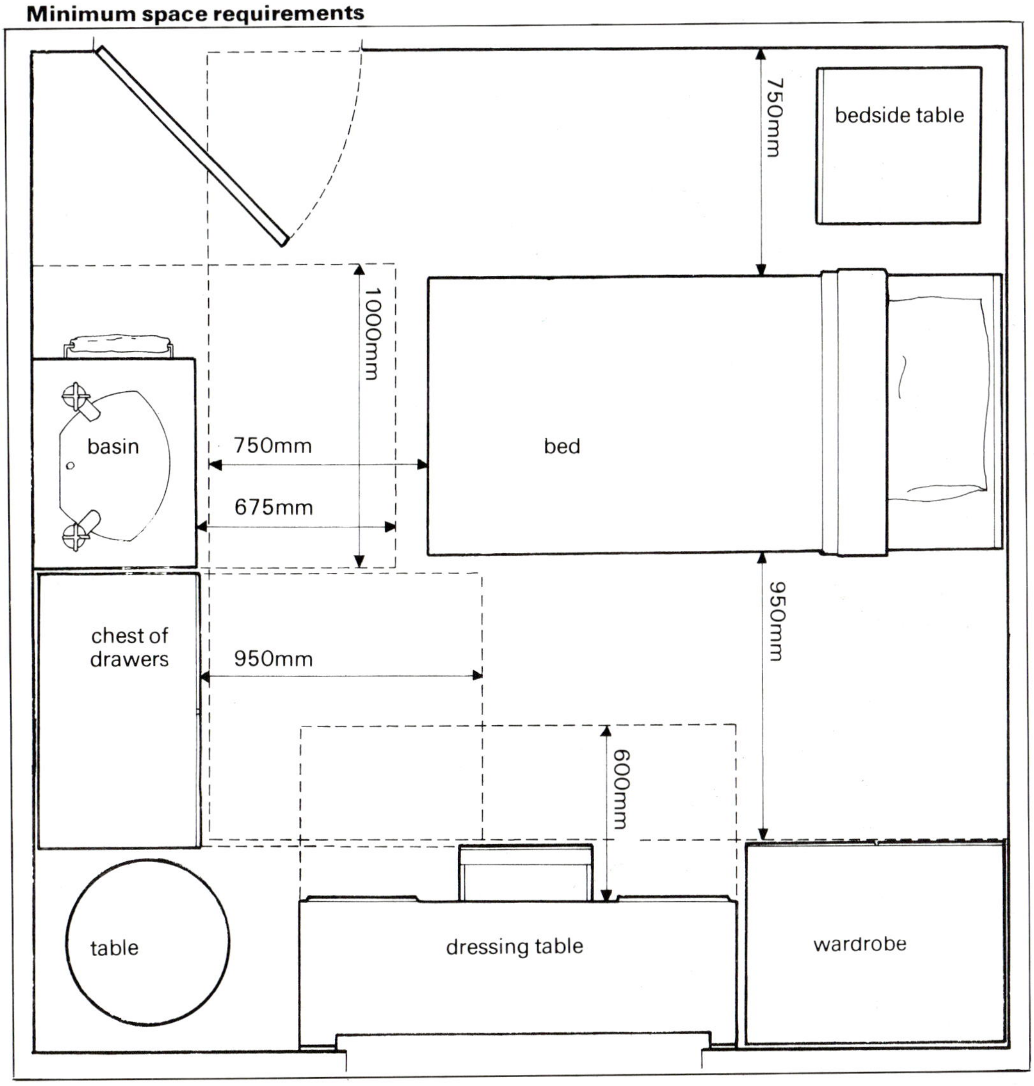

Far left If you are using small patterns, keep the colour scheme simple to avoid an overpowering effect
Left Arrange your furniture to allow as much room as possible around each item
Below left With careful planning, a treasured piece of old furniture can be incorporated in a run of modern units

Make a plan

Once you have defined the area of your room, make a scale plan on graph paper to show doors, windows, electrical outlets, water pipes and any permanent fittings. Cut out similarly scaled models of existing furniture and move them around until you arrive at the best possible use of the space. If you are planning to buy additional pieces, you will then know how much room you have for them. The important thing is to allow enough space around each piece of furniture so it can be used comfortably.

The 'corridor' around a bed should be at least 750mm (30in), or 950mm (37in) if the doors of a storage unit open into it as well. Twin beds should have 500mm (20in) between them. A dressing table needs 600mm (24in) if it has a knee recess, and 900mm (36in) if not. Your chest of drawers will need 950mm (37in) clearance and a basin area should have a total width of 1000mm (39in), with 675mm (27in) in front to allow room for washing hair.

Use that space

At this stage, think about extending the use of the bedroom. When you consider how many family activities are crammed into the living area – and how inconvenient this can be if the ground floor is small or open plan – you will see the advantages of utilizing fully a room which is often empty for 16 hours or more a day. Even the addition of a bookshelf and a comfortable chair can provide a place to read quietly away from the television.

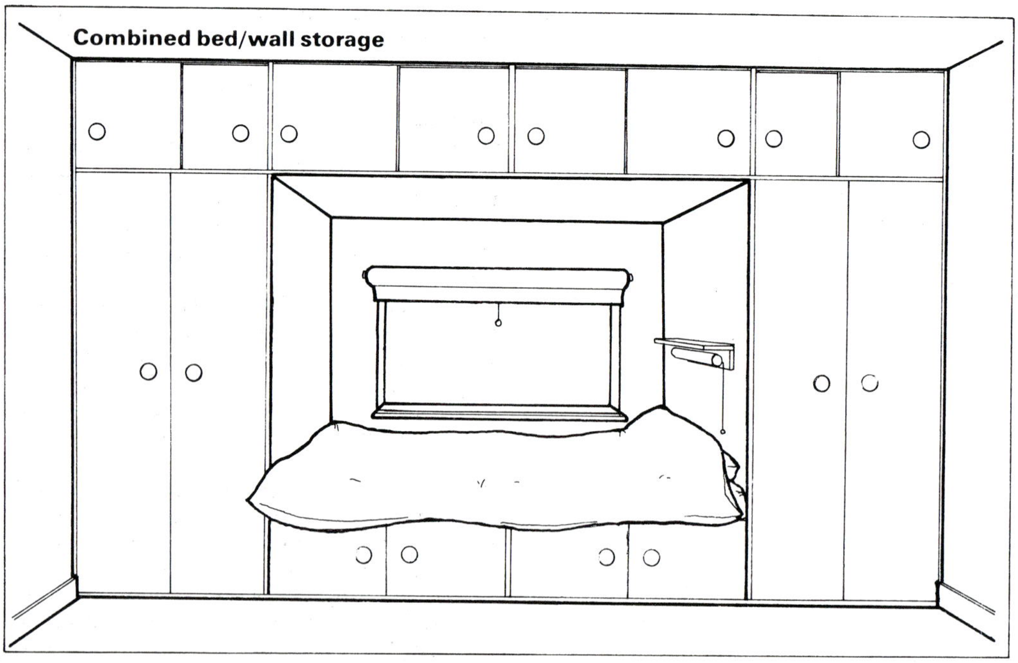

Left Young children might enjoy this arrangement because of its resemblance to a ship's cabin
Below left A study can often double as a sitting room or bedroom for guests
Top right Put away the bedclothes to provide extra seating in this work/leisure area
Centre right This arrangement gives maximum work and storage facilities
Below right Muted colours and subtle lighting give the bedroom a calm and peaceful atmosphere

Add a work surface, a few more shelves and a filing system and you have a purpose-built study – somewhere to write letters and deal with the family accounts. Other hobbies, like sewing and stamp collecting, can be catered for in the same way. If space is at a premium, gather all your equipment together on a trolley and install a simple flap-down table, which folds away when not in use.

Where to sleep

When you have decided what furniture you want in the room, the major consideration will be where to put the bed. If you do not enjoy the early morning sun, you will not want to position the bed so it faces a window. In a draughty room, avoid setting it directly under a window or in the path between the window and door. Where windows are draught-free and you like the idea of a closed-in feeling when you are asleep, combine the bed and storage areas on one wall. If you have a single bed, make the two end cupboards into ordinary wardrobes; if the bed is a double one, you will be able to install two large, walk-in storage units.

Although sleeping against a wall does save space, make sure this arrangement will not make you feel hemmed in and check on any noise that might come through from an adjoining room or a neighbouring house. Any bed in this position should have castors and a fitted undersheet and duvet to make bedmaking easier.

If you do not want the head of the bed against a chimney-breast, this wall is an excellent place for storage. Fit floor-to-ceiling units right across; those in front of the alcoves will be wide enough to take hanging rails for your clothes and the centre section – over the breast itself – will take narrower shelves for shoes, bags and accessories. The top shelves will be useful for sports equipment, luggage and out-of-season clothes.

If you are lucky enough to have a guest room, this is a good place to plan a study/hobby area. Two single beds here are more flexible than a double one and, if you choose a plain design without headboards, you can arrange the beds in an L-shape against the wall and add a few cushions to provide extra seating. Even a tiny spare room with one

Working bedroom

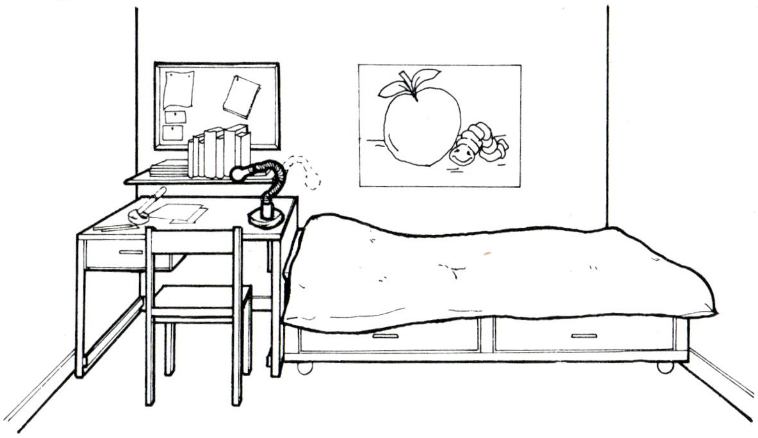

Storage units round window

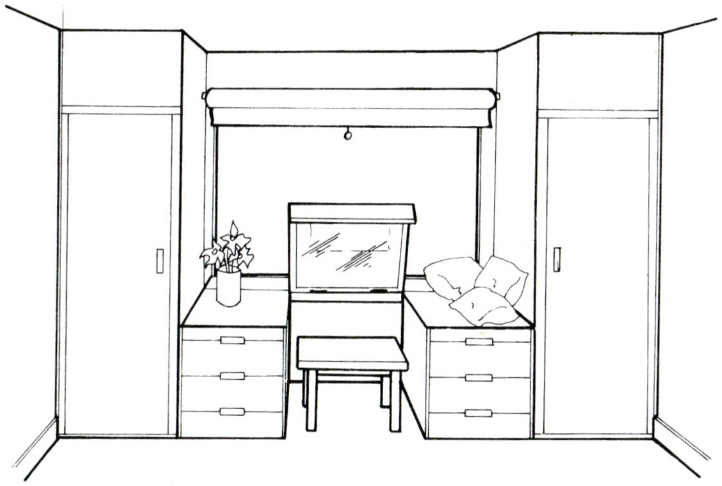

single bed should provide plenty of work space if you organize it wisely and plan so several fittings serve a double purpose.

Other facilities

If you want a dressing table, try to follow the Victorian tradition of putting it under or in front of a window so your face is well lit. Choose a design which has its mirror on the inside of a hinged lid so you can pull it down to hide your clutter under a useful work surface.

An extra wash-basin is always handy in the bedroom, especially if there is only one bathroom for the whole family. Tuck it away in a corner or hide it behind doors which match those on a fitted storage system. You may find an L-shaped bedroom allows for the installation of an extra bathroom in the smaller section, if the necessary plumbing connections are possible and your local authority approves your plans. If your room is large enough, you might consider an open-plan bedroom/bathroom with a WC elsewhere.

If you enjoy watching television in bed make sure you position it wisely to avoid neck and eye strain. The ideal place is at the foot of the bed, up to about one metre (or three feet) above eye level.

Colour and pattern

Your bedroom should, above all, provide a restful retreat for you at the end of each day. This is not the place to try out a dramatic colour scheme or exotic wallpaper. Stick to one or two colours and small patterns which do not dazzle the eye. A sunny room will take cool blues or greens, but choose warmer colours for a north-facing bedroom. Small or dark rooms are not necessarily improved by a coat of brilliant white paint – this treatment often results in a chilly grey appearance and you might find slightly darker, muted shades will give an air of cosiness and sophistication.

Choosing beds

Beds are such a standard piece of furniture in the home that often we pay far too little attention to the type or design. Because a good night's sleep is crucial if your body is to function properly, make sure you choose a quality bed that is not only comfortable but also gives you the right kind of support for tired limbs.

With many pieces of furniture you can save money by being imaginative, by improvising, restoring and generally 'making do'; but when it comes to the very important question of choosing a bed, there are no short cuts. After all, you spend about a third of your life there. A poor quality or worn-out model can lead to chronic backache, tiredness, tension and a general inability to function at your best, while a good quality bed, chosen to suit your needs, should cradle your body gently so the muscles can relax and allow you the deep and restorative sleep that is so important to your physical and mental well-being.

How long is it since you examined your bed closely? Does it feel lumpy and matted? Does it sag in the middle? Can you feel the springs? Have the edges lost their firmness? Is your divan base soft and uneven? If any of these symptoms are present, you should buy a new bed. When that arrives, never put the old one in a child's room since it can impair the correct development of bones and muscles. Try to avoid putting it in the guest room – this can be very unfair on visitors. You should throw it – and its divan base – away; you will be wasting your money if you put a new mattress on an old divan. They are made to function together, so if the base is saggy and lumpy, the new mattress will very soon look the same. Avoid getting a second-hand bed – even if it belonged to your best friend. When you consider you lose 50 litre (or $10\frac{1}{2}$gal) of moisture and about 500g (or 1lb) of skin cells into your bed every year, you will realize that, apart from leaving you with a bed moulded to someones else's body, this arrangement is incredibly unhygienic.

A bed raised well clear of the ground enables the area underneath to be cleaned easily

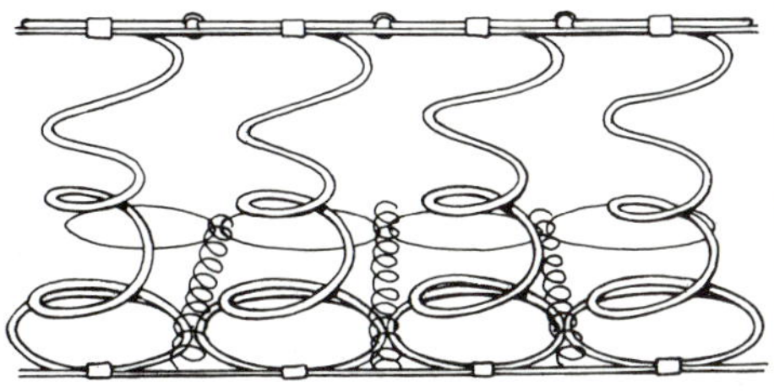
Open springs

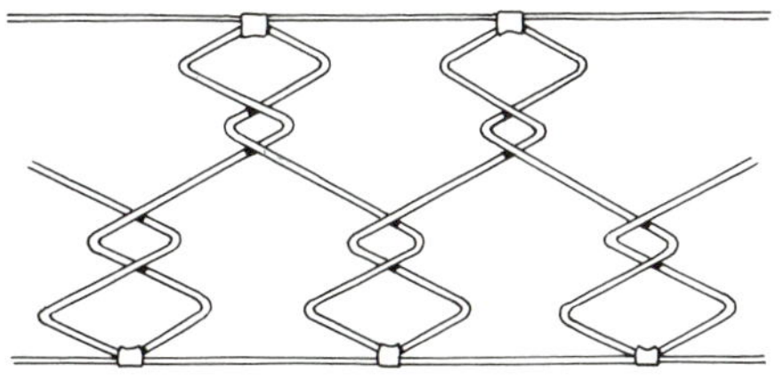
Linked springs

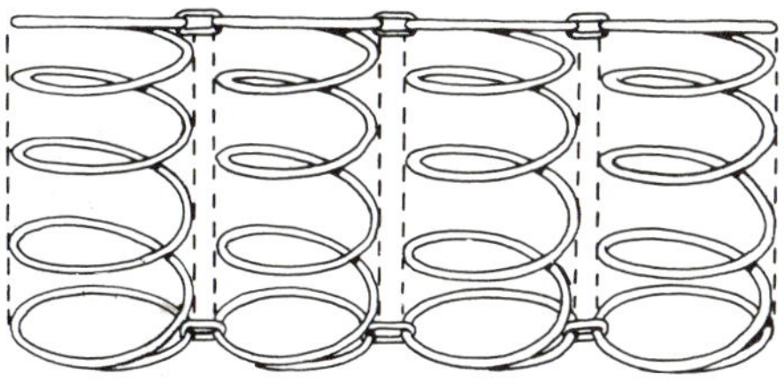
Pocket springs

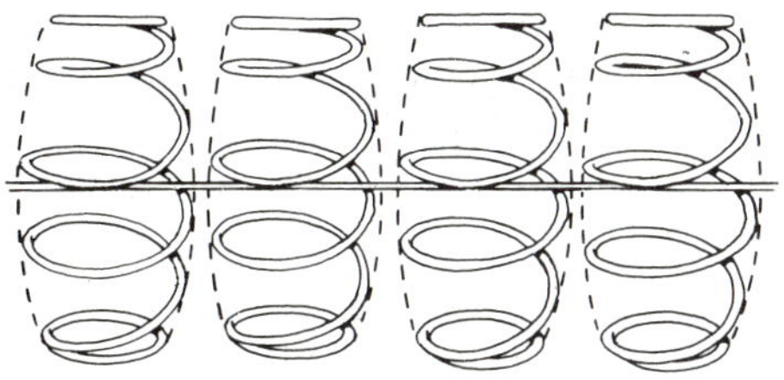
Barrel-shaped pocket springs

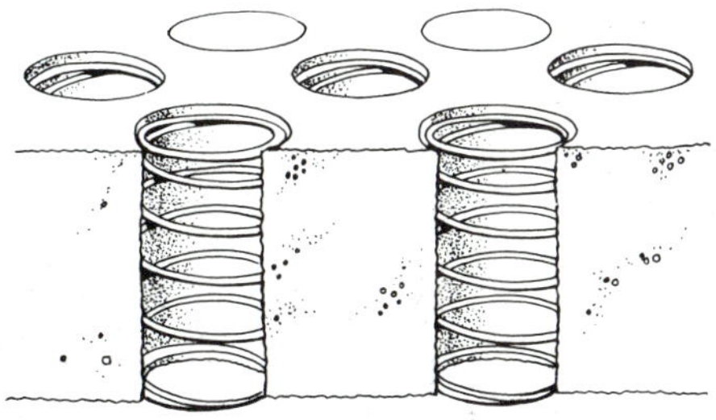
Separate springs in foam

The first task when buying a new bed is to find a reputable dealer – one with experience and a reputation for fair dealing. Ask his advice and tell him the size, weight and any special infirmity of the person or persons who will be using it. This kind of transaction requires a great deal of trust and faith on the part of the consumer, since the most important part of the article – the inside – is impossible to see. A surprising number of people fall into the trap of making their choice on the basis of the external covering, which is after all on view only when you are changing the bedlinen. Investigate any massive discounts carefully; are they genuine ends of line or special promotions, or is the 'original' price an unreasonably inflated figure displayed prominently to confuse the customer? Here price is a very good guide to quality and the old saying 'you get only what you pay for' usually applies.

Above Single models joined together to make a double bed are the ideal solution if one partner prefers a firmer mattress than the other
Left Types of spring found in mattresses

Choosing a mattress

There are four main types of sprung mattress, so you must first decide which one you want. A common and inexpensive type, called 'open' springing, consists of rows of hourglass-shaped springs joined together at the top and bottom with wire. A similar, joined, method involves a continuous run of springs all made from one piece of wire, rather like knitting. Individual or 'pocketed' springing will usually give you greater support than either of these because each unit is enclosed in a separate fabric 'pocket', so it acts more independently under pressure; but since they are joined at the top and bottom, there will still be some interaction. Probably the most efficient springs are those pocketed ones which are joined only at the waist so each one can be compressed to its halfway point without affecting its neighbours – one company makes them barrel-shaped so each ring telescopes into the one below without touching it. This method does away with any twanging, metal-on-metal sounds and reduces wear when pressure is applied.

All sprung mattresses have upholstery to protect you from the hard springs. This is usually made from coconut (coir) fibre, curled black hair sewn onto hessian, cotton, or a wire cord insulator. On top of this is a surface layer made from wool, cotton, hair or a man-made material such as foam. Mattresses made entirely from foam are light and easy-to-handle since they consist of rubber or plastic formed into a honeycomb structure. They distribute weight evenly and should not lose their shape with use as long as they are at least 115mm ($4\frac{1}{2}$in) thick. Some newer models have a basic construction of foam with interspersed separate springs.

Try out all the different types by lying down on them full-stretch – sitting on the edge or prodding them with your finger will not tell you anything. Back sufferers, heavier people and those who are chronically bedridden should choose a firm or orthopaedic bed, but remember that firm is not the same as hard; a hard model – one that is solid and unyielding – is not good for anyone. Older people often prefer a softer version and one that is high enough for them to get in and out of easily.

Types of divan

Divans also have different constructions. Some, called 'firm-edge', have a piece of wood around the

perimeter which makes the edges quite hard. The 'sprung-edge' type will give more even and flexible support, but if you need a really firm base, choose a 'non-sprung' model. Castors are always useful so you can move the bed to make it or clean around it – especially if it is set against a wall. If you are short on space, find a base with drawers or a top which lifts to give access to a storage area under the mattress.

The right size

Once you have selected the type of mattress and divan you want, decide which size will be best, bearing in mind that metric ones vary slightly from the traditional sizes. Again, this is no place to skimp, particularly on a double bed. A small double measures 1350mm × 1900mm (4ft 6in × 6ft 3in), but what has now become a standard double is only 1500mm × 2000mm (5ft × 6ft 6in) leaving 760mm (2ft 6in) for each sleeper – the size of a child's bunk bed. To make sure a bed is wide enough, lie on it with your partner, hands clasped behind your head. If your elbows touch, look for a bigger bed. Lone sleepers can choose between a small single, 900 × 1900mm (3ft × 6ft 3in), or a standard single, 1000 × 2000mm (3ft 3in × 6ft 6in).

Care of the bed

Whichever type and size you choose, you will probably have to reconcile yourself to the fact that this piece of furniture will cost more than you expected. It is a major investment and one you might not have thought about in years, so the price is bound to come as a shock. Even so, bear in mind that even a top quality model will wear out in about ten years, so make a mental note to examine it periodically to make sure it is still in good condition. You will get more wear out of your new bed if you take good care of it, so follow a few simple rules to keep it at its best.

- Never put a mattress directly on the floor. It needs proper ventilation so if you want the exotic effect of a low bed, raise it slightly by placing it on a plinth drilled with large holes.
- Don't leave the protective wrapping on a new mattress or divan base. When you sleep on it, the warmth from your body traps moisture inside the bag and leads to a damp bed, mildew and eventual rotting.
- When you get up in the morning, throw the bedclothes back so the bed can air for at least 20 minutes. This will get rid of some of the dampness that may have accumulated during the night.
- Don't make a habit of sitting on the edge of the bed – pressure concentrated on the same small area weakens the edge of the mattress and the base.
- Turn the sprung mattress over and swing it round on the bed to reverse head and foot ends every week for the first month, then at three-month intervals to help the filling to settle evenly. Try not to bend the mattress when you do this (and make sure when you move house the movers do not roll and tie it to cram it into the van).
- Check your hot water bottle frequently to make sure it has no leaks. If a young child or an incontinent adult is to use the bed, protect it with a rubber sheet.
- Don't let children bounce up and down on any bed. It is dangerous for them and very bad for the mattress.
- Clean the bed every few months with a soft brush to remove dust and fluff. Don't use a vacuum cleaner unless your mattress is made of foam since this can disturb the filling of a sprung mattress.

Above If you choose a divan base with drawers, make sure you allow sufficient clearance all round for easy access

Special beds

There are many variations on the basic bed. Some, like convertibles, have a special, practical purpose; others, like four-poster, round, oval and heart-shaped varieties, are purely for decoration.

Convertibles Although handy for a guestroom/study or a sitting room, these may not prove suitable for constant use. They often make an unsatisfactory sofa as well as an uncomfortable bed and you may find it a chore to make them up each evening and pack them away in the morning.

Folding These range from the simple camp bed to more sophisticated models incorporated in bedroom storage systems. Avoid any bed with a mattress or divan which will be constantly creased when not in use.

Water Said to support the body with the minimum amount of pressure from below on small blood vessels, which often become constricted during sleep, this type is very expensive and very heavy. If you are not sure about the weight load of your floors, ask an architect or surveyor to check this.

Four posters Fashionable in the days when servants were plentiful, this type collects a great deal of dust and is often impractical for smaller, modern homes. You can create a similar, tented effect by hanging a length of soft fabric from the ceiling by each of its four corners.

Bunk A wise choice for young children, this type can often be separated when the children get older. Bunk beds will be covered more thoroughly later in this book when we deal with the planning aspects of children's rooms.

Opposite page

Above Old people may find it easier to get in and out of a high bed than a low one

Below A mattress which lifts up to reveal space underneath is ideal for storing spare linen

Housing bedroom clutter

For those who like their bedroom smart, sleek and uncluttered, efficient storage is often a problem. This is particularly true beside the bed where such things as clock, lamp, reading material and tissues should be close at hand so you do not have to get them out every evening and put them away again in the morning.

This row of adjustable bedside shelves has been tucked on the side of a small wardrobe and partly hidden behind its extended facade. All the control switches for the room are below the bottom shelf, making them easily accessible from the bed.

Bedroom storage

If your bedrooms are filled with clutter, take a good look at the storage facilities before you start tidying up yet again. Are you making the most of the space available? Your problems could be solved with a multi-purpose fitted system or functional individual units.

When you are planning the storage areas in your bedroom, the first thing to work out is the exact amount and type of things you want to accommodate. Will you need to house the family linen or is there a separate cupboard for it elsewhere? Are you lucky enough to have a spare room, attic or basement for family treasures, bulky luggage and old clothes – or will you have to find a place for these in the bedroom as well? It is always better to overestimate the amount of space you need, since possessions tend to accumulate; it would be a great shame to fit expensive storage units, only to find in a few years you have to rip them out and replace them with a larger system.

Decide whether you want fitted storage or separate pieces of furniture – if your room is an old one with traditional moulding and classical proportions, you might spoil it with a floor-to-ceiling run of cupboards. Remember too that although this type of storage always makes good use of space, it

A flexible system like this can be adjusted to give more hanging, shelf or drawer space. Wire baskets make it easy to find what you need in a hurry

looks best when it covers an entire wall, since smaller sections tend to give a half-finished appearance. Make sure any set of drawers you choose – whether in a fitted or separate unit – includes several different sizes. Deep ones are useful for sweaters, nightwear and folded shirts, while it is much easier to find underwear, socks, stockings and jewellery in a shallow drawer. Belts, scarves and ties are easy to get at if you hang them on a coat rack or on the back of a door; this is often a good place for a shoe bag or rack as well.

Hanging rails should have at least 1700mm (5ft 6in) clearance to take long dresses and coats and should be supported by brackets every 750mm (2ft 6in) to prevent the middle sagging. Jackets or skirts need only 1000mm (3ft 3in) clearance, so put these things all together to make room for boxes, boots, shelves or another hanging unit underneath. Most rails are fixed from one side of the unit to the other, but if you find this does not leave sufficient room for your clothes widthways, fit two rails running from front to back instead.

Fitted storage

If you decide on this type of system, make sure you measure very carefully since an error of a few millimetres may mean you are left with a costly piece of furniture which you cannot fit in. For rooms slightly higher or wider than the standard unit, filler panels are usually available to make up any left-over space on top of or alongside the cupboards.

Fitted systems, whether horizontal or vertical, are normally in single, double or triple units of a standard size. This kind of furniture is commonly made of chipboard, hardboard or plywood with a laminate or veneer finish; some do come with plain doors, which you paint yourself, or removable panels, which lift out of an aluminium frame so you can cover them in a paper or fabric of your choice. The latter arrangement does not usually require screws or other fixing materials. It is very important the units are clearly marked so you know what the finish is and are able to care for it correctly.

Make sure the range you choose includes the pieces you need: wardrobes, cupboards which fit above them, dressing tables, drawers, bedside tables and lights, corner units and headboards are all available as modular units.

Your chosen furniture should be deep enough to hang your clothes easily without crushing the shoulders. Check, if you buy wall units, that there is a wide range of adjustable internal fittings and a movable hanging rail. All drawers should run smoothly on their plastic or nylon runners. Some manufacturers supply wire baskets which are very light and allow you to see what it inside, but conventional drawers in wood or plastic might be better for articles of clothing not worn regularly, since these tend to get dusty in open baskets.

When choosing ready-made units, make sure they are structurally sound. Examine all joints closely – give them a gentle pull and if you feel any weakness, look for another range. To save money, go for backless units; these are not free-standing, but fixed securely to the wall to make them rigid and stable. If you decide on this arrangement, make sure the wall behind the fitting is strong enough to take the load and is covered with a paper or paint which will not rub off on your clothes; white distemper, for example, could ruin the contents of your wardrobe.

Above left Fit traditionally styled storage units if you want to retain the atmosphere of a period house **Left** Some units come with removable panels which you can paint, paper or cover with fabric to co-ordinate with the rest of the room **Above** Plain pine units will not detract from the rustic look of an old beamed cottage

Choose an extra deep system – or make one yourself. If you are stuck with a battered or ugly chest of drawers you do not want to throw out, hide it inside the wardrobe section so it is covered by the doors of the unit.

Many fitted systems come in KD (knock-down) or QA (quick assembly) form. If this is the case with the one you have chosen, make sure you understand the manufacturer's instructions completely before you take your furniture home – and follow the specifications for screws and other fixing materials.

You can often save a great deal of money by making fitted cupboards yourself – and this is often satisfying and not very difficult to do. If you want them to span an entire wall and to fit from floor to ceiling, you will not have to provide a top, bottom or any sides for your units; all you will need is a basic frame, inside fittings and doors which can be bought ready-made in standard sizes from a builder's merchant.

Whether you are looking for ready-made, self-assembly or DIY units, it is best to stick to fairly plain designs. The units are an expensive investment and you will want to use them for a long time; elaborate mouldings and handles may not blend with the style you want ten years from now. In addition, the room will look bigger with simple furniture; and a range which includes mirrored doors will help you achieve an even greater magnifying effect.

When your storage system has been assembled, think about how you will organize the inside fittings. Shelves should not be too widely spaced since items at the bottom of a large pile will be difficult to remove quickly and neatly. Keep anything that is in constant use close to the middle of the unit so you do not have to keep stretching or stooping to remove them.

Separate storage furniture

This type of furniture is often cheaper than the fitted variety and always more flexible, provided you have the space. There is a much greater range of styles to choose from and you can take it all with you when you move home.

If you are working within a strict budget, a junk shop will often provide you with a solid, well made wardrobe or chest of drawers. These are preferable to a new piece, which might involve a greater outlay for something which could be flimsy and poorly built. Put up good quality open shelves rather than cheap cupboards; you can always add doors later, when you can afford them.

A bay window might provide an ideal space for a window seat with a lid, which is hinged so you can store bulky linen or clothes underneath. Choose a bed with space for additional storage underneath, but remember two or three smaller drawers will be easier to manoeuvre than one large one. If your work surface or dressing table top will have to double as a home office, a trolley with several shelves could solve many storage problems. Fit it with a table-sized filing cabinet, letter and magazine racks, pen holders and a couple of attractive filing baskets to keep office or grooming clutter out of the way yet easily accessible.

Lighting, heating and safety in the bedroom

The often overlooked aspects of the bedroom, such as lighting, heating and safety, can contribute more than any article of furniture or furnishings towards making the bedroom a comfortable and relaxing, yet functional, place.

Lighting

Good lighting in the bedroom can flatter you and improve the look of the room as well as making it efficient and, perhaps most important, safe. If you are planning your wiring from scratch, make sure all the lights in the room can be controlled from the bedside so you do not have to get out of bed to turn fittings on or off. (While you are planning your lighting requirements, you might also consider any other electrical appliances you are likely to need – and where they will be used – and site the socket outlets in the most sensible places.)

Avoid any kind of glare; you will need a general light for dressing and getting ready for bed, but it should be soft and warm. Central ceiling fixtures can flatten a room and make it look dull and uninteresting, so be careful what style of light and shade you choose. Ceiling or wall lights are often more effective when they are controlled with a dimmer switch to give you the exact intensity of light you need at any given time. Bedside lamps are more practical if they can be angled so one partner can sleep undisturbed while the other reads or writes late into the night.

If you make up or shave in your bedroom, you will need a good strong light by the dressing table. The requirements here are very much the same as those in the bathroom; light above, around or down both sides of the mirror should be directed at you rather than at the glass. The same principle applies when you are planning the lighting for a full length mirror; ideally the source should be between you and the mirror, pointing at you. Some wardrobe units have built-in lights which come on when you open the doors. If you do not have this arrangement, try fixing a wall or ceiling spotlight nearby which can be angled to illuminate the contents of a wardrobe or cupboard when the doors are opened.

An office/study area should have its own lighting arrangements. If you have plenty of space, a plain table lamp is ideal as long as its shade is not too dark or too large to let out sufficient light. A desk

Above If your window has a radiator underneath, choose blinds or short curtains which will not block out the heat
Above right Here the paint treatment and the round topped mirror have been chosen to complement the efficient dressing table lighting and prevent it looking clinical
Right Concealed tungsten strips give a soft, strong light and are useful where there is a shortage of bedside space

clamp version is a great space-saver here, as is a tungsten striplight concealed under a shelf above the work surface. A comfortable reading chair will need a light to go with it; a standard or table lamp might be the answer – or a wall or ceiling track spotlight which can be turned towards the chair when you need extra brightness.

Heating

Normally your bedrooms will be immediately below the loft area and your first concern will be efficient insulation, since the heat in the room will naturally go straight up and out through the roof if you are not careful. Make sure the loft is properly insulated and fit double-glazing or draught excluders to the windows; also line and interline your curtains to keep out the cold.

Most people sleep quite happily in a lower temperature than they are comfortable with during the day. The ideal set-up is a central heating system with a thermostat and timer, so you can set the heating to go off just before you turn in for the night and to come on again before you get up in the morning; there is nothing more daunting than having to crawl out of a warm bed into a freezing room. If possible, try to keep a minimum background level of warmth all the time; if you let the room get very cold, it will take longer to warm up and a great deal more fuel will be used. Condensation will also be a problem if you have a large variation in temperature. Those people who find their heating system is drying should consider a humidifier in the bedroom. Sleeping in constantly desiccated air is very bad for the skin and can result in an uncomfortable parched feeling in the mouth and throat when you wake up. Dry air can also be very damaging to your furniture.

Safety

The bedroom is one of the most vulnerable areas for accidents in the home. We are unconscious most of the time we spend there and any moving around during the night tends to be done in the dark, especially if we are afraid of waking a sleeping partner.

One of the most obvious and commonly heard warnings about bedroom safety concerns smoking in bed. Ideally you should refrain from doing it altogether; but if you must, take a few sensible precautions. Never smoke when you feel drowsy since you are very likely to fall asleep holding the lighted cigarette. Make sure your ashtray is large and stable; if necessary, stick it to the bedside table with adhesive pads. Before you turn out the light, check every butt is completely extinguished and there are no ashes on the floor or the bedcovers – or on you. Choose nightwear which is flame-resistant or flame proof. It is possible to treat your clothes and bedlinen with a special fluid so they cannot catch fire; but since the ingredients are soluble in water you will have to re-treat every item each time it is washed.

If you have an electric blanket, be sure to follow the manufacturer's instructions to the letter. Check frequently for loose connections or frayed wires and don't ever switch on the blanket if you are going out. Send it back to the manufacturer every two years for a service, even if you are not having any particular problems with it.

Low wattage or night lights are a good idea, especially for young children or elderly relatives, or where there is a long and circuitous route to the bathroom. Make sure there are no flexes trailing around the room, which you might trip over in the dark. Wall or clamp lights are ideal for bedside use since you are not likely to knock them over and set light to the bedlinen. Table lamps, like ashtrays, should be heavy and stable and, here again, strong adhesive pads could prevent a serious accident. If you like to watch television from your bed, beware of dropping off while the set is still on. Before you reach that stage, switch the set off and pull the plug from the socket to be absolutely safe.

Make sure all backless storage units are fixed securely to the wall since they are not naturally as stable as complete units. Don't fill your shelves with great unwieldy piles of heavy objects which could come crashing down on you when you open the door.

All free-standing gas, electric or paraffin heaters should be positioned far from curtains, bedclothes, furniture or anything else which may catch fire. Keep them well away from the sides or the foot of the bed where a restless sleeper might unknowingly kick them over. And never dress or undress near them, since clothes can catch light and burn up in seconds – another common instance of accidents in the bedroom.

Any loose rugs laid on a highly polished floor should have a mat of rubber webbing put underneath them so there is no chance that anyone will slip and fall. Take this webbing right to the edges of the rug since loose corners are very easy to trip on, especially in the dark or first thing in the morning before you are properly awake.

Top A small, unobtrusive radiator will provide efficient heating without affecting the look of your bedroom
Above Choose wall-fixed lights beside the bed to be completely safe
Left To eliminate accidents, make sure any loose rugs will not slip

Choosing bed-linen

The personal atmosphere of the bedroom will be affected to a great extent by your choice of bedlinen, one aspect of decoration now particularly relevant with the emergence of a large range of colours, patterns and designs.

Although the care of household linen has been greatly simplified since our grandmothers boiled up the family sheets every Monday, the choice has become much wider and more confusing. To get the best value for your money, postpone any major purchases until sale times, when second quality goods, manufacturers' samples and ends of lines are offered at quite dramatic reductions.

Sheets and pillow cases

At one time, there was no question of 'design' in sheets and pillowcases – they were plain and white. But in the last few years stripes, flowers and geometric shapes have made these items an important part in bedroom decoration.

Types of material
Traditionally made from natural fibres like linen and cotton, the material for – and manufacture of – sheets has changed drastically with the development of man-made fabrics.

Linen Although they are sometimes difficult to find and always very costly, linen sheets are hard-wearing, easy to wash, and because of their smooth surface, resistant to dirt. However, unless you have a spartan nature or a good electric blanket, you may find them chilly to crawl between on a cold night.

Cotton Also increasingly rare in the shops, cotton sheets remain the first choice of many people. Ranging from fine percale to coarser Egyptian fabric, they are soft and absorbent and tend not to show dirt easily. Cotton sheets are, however, becoming increasingly expensive – and they require ironing after each wash.

The use of duvets is becoming increasingly widespread and their covers are often so attractive you do not need a separate bedcover (Dorma bedlinen and scheme)

Above Plain wool blankets are still the first choice for many people
Above right More sophisticated electric overblankets have an automatically monitored system which keeps you warm throughout the night despite any fluctuation in room temperature (Monogram overblanket, John Lewis linen)
Right Cellular blankets wash easily and provide excellent insulation on the same principle as a string vest (John Lewis blanket and linen)

Synthetic fabrics These, which include nylon, certainly make sheets easy to care for. They do not wrinkle and are usually strong, easy to wash and quick to dry. Unfortunately this type often has a permanently damp feel and smell which many people find unpleasant.
Cotton and synthetic mixes Most sheets and pillowcases sold today are made from 50 percent cotton and 50 percent man-made material such as vincel, terylene or polyester. They are often the most practical type since they combine the smooth, soft feeling of cotton with the easy wash-and-dry properties of synthetics.
Flannelette Beautifully warm, cosy and highly absorbent, sheets made from this material are usually inexpensive as well. Their main drawback is their unfortunate tendency to show every bit of dirt and dust, so they require very frequent washing.

Checking quality
Look for an even, regular weave in the cloth and remember the smooth, firm feel of good sheets should be in the fibre itself. Manufacturers of poor quality linen often add a fine white powder or 'dressing' to the finished product before it is put on display to make it look and feel more attractive. Rub the fabric between your fingers; if you see evidence of this powder, you can be sure after its first washing your sheet will feel thin and limp.

What size to buy
Few things are more irritating than a sheet which is too small pulling out and leaving your feet uncovered. Always check the actual measurements; don't rely on labels which say 'single' or 'double' – especially on cheaper products. All flat sheets should have 610mm (24in) extra on the length and width to give a generous tuck in and to allow for shrinkage, since even the best quality cotton will shrink a little. Pillowcases are sold in fairly standard sizes to fit most pillows.

Style and design
A major improvement in bedlinen during recent years has been the invention of fitted bottom sheets; they make the bed look much neater and save untold time and effort making it up. If you have trouble sorting out the different kinds of sheets in your linen cupboard, choose plain bottom sheets and top sheets in complementary colours or co-ordinating designs. It is usually a good idea to buy all one colour or pattern combination for one size of bed, since printed sets which look lovely when new and complete can quickly become a motley collection of odd bits when some of the pieces are damaged, lost at the laundry or worn out. White sheets on the other hand always look crisp and clean, wash well and present no matching problems.

Looking after material
Always mend small holes or tears before you wash sheets and pillowcases or send them to the laundry, since what started as a minute rip may end up as a major repair job. If you have dark, deep-dyed linen, wash it alone for the first few times since it is bound to shed some of the excess dye necessary to achieve the depth of colour. Strong bleach is not good for coloured or man-made fabrics, although white cotton responds well to this treatment as long as you do not add so much bleach that the fibres are weakened. Use hot water for white linen or cotton sheets and warm water for all other types.

Blankets
Although the popularity of the blanket has declined a little in recent years due to the increasing use of the duvet, many people do prefer them and a large comprehensive range is still available. Whichever type of blanket you choose, make sure the ones you buy are moth-proof and will not shrink.

Types of material
Most blankets are made of wool – or a mixture of wool with a man-made fibre. This type is very warm and wears extremely well, the softest and most expensive ones being made from merino or cashmere. Don't wash a wool blanket – send it to the dry-cleaners before it gets heavily soiled to prolong its life. Brush it often to remove dust and dirt and to fluff up the nap so it insulates more effectively and provides greater warmth; work from the top to the bottom, never across the width, and use a clean, semi-stiff brush. Never store a wool blanket at the bottom of a pile of household linen since this will flatten its pile.

Blankets made entirely from a man-made material such as Acrilan are less costly than those made from pure wool, but you may also find them less warm. They are usually washable, shrink-proof and quick to dry – with a built-in resistance to moths.

Cotton blankets are much less warm; but they wash easily and quickly, making them ideal for children's beds. They are very light in weight, so you can use several on the bed at a time.

Also light and easy to wash are cellular blankets. These consist of a series of pockets which trap warm air on the same principle as a string vest, making them excellent insulators especially when used under an ordinary blanket.

What size to buy
To determine what size of blanket you need, add 750mm (or 30in) to the width of your bed and 500mm (or 20in) to its length to allow for the thickness of the mattress and plenty of 'tuck in'. Blankets are often sold in 250mm (or 10in)

multiples, so choose one to the nearest 250mm (or 10in) above for a generous fit.

Electric blankets

Electric blankets cost very little to run and can add considerably to your comfort. They are ideal for beds not often used, such as those in a spare room or weekend cottage, since they quickly dry out any damp feeling. A pre-heating underblanket is the least expensive to buy, but it means what it says; turn it on to the correct temperature an hour or two before bedtime, and turn it off again before you retire – don't leave it switched on.

Warning The blanket should never be on while the bed is occupied, although there are special low wattage models which are rather more expensive and allow you to leave the blanket on all night in complete safety.

Place it under the bottom sheet and fasten it securely to the mattress with a series of tapes tied around its corners. Some models come with multiple heat settings and double ones are available with separate controls for each side of the bed. In warm weather the easiest place to store your under-

blanket is on the bed; there is no need to remove it and it should not be folded or creased in any case.

Overblankets cost more than underblankets because they have a special system which lets you leave them on while you are in bed. This protective system also maintains the inside of the bed at a constant temperature no matter how cold the bedroom gets. Like underblankets, some double versions have dual controls for those couples who like to sleep at different temperatures. Overblankets should be at least 500mm (or 20in) longer and wider than your bed to keep you warm efficiently; and they should be put over the top sheet, with a light covering on top to keep in the heat. Most of them you can machine-wash, but always follow carefully the directions on the manufacturer's label. Store your overblanket rolled or folded with a minimum of creases – or better still, hang it up open at the back of a cupboard or lay it flat on a spare bed.

Looking after electric blankets

Take proper care of your blanket and it will not only last longer, but also remain safe; read the maker's instructions and always follow them carefully. Your blanket should be serviced regularly, so return it to the maker for an overhaul about every two years. Never use it when it is wet; and let it dry naturally – never turn it on to speed up this process.

Check frequently for frayed edges, worn fabric, scorches, damage to the flex or loose connections at the control or plug. Hold the blanket up to the light and look for wires bunching up or touching; if they are, return the blanket to the manufacturer for servicing.

Duvets

The greatest innovation in bedmaking in recent years has been the duvet (or continental quilt) which is increasingly widely used. Warmer than the conventional blanket and topsheet arrangement which it replaces, a duvet works on the principle of retaining body heat with a covering of bulky, yet almost weightless, material sewn into cleverly constructed channels between two layers of a very fine material such as cambric. Duvets are not cheap, but they do work out less expensive than the sheet and three blankets which you would need to buy in order to get an equal amount of warmth.

If you use a fitted bottom sheet with your continental quilt, your bedmaking time should be less than one minute; shake your quilt out, put it back on the bed and the job is done. You will have no restricted 'tucked in' feeling in bed and your housework will be easier because a quilt does not give off the dust and fluff normally associated with wool blankets. The warmth of each quilt is measured in togs, of which there are four categories: 7.5, 8.5, 9.5, and 10.5. However you will probably find a quilt of the highest rating too hot, unless you feel the cold badly or sleep in a very chilly room.

Types of material

Duvets are filled with either natural or man-made materials. Pure down is the lightest, warmest and most expensive filling, but don't assume you can use an old eiderdown as a duvet – the loose pocketed construction is unique and largely responsible for the duvet's efficient action.

A product marked 'down and feather' must by

law consist of more than 51 percent down. 'Feather and down' describes the least expensive type of natural quilt which is mainly feathers, but it must have 15 percent down in its filling. No duvet filled with natural materials can be washed or cleaned in the normal way, so you should always enclose yours in a special cover, like a giant pillowslip, to protect it so it never needs cleaning. If an accident should happen, send the duvet to the manufacturer or a specialist cleaner for treatment.

Continental quilts filled with man-made material cost less, but they also have a lower warmth/weight ratio. Excellent for allergy sufferers because of their filling, and for children because they are completely washable, they are the only type recommended for very small babies. Never send any synthetic-filled duvet to the dry-cleaners since the fumes will stay inside the bulky filling and may be breathed in during the night.

Choose a well-known brand to be sure you are getting a good quality filling; terylene P3 is excellent and often specified for use in hospitals. Some newer quilts are being manufactured with a combined feather/down/synthetic filling which reduces cost, although these are not, of course, washable.

Check whichever kind of duvet you choose conforms to British Standards for content or cleanliness or both. Sticking to British Standards codes will also ensure the quilt you buy is filled with new, rather than reconditioned material.

You can make your own duvet from either an old eiderdown or a ready-assembled kit, but this is a very fiddly and messy job and you may find the extra cost of having it done professionally is well worth it.

What size to buy

The size of your quilt should depend on the number of people sleeping under it – not on the size of the bed. A single person needs a duvet at least 1370mm (or 54in) wide, while two people need one of 1830mm (or 72in). On a large bed, you may find two single quilts easier to manage and this is often a good solution if one person is restless in bed or likes to sleep at a different temperature from his partner. Always check the size of the duvet rather than trusting any manufacturer's designations of 'single' or 'double'. The usual length of a continental quilt is 2000m (or 6ft 6in), although some companies make them 2200mm (or 7ft 4in) long for tall people.

Covering a duvet

A continental quilt cover is necessary to increase insulation and to protect the quilt from dust, dirt and accidental spills. Choose one the same size or slightly larger than the quilt and make sure it is easily removable for washing, with an opening either at one end or along the side and fastened with ties, nylon press studs, Velcro or a zip fastener.

Quilt covers come separately or as part of a range with matching sheets, pillowslips and valances, in light washable fabrics such as seersucker and polyester cotton. They are fairly easy to make – try using two old sheets which became redundant when you bought your quilt. The selection of attractive covers is so large and varied you will probably find you have no need of a bedcover.

Bedcovers

The design of a bedcover – whether it is pink and frilly or tailored and plain – can establish the entire feeling of your bedroom, so choose it with care.

Because a bedcover is mainly decorative rather than functional, the range of materials and styles is enormous; traditional crochet, candlewick and patchwork spreads are still widely used, as well as more recent additions to the range such as the Indian cotton type which is such good value for money. A small rug makes an exotic bedcover; but before you opt for something like this, make sure you can lift it easily so that turning the bed down at night and making it up in the morning do not become major tasks. If your bedrooms will double as a study or workroom, or if you simply want it to look sleek and tailored, wool, tweed, cord or any other upholstery fabric would be an excellent choice.

Decide whether you want a plain throw-over cover or one that is fitted to the bed and piped along the edges. The sides can be frilled, pleated, or left flat with a kick pleat at each corner so you can remove the cover easily. If your bed is sited against a wall, a simple cover plus a collection of scatter cushions will give you an extra seating area during the day.

Valances

If you want your divan covered even when the bedspread is turned back, think about fitting a bedbase cover – or valance. Often available in the same ranges as sheets, pillowcases and duvet covers, they usually give a frilled or pleated effect around the bottom of the bed. One company makes a valance attached to a fitted bottom sheet, but if you tend to iron all bedlinen – even those things which are claimed not to need it – you may find it a little tedious to press yards of gathered fabric each time you wash the bottom sheet.

A flat, fitted bedbase cover is fairly easy to make; just attach it to a large piece of curtain lining fabric which you then place between the mattress and the divan base. If you are not skilled with a needle, any large or specialist shop should do this for you.

Above left A plain bedcover made up in woollen upholstery fabric will give your room a neat, tailored look
Left Traditional candlewick bedspreads give an extra layer of warmth and are very easy to launder (Incover)
Above If you want your divan base to be covered, choose a fitted bottom sheet with a valance attached (Dorma)

General bedroom furniture

Once you have your bed and large storage furniture sorted out, there are still several smaller items to consider; and it is often these, along with the soft furnishings and accessories, which will give your bedroom its distinctive appearance and character.

Bedsteads

Old-fashioned solid brass bedsteads are becoming more and more difficult to find – and are prohibitively expensive. Some shops sell only old and reproduction beds so go to one of these places if this is the type of bed you want. If you are lucky

Left An original or reproduction brass bedstead gives a traditional look to any design scheme
Below left Small chests of drawers make excellent bedside tables since they provide a great deal of extra storage space
Below This striking headboard is an extension of the stained tongued and grooved cladding fixed below window sill height
Right Choose a practical, wipe-clean surface, like glass or laminate, for your dressing table

enough to inherit a brass bed, you will find the finish fairly easy to restore; keep it bright and untarnished by applying a coat of lacquer.

More common are iron bedsteads with brass finish or detailing. These are less expensive and you might be fortunate enough to pick one up in a junk or second-hand shop. If you find one you like which is in poor condition, give it a new look by sanding it with emery cloth, priming it with red oxide to prevent rust and applying undercoat and gloss paint in the usual way.

Old wood bedsteads are still widely available; here again, choose one with a style you like and, if necessary, refinish or paint it.

Headboards

First decide whether you really need one; few come high enough to protect the wall from head marks and a solid mattress/divan set is quite firm enough to stay in place if you lean on a pillow propped up against the wall. Headboards are often bought for their decorative value; but an attractive picture or wall-hanging will give you a similar effect and one which is more flexible as well as being less costly.

If you do make up your mind to buy a headboard, look for a design that is practical as well as good

looking and avoid metal ones since they can feel chilly against your back on a cold morning. Choose something sturdy, comfortable and easy to clean – a plain headboard to which you add a removable home-made cover is an excellent choice since you can wash it when it looks grubby and change it if you redecorate.

If you do not sit up to read or eat in bed, choose an antique or junk shop mantle mirror which makes a striking headboard and can often be bought the same width as a small double bed.

You can save money and space if you choose a headboard that incorporates bedside storage in its design, in which case you will not need separate bedside units. Some even have light fixtures as well. This type is not just space-saving; it also leaves the floor clear so you can make the bed and clean round it more easily.

Bedside tables

Some people like a great many things beside them when they go to bed – clock, tissues, reading material, cigarettes, lighter and ashtray, water jug, glass and so on. If you are one of these, choose a bedside table with plenty of storage space – a minimum of two drawers plus a shelf for books and magazines – so at least some of the normal clutter is kept out of sight. If your bedtime requirements are simple, you can save money by having an ordinary small low table, possibly a whitewood one which you can finish off yourself. Extra room for small items of household linen would be provided by metal, wood or cane trunks that give a similar table top area while having the added advantage of offering lots more storage underneath.

Right A comfortable chair in the bedroom gives you an additional place to read and rest during the day
Below A large picture or wall hanging creates the same effect as a headboard, but is more flexible and often less costly
Bottom Give your bedroom a co-ordinated look by covering a plain headboard with a fabric used elsewhere in the room
Opposite If you can sew, consider making ruffled and swathed four-poster curtains for the ultimate in feminine bedroom design

Dressing tables

If you do all your grooming in the bedroom, you should provide a place where all the necessary equipment can be stored out of sight, since nothing makes the bedroom look messier than a collection of half-filled, odd shaped bottles, jars and tubes or brushes and combs. The neatest solution is a dressing table with a hinged lid (and preferably a mirror on the inside) so you can put all these items away under a flat clear surface.

Your dressing table can double as a home office if it has several drawers for paperwork, pens and files. The most practical surface for either of these purposes is glass or laminate, since they are the only finishes which will stand up to things like nail varnish remover and biro ink.

Those who prefer something more traditional could look for an old dressing table or desk and perhaps a pivoting mirror with drawers underneath; these are still quite common in second-hand, junk or antique shops.

Whichever type you choose, the lighting arrangements are very important. New models sometimes come with built-in tungsten striplights; but if this is not the case you should fit table, wall or clamp lights on each side of the mirror.

Chairs

Although we all intend to hang up or put away our clothes as soon as we take them off, they usually end up in a heap somewhere until we get round to sorting them out; if there is a chair handy, then at least the bed can remain uncluttered. Choose a comfortable cane or upholstered style so you can sit in it to read or rest during the day.

Bedroom wall and floor coverings

Above Use fabric and wallpaper from the same range for a neat, co-ordinated look
Top right An all-over treatment on walls and ceilings will help disguise any irregularities in the shape of the room
Above right Long pile carpet is comfortable and practical in a bedroom

Finding the right bedroom wall and floor coverings is not easy because there is such a wide range to choose from. We describe what works well and how to use it to get the best effect.

Because the bedroom gets less frequent and less demanding use than many other areas in the home, you do not have to be quite so practical in your choice of floor, wall and window coverings and therefore you have a much wider range from which to make your selection.

On the walls

You should not need to wash the walls in your bedroom and, unless your home is very damp, you should have no problems with moisture at all. This means you can choose flat or silk paint or any sort of wall covering you like, from the cheapest paper to luxurious materials such as suede, felt, hessian or silk. Try using fabric as a wall covering, fixing it to narrow timber battens at the top and bottom of the wall and at intervals vertically. Printed sheets and cotton bedspreads are a good size and quality for this treatment and they are likely to be much cheaper than fabric bought by the metre. Cork and wood panelling cost more than paint or most papers, but they both absorb sound efficiently and make excellent insulators against cold.

If you want a headboard for your bed but cannot manage the expense, paint one on the wall trompe-l'oeil fashion so you will be able to obliterate it when you can afford the real thing.

Paint or paper the ceiling to match the walls; this gives a cosy feeling and helps to 'lower' a very high room. A darker coat of paint continued down to picture rail height will have the same effect, but be careful of using a very dark shade since this will

make the ceiling seem to recede. For an exotic effect make a canopy by attaching long lengths of cloth to the ceiling rose and draping them over the room to the ceiling-to-wall angle.

On the floor

There is a strong case for laying fitted carpet in your bedroom even if the rest of the home has to do without. Because this room gets less use than heavy traffic areas such as halls and living rooms, a cheap 'light domestic' grade will be perfectly adequate and make a remarkable difference to your personal comfort as well as improving both heat and sound insulation.

Long pile shag carpet is the ultimate in luxury, but even flooring felt bought cheaply from an ex-exhibition dealer would be an improvement on a cold, hard floor. In any case it would be wise to put down a few small rugs in areas of heavy wear such as those at the side of the bed or in front of the wardrobe. If your bedroom serves more than one purpose and is in constant use during the day, you will have to invest in something more durable to avoid the necessity of replacing it in two or three years. Whatever carpeting you choose, be sure to invest in a good quality, thick underlay to prolong the life of the carpet and improve its performance as an insulator.

Where a bedroom leads straight into a bathroom or dressing room choose the same floor covering, or at least the same colour of floor covering, for both areas to link them together visually. Covering the bedroom floors with the same carpet as that on the landing or in the hall will make any home seem larger and more co-ordinated.

If you choose not to carpet this room, you will have to opt for one of the forms of hard covering. Floorboards are often in better condition here than they are in the rest of the house, so you may be able

If you choose vinyl flooring in your bedroom, put a rug beside the bed so you do not have to step onto a cold, hard surface first thing in the morning

Top left Bedroom walls painted in a subtle colour help provide a relaxing atmosphere
Top right Luxurious silk wallpaper is ideal for bedroom use
Above left Ceramic tiles can be used where the bathroom leads off the bedroom
Above right Blinds are a good idea when you want to put a dressing table or any other piece of furniture in front of the window, where curtains would get in the way

to sand and seal them without much difficulty or treat them with a special hard-wearing floor paint which comes in bright, muted or neutral colours.

You can cover boards that are badly marked with vinyl or cork, but avoid really hard surfaces like ceramic or quarry tiles unless you have underfloor heating or where you are covering a bathroom/bedroom area. With cold surfaces, try to find a scatter rug for each side of the bed so you will not be rudely awakened when your feet touch the floor first thing in the morning. Alternatively construct a timber platform, cover it with carpet and put the bed on this; if planned cleverly this could give you additional seating as well.

At the window

Before you choose any covering for your bedroom windows, think about installing double glazing to keep the warmth in and the noise out – you will appreciate quiet here more than in any other room in your home.

If you like the sun streaming into your room early in the morning, go for unlined curtains; but if you would rather wake up gradually, invest in lined or interlined ones which will improve the insulation of the room as well. Choose a fabric to match the wallpaper or bedcover, or one in a co-ordinating colour or print. Net curtains will let in light during the day while giving the maximum amount of privacy, but they tend to look grey and grubby in a very short time. Try thick cotton lace ones instead, or those made from lightweight, white-on-white printed fabric.

Blinds are perfectly suitable for the bedroom as long as they prevent neighbours looking in; choose any type except cane or pinoleum which are transparent from the side which has the least amount of light. If, however, you fix curtains as well as a blind, this will not be a problem.

The Bedroom: Top Designers' Tips

1. Enliven a dull boxy room with a **pretty paper border** along the tops of the walls and round the door frames.

2. Try the luxurious effect of a room done in many **different shades and textures** of the same colour: cream or green, for example, have infinite variations.

3. **Festoon curtains** give a **sumptuous appearance** to any bedroom and are particularly effective for hiding ugly windows. Special tapes and instructions for making them are now widely available.

4. If you are short of space, **fix bedside lights to the walls** rather than have table lamps on bedside tables.

5. With a steady hand, you can **stencil cheap and pretty patterns** on plain walls.

6. Co-ordinating curtains, blinds, bedcovers and sheets give an instant **feeling of luxury** to a room at a relatively low cost. Several manufacturers produce co-ordinating sets.

7. Fabric wall coverings (paper backed for easy application) not only look **elegant** and make a bedroom **quiet and tranquil**, but conceal minor deficiencies in the plasterwork. Hessian, felt, silk, stranded wool and even cork are available in this form.

8. Clothes racks (the sort used by dress manufacturers) make an **inexpensive and mobile place to hang clothes** if you live in a dust-free country area.

9. Modern pine four posters can be hung with inexpensive printed cotton to give a **decorative country quality** to the room.

10. **Large arrangements of dried flowers** can complement your bedroom colour scheme.

11. For a genuine period feel, look for an old-fashioned **cheval mirror** in the second hand shops.

12. Increase your enjoyment of a beautiful view by **lining the window reveals** with mirror glass.

THE LIVING ROOM

WITH THE EMERGENCE OF THE KITCHEN AS a focus of family life, plus the fact that many homes now have central heating so that bedrooms can be used for homework and such mess-inducing hobbies as model-making and sewing, the living room has assumed its rightful place as the room where family and friends can gather together for a little civilized living.

Plan it with three things in mind: comfort, good looks and hard wear. Comfort is essential, because this is a room where everyone will come to relax after a hard day, whether this was spent at school, at work or at home. A room where the chairs are hard and upright, the furniture is awkwardly arranged and cold draughts twirl round your ankles will give no pleasure to anyone.

Choose chairs which are soft to collapse into but firm enough to give support to tired bodies, and if there is a knitter in the family be sure to have at least one which has arms low enough to accommodate busy elbows. Arrange the seats intelligently with a wide group round the fireplace if you have one, and the television placed so that as large a number of people as possible can see it. In a room of ample size, try to have a separate seating arrangement elsewhere in the room, preferably with its own low table for those who do not want to watch television, but prefer to play a game, chat or read.

Arrange bookshelves and other storage on an accessible wall, not for instance behind the television or the sofa, so that members of the family do not have to disturb each other to get at books, records and other possessions.

Good looks are a rather more subjective topic, but whatever style you prefer, beware the discordance caused by too many colours, too many conflicting patterns or too many diverse materials. Keep the furnishing simple, putting all the personality, character and idiosyncratic quirks into the room with accessories. Prints, ornaments, cushions, rugs, plants and curtains are changed more easily than the main pieces of furniture; rearrange them to suit your mood and to bring colour to a room, thus providing you with change at no vast capital outlay. Large items of furniture, however, should be chosen in the sure knowledge that they will please you for a long time.

Everything in the living room should be selected for its hard wearing qualities; if you insist on pale colours on your seating, at least have loose covers which are fairly easily cleaned or washed. Curtains can be hugely costly, but you will get far better value from cheap material, lined so that it lasts longer and hangs better, than from better quality material unlined.

A separate dining room, which by its nature is used only for limited periods of time, can be treated very dramatically with splendidly rich colour schemes, unusual (even bizarre if your taste runs in that direction) furniture, and lighting which contributes to the sense of theatre. Again though, do not forget that all this must be hard wearing and easily cleaned.

A real fire and soothing colours make this living room a haven after a hard day's work.

Planning living rooms

The main activities of the household usually take place in the living room, where members of the family meet, work, read, pursue hobbies, listen to music, watch television or entertain friends. If it is going to accommodate all these comfortably, it must be efficient and adaptable; so choose the room you want to use – and all its components – with great care.

Creating space

First look closely at the existing living area and decide whether this could be allocated to a more suitable room in the house. Up to the time of our grandparents, sitting rooms were often on an upper floor and work areas were consigned to the lower level where there was less light and more noise and fumes. If your ground floor comprises a kitchen, living room and dining room, it might be possible for the living room to change places with the first floor master bedroom where daylight is not so necessary. A downstairs bedroom, if used by adults, will not be affected so much by traffic and other outside noise since it will normally be in use only from the late evening onwards.

Structural alterations require more money and trouble (and, of course, must always comply with local building regulations); but you can often get quite dramatic results by removing a wall altogether where possible. For example, a dining room is used only for short periods each day – and perhaps not at all some days if meals are taken in the kitchen. See if you can take down the wall separating the dining room from the living area; this will give you one room which seems much larger than the total of the two smaller original areas. In addition the dining table can be used for other activities such as sewing or letter-writing without the person involved having to be separated from the rest of the household.

You may also be able to remove the wall which separates the living room from the hall; this will give you a greater area of living space without sacrificing any other rooms in the home. You could remove both the dining room and hall walls to increase your living area further.

Of course if either of these are supporting walls, they will have to be replaced with a rolled steel joist (RSJ) or some other suitable support; so

Above left Adaptable unit seating forms easily into a neat and convenient L-shaped arrangement
Left Heavy curtains hung to cover both door and window minimize draughts
Top right Small patterns, bright colours and a collection of plants and cane accessories transform a dark basement into a cheerful living area
Centre right Plain sofas and chairs set at right-angles make a workable U-shaped seating arrangement in this large and formal sitting room
Right The design of these stairs maintains the open aspect of this through room

always contact a surveyor or architect before you attempt such a scheme. Other than this the only real problems involved in knocking two rooms into one are those of heating and insulation; but these can be partly overcome by draughtproofing the windows and the front door – and even by extending a run of full-length curtains to cover the whole of the external wall, including the door.

You can create extra space by rehanging a door to open outwards or replace it with a folding or sliding version. If possible, reposition any radiators where they interfere with an efficient arrangement of furniture and add electrical outlets so you are not stuck with a particularly unsuitable location for the lighting, television or hi-fi.

Taking away a chimney-breast will also add space; but before you do this, be absolutely sure you get expert advice on any structural problems which could arise. Also make sure you will never want an open fire again – and remember that a working fireplace is a much better focal point for a room than a television set, which should be only an accessory. If you cannot remove the entire breast, at least take away the surround and plaster over the opening. Nothing looks sadder than a bare, blocked-up fireplace. Alternatively leave the recess and use it to house an ornament or large plant and retain a focal point.

Using colour

Colour can make a great difference to the feeling of any room; but the important thing with the living room is to decorate with shades and patterns that are relaxing and easy to live with. This is not the place to indulge your fantasy for dark brown or bright pink walls – the immediate effect might be dazzling, but it is unlikely you will be comfortable with it for several hours each day and over a long period of time.

Choosing furniture

The particular pieces of furniture needed for this room will differ widely with the age, interests and number of people who will be using it; the needs of a young couple in their first home will be very different from those of a large family plus, possibly, an elderly relative. The basic requirements are seating, storage, occasional tables and any equipment needed for entertaining such as a television, record player, tape recorder or radio.

The best way to plan is with the help of a scale drawing of the room on graph paper and cut-out shapes to represent existing and planned pieces of furniture. This paperwork might save you a great deal of time and money if it teaches you that the sofa you saw in the sales will be just that bit too long for the recess you had in mind for it, or that the huge bookcase which took three of you half an hour to move will not fit after all.

Even after the most meticulous planning you may find, with such a complex room, you can arrive at the optimum arrangement only after living in it for a time. If you need extra furniture or furnishings, you do not have to rush out and buy them all at once. Start with the bare necessities and add only those items you really need or like very much. For example, if you are not sure about material for curtains, first fix cheap white or cream blinds which will always be useful and will give you sufficient privacy; postpone the final choice until you are quite sure what you want. You will find the finished room is much more efficient and pleasant

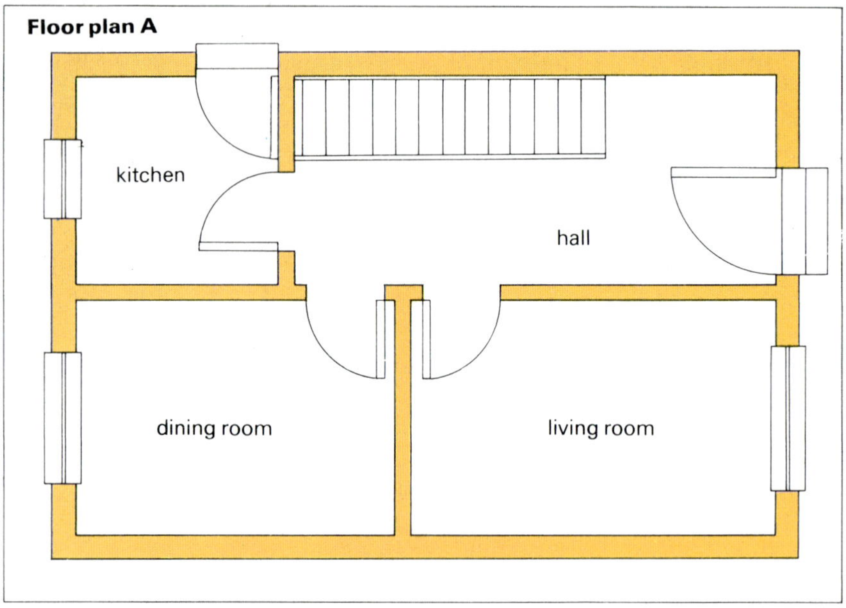

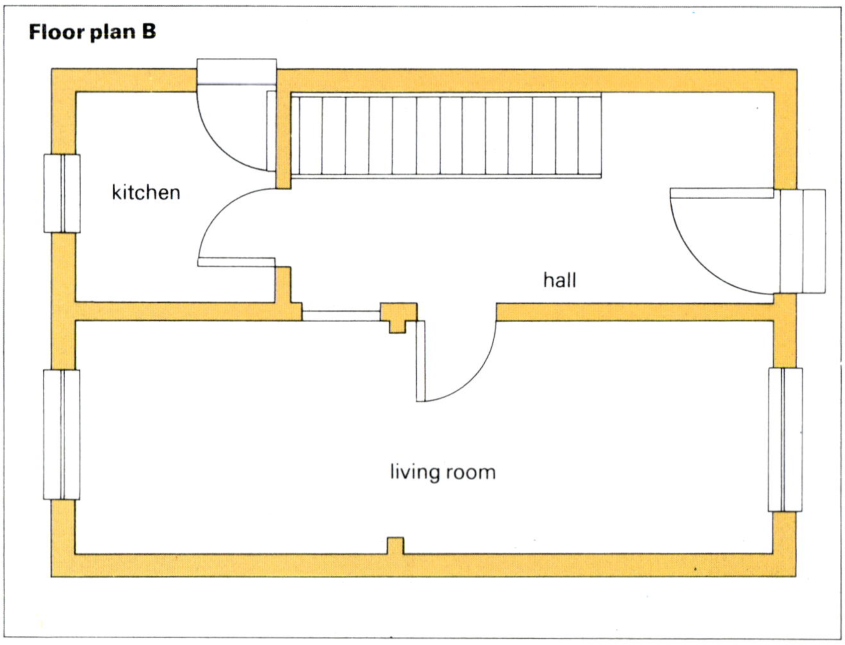

to be in if you take a great deal of time and thought over everything that goes into it.

Seating The main sitting area should be your first consideration. There is no reason to line the walls with furniture like a public waiting room; people probably converse most comfortably when sitting at right-angles to each other, so some kind of 'L' or 'U' shape arrangement is ideal. Where possible make sure people do not have to walk through or near this area to cross the room and check it is free from draughts and excessive noise. You might like to plan your seating arrangements to take advantage of such features as a working fireplace or a window with a particularly appealing view.

You will need at least one accessible low table so people do not have to balance a cup or glass on their knee or leave it on the floor where it might get knocked over. Incidentally, it should follow that any arrangement which is comfortable for those who live with it will be right for any visitors using it as well.

Storage Needs will vary enormously according to the household – and the use of the room. Try to be

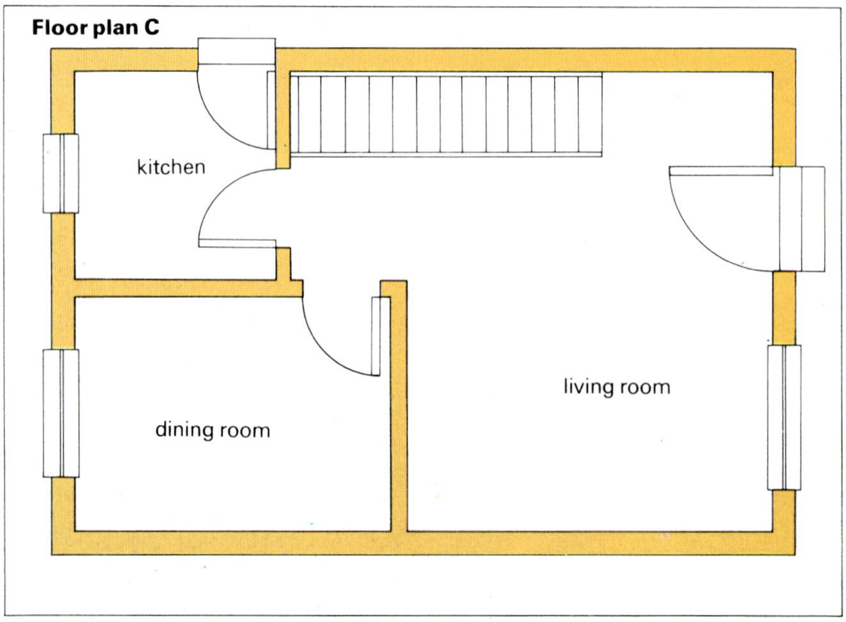

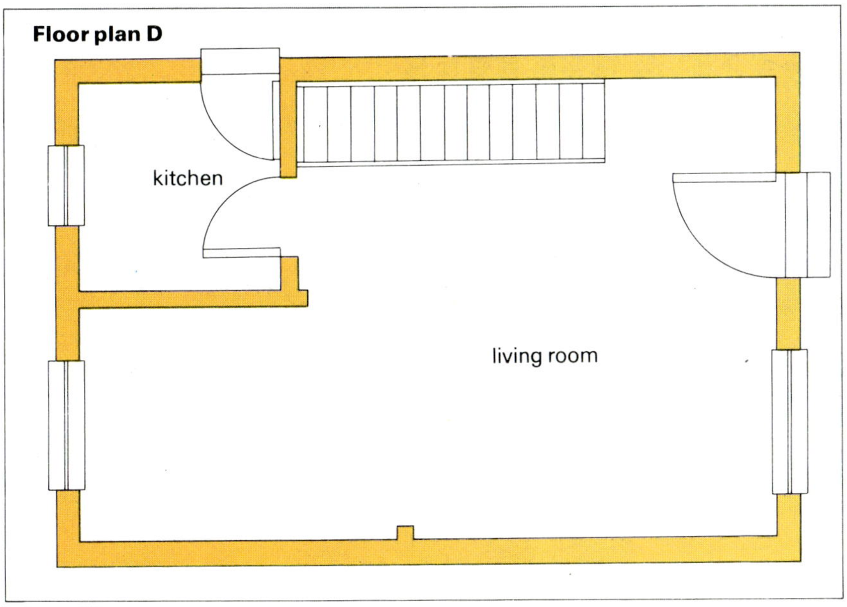

Opposite page
Top left An unused fireplace makes the ideal setting for plants or ornaments
Centre left A large glass table takes plenty of clutter and highlights the floor covering underneath
Top Original ground floor plan
Centre Wall removed between living room and dining room
Bottom Wall removed between living room and hall

Top Wall between dining room, living room and hall removed to create one through area
Centre Seating arranged in an 'L' shape
Bottom Seating arranged in a 'U' shape
Top right Neutral colours create a restful atmosphere
Centre right Start furnishing with essential items and add to them gradually

flexible in terms of location. An empty wall is the obvious place for books, hi-fi equipment and drinks, but you may find a run of open shelves for these things will make an efficient room divider to cut off a dining or sitting area from the place where children watch television or where the telephone is located. Look for double-duty furniture such as seating with storage underneath or tables with a lower shelf as well as the top surface.

Make sure the dining table, if it is to be in the living room, is close to the kitchen. When you have guests, you will not want to be carrying dishes and pots of food past them while you are preparing the table. Ideally there should be a hatch from the kitchen through to the serving area; otherwise try to make the route between the two as short as possible.

Above all, plan a living room for the people who will be using it. Although you will always gain by reading decorating books and articles and gleaning ideas from them, in the end it is your own needs and preferences which must come first – not any fancy designs or special effects.

General living room furniture

If your living room is going to be a comfortable and efficient centre for family activities – as well as a place where all the members can relax or entertain friends – the furniture will have to be adaptable for a whole range of different uses.

Tables and chairs

Although a smaller part of living room design than major seating and storage systems, the occasional tables and chairs in the room contribute just as much to its appearance and efficiency.

Arrange to have coffee or occasional tables conveniently located near seating units. Those in front of seats should be no higher than 50mm (2in) above the seat height of the surrounding chairs, while side tables should be approximately the same height as the arms of the adjacent seating (unless of course the seating has no arms, in which case the first rule applies).

The shape of the table should correspond to the shape formed by the seating arrangement – square (or round) or rectangular as the case may be. If you are short of storage space, look for tables

with an extra shelf underneath for books, magazines and newspapers – or nesting tables which provide extra surfaces when needed for games, meals in front of the television or when entertaining guests.

Materials For something which is strong and reasonably easy to clean, varnished or lacquered wood is a good choice; but make sure you choose a surface without any mouldings or crevices to hold dirt. Plastic tables are inexpensive, sturdy and very light so you can move them about; and they are particularly easy to look after. You may find some acrylic finishes have a tendency to attract dust (like a television screen), but a special anti-static polish will solve this problem for you. Cane tables and chairs can often be bought quite cheaply, in a wide range of styles, and will give an outdoor look to a room. Glass is a versatile surface and particularly suitable for a very small room since transparent furniture will give a more open and less cluttered appearance; it does, however, need constant care because it will show finger marks or rings left from glasses or dishes more than any other surface – and it can be scratched.

Entertaining Some people find a wheeled trolley useful, either as a stand for the television – making it possible to store the set away when it is not being watched – or as a portable bar holding bottles, cans and glasses. Cocktail cabinets and even fitted bars can be included in living room areas, but they tend to be bulky and limited in their use and will pose space problems in most modern living areas.

Flexibility If your living area does not include a dining area – leaving you without a general purpose table – you may need a separate desk-height table for paperwork, hobbies and children's homework. Select a design with drawers so you can clear away clutter when the surface is not being used. If you want a desk chair as well, choose one which is comfortable enough to double as extra general seating when necessary.

An eating area in a combined living/dining room will be more flexible if the table and chairs you select for it are not an obviously purpose-designed suite. Choose a simple strong table with a surface durable enough to withstand the punishment which will be imposed on it by children playing,

Above left Choose a coffee table which is approximately the same height as the seats of surrounding chairs or sofas. A shelf underneath allows for extra storage
Left You can use simple bracket shelving in an alcove of any width
Top If your dining area is in the living room, choose plain furniture which can be put to other uses
Above A desk with drawers is especially useful if you have no other suitable working surface in the living room
Right A purpose-built shelving unit will hold your hi-fi equipment and leave other useful surfaces free for drinks, books or ornaments

Above Extend an adjustable shelving system to include a work surface which is at a practical height and slightly wider than the other shelves
Above right The alcove beside this chimney-breast has had shelves and cupboards built in to provide not only different size storage compartments, but also space to hide away general paraphernalia
Right This free-standing storage unit, which is attractive and flexible, also acts as a partial room divider

dressmaking and any other family activity that may be carried on there. Again, select dining chairs which are suitable for use in the living area when you have visitors. Flexibility is most important; space is all too valuable in most homes and large pieces of furniture too expensive for either of these to be wasted on just occasional use.

Storage furniture

As with the storage area in any other room, you must first work out what things need to be housed. Most people keep books in the living room and these could require anything from a floor-to-ceiling cabinet to a couple of shelves for paperbacks. Equipment for family entertainment must be allowed for, but again, the quantity varies enormously. Television, radio, tape recorder, stereo and records all need plenty of space and you should decide whether you want them on view or discreetly hidden away. Hi-fi addicts will not mind if speakers, deck, tuner, amplifier, headphones and connecting wires are in evidence, but less committed listeners may want to store some of these items out of sight.

If you like serving drinks in the living room, but do not want to go to the lengths of using a cocktail cabinet or bar, decide whether you would prefer to display the different shapes and colours of the bottles on open shelves to add colour to the room or hide away all the alcoholic paraphernalia. Glasses are best stored behind closed doors to avoid dusty gin and tonics. You may wish to show off handicraft work you have done, a cherished collection of china, glass, pottery or silver, or a selection of family photographs as well as more practical items. But whatever you have to accommodate, remember you will always need more room than you bargained for and that possessions have a way of increasing at an alarming rate. So be very generous with your storage allowance.

Once you have worked out how much space you need, you will have to decide what type of storage will be most suitable for your possessions, your home and your budget. Whichever type you choose, keep the design simple since the objects on display will provide all the visual interest you require.

Wall shelves These are one of the cheapest methods of storage; they include systems supported by fixed or adjustable brackets or by battens fitted to the wall. Although shelves are perfect for a contained area such as a chimney recess, they can prove inflexible. You may find, if you move house, that the shelves you have taken with you are too short for a recess in your new home. They can sometimes be difficult to dismantle and you may have to make good the area exposed afterwards.

Make sure your walls are strong enough to take a loaded storage system – partition or hollow walls, for example, might not take the extra weight. It is best to choose an adjustable system so you can rearrange the shelves if you want a change at some time in the future. Unless you are working in a very tight corner, fit fairly wide shelves so you can use them for items of varying sizes.

If the goods to be stored on a bracket-supported system are very heavy, you will need to position your brackets closer together than if you are catering for just a few ornaments and plants. Always check on the strength of the material you are using for your shelves and the load they will have to support. Make sure any timber you use is suitable for the purpose; if it is too weak, it will buckle under the weight of books and records. If you choose a material faced with laminate, fix matching self-adhesive edging strips for a neat finish on the shelves. For enclosed storage space you can buy ready-made doors in a wide range of sizes to incorporate into a shelving system.

Purpose-built storage This type represents a greater financial outlay than wall shelves, but it does have some advantages. It is easy to pack up and take with you when you move and it can be used against a wall or in the middle of the room to give privacy or divide areas with separate functions, while providing an attractive and useful display which can be appreciated from both sides.

It is most often available in modular units, which usually have a standard height and depth. This type is available in such a wide selection of shapes and sizes you are sure to find something to fill your particular area. These ranges usually have many different designs to suit every possible storage requirement – some even have panels which swing open to reveal a single bed. Any combination of shelves, drawers, cupboards and flap-down working surfaces can be accommodated and some models have striplighting concealed inside cupboards and above shelves. Bear in mind anything which extends out from the unit such as a door, flap or drawer needs 900mm (or 3ft) clearance to operate easily.

Some of the newer storage units are available in cube form; these are all varying forms of one basic cube, with various combinations of small and large shelves, doors, drawers and compartments. Although very expensive as a simple shelving system, this type of furniture repays its initial cost by being totally flexible. A plain cube can be a storage box, a plant holder or even a small table, depending on which way up you use it. Four cubes together make a good size coffee table with storage underneath, while you can make a simple desk by spanning stacked units with a worktop. Since storage requirements throughout the home change, use these cubes in different rooms for varying purposes or join them together to make one large, comprehensive system.

Study all the manufacturers' catalogues carefully before you decide on what range to buy; check to see if any system has to be fixed to a wall or whether it is equally suitable to be completely free-standing, since you may want to use your storage units as a room divider.

Keep an open mind and look at all kinds of furniture; you may find simple wood or laminated storage items designed for use in a kitchen could work equally well in a living room. With plain wood, you can decorate to match the colour scheme in the living room; you may find this type of furniture less costly as well. In small homes it is often a good idea to choose all your storage furniture from the same range to give a feeling of continuity in otherwise confined areas.

Separate storage If a modern system does not fit in with your personal taste or the style of your home, look around for antique, restorable or reproduction pieces of separate storage furniture such as tallboys and wall-mounted or corner cabinets, which will fill otherwise wasted areas of space. You can get cabinets which are glass-fronted to display treasured articles of silver, china, glass and other ornaments.

Top A cube style storage system is extremely adaptable, can be moved easily from one room to another and added to as space and budget permit. Transparent glass or plastic units are particularly effective in a small room where a solid piece of furniture of this size could look clumsy and overpowering

Above If you prefer traditional furniture to more modern designs, you can still find older storage pieces in antique and junk shops and renovate them. This type of furniture, although it can mix happily with more modern styles, usually looks best in a large, high room which will help to complement its proportions

Dining rooms

Many older homes – and some newer ones – have a purpose-built dining area; if your home has one, you must first decide whether you want to devote so much space to a room which is used only at certain times during the day.

If the dining room is next to the living room or kitchen, you may prefer to knock down a wall, thus forming a living/dining or kitchen/dining room for a more open, larger effect. If you like the idea of having a separate eating area for dinner parties and special occasions, consider sliding or folding doors between adjoining rooms which will make it possible to have the best of both arrangements.

Before making structural alterations of any kind, however, check with a builder or architect to be sure no load-bearing wall is removed without being replaced by a suitable support system. Any work of this nature must comply with Building Regulations.

Try to make sure the dining area you choose is easily accessible from the kitchen; you will not want to carry hot, heavy dishes of food very far or push past guests when you are laden down with cutlery, glass and china. If possible, cut a serving hatch through from the kitchen to the dining area to save a lot of walking backwards and forwards and ensure food can be served quickly and efficiently. A well designed serving hatch should be at least 600mm (or 24in) wide and 450mm (or 18in) high – and ideally its base should be level with the kitchen work surface. On the dining room side, it is a good idea to have a serving counter – possibly a small table or the top of a sideboard, if suitably protected to take hot dishes – or a hinged flap which can be raised or lowered when required.

Furniture

Since a separate dining room is normally used for one purpose only, planning here is more straightforward than in other areas where many activities must be catered for. Essential furniture – dining table and chairs, plus some form of storage – should be positioned according to your family's requirements and the size and shape of the room. If you prefer to keep such items as cutlery, crockery, linen and place mats in the kitchen, you might be able to get away without a storage unit; but try to have a trolley or serving area which you can use to put out other courses of food or stack dirty plates.

If your home is small and generally short of storage space, you may find a built-in corner cupboard in this room will hold a great many items without interfering with the room's main function or taking up valuable space.

Below A serving hatch could save unnecessary traffic between the kitchen and the dining room. Note the practical and warm-looking timber floor
Right This simple brass chandelier gives effective, atmospheric light and is quite in keeping with this traditional, stone-floored dining room
Far right Slim radiators will keep the room comfortably warm without taking up valuable space
Bottom right The chairs in this screened off dining area fold up and hang on the wall when not in use

Tables

The size of the table will be determined by the number of people in the family, the amount of entertaining to be allowed for and, of course, the size of the room. The shape of the table is another factor affected by the dimensions of the room, although there are some practical guidelines you should consider before buying a table.

Since each person needs approximately 700mm (or 28in) elbow room and 300mm (or 12in) knee space, a small square or round table is comfortable for only four people; the average family would probably need one which extends to a rectangular or oval shape capable of accommodating at least six people. If you have a large household or are in the habit of entertaining a number of guests at any one time, go for a larger version which will seat at least eight. The extra money you will have to pay for a table which includes a drop end or a removable leaf is well worth the convenience it provides.

When considering the size of your dining room table, always keep in mind the fact that you will need at least 900mm (or 36in) corridor space between the table and the nearest wall – more if you plan to have an adjacent sideboard or serving area. Also make sure the legs of the table are not in an awkward position where they might get in the way of those sitting nearby. This is often a problem when an extension is in use, so try out any table fully extended before you buy it. Those models with a central pedestal base avoid this kind of problem altogether, but they do not usually lend themselves to extension systems. Whatever its style and size, your table should be about 750mm (or 30in) high for most to eat comfortably at it.

Left This stylish dining furniture is made from lightweight and practical plastic
Below left If there is a pendant light over your dining table, make sure it is high enough to allow an easy flow of conversation and its lamp is completely hidden

Chairs
In addition to having enough chairs for all the family, be sure to allow a few additional ones for guests. They do not have to be part of a set or even situated in the same room, as long as you can press them into service easily when visitors are expected.

Chair seats should be about 400mm (or 16in) above the floor, with backs at least 400mm (or 16in) high to give adequate support. Some people find dining chairs with arms more comfortable than ordinary ones, but these tend to be too bulky to slide under the table and therefore take up more space. If you have a very small room, look for chairs which stack neatly when not in use – some can even hang on a matching wall bracket which will hold up to four chairs. One solution could be to have bench seating, if you have a long table; but make sure the people who are going to use it do not object to this rather informal type of seating.

Lighting

One of the most practical lighting arrangements for the dining room is a rise and fall pendant over the table. This type of lighting will usually retract fairly close to the ceiling when the table is being set and can be lowered down over the table to create a warm and intimate atmosphere while still providing adequate light during the meal.

Make sure with any lowered pendant that the lamp cannot be seen by those people seated at the table and that the pendant is not at eye level so it does not interfere with conversation. If you have a very long table, you may need two fittings – one at each end.

An informal atmosphere can also be created by using candles instead of electric lights. Candlesticks not only help to dress a table, but can also set off a sideboard. Make sure they sit firmly and are not placed where they could be knocked over.

Alternatives to pendants are surface-mounted or recessed downlights; the quantity and strength of the lamps used will depend on the size of the room and the effect you want to create. If you prefer something more ornate, choose a decorative chandelier; a typical version will contain six lights.

Depending on the type of main lighting you decide to use in the dining room, you may want to

Right You can afford to be daring with a dining room colour scheme since you spend comparatively little time there
Below Old-fashioned wall lights are effective and appropriate in a period room, but you may need to supplement them with another form of lighting

supplement it with some form of background lighting. Table lights are one possibility, but make sure there is enough room on a sideboard or edge-of-room work surface so this type of light will not get in the way or take up valuable space. A further point to bear in mind is that you must not have any trailing flex which could be a hazard, especially when someone is walking past carrying plates of hot food.

A floor standard in the corner of the room can provide effective additional lighting or you may prefer to fit wall lights; again the quantity and strength of the lamps in these will depend on the size of the room and the amount of light you want them to provide.

Warning When using shades, particularly those made of fabric, check on the recommended maximum strength of lamp to avoid the risk of burning the shade.

Dimmers Ideally you should be able to vary the intensity of light in the dining room and dimmer switches are particularly useful here. They are very effective, for example, when controlling a rise and fall pendant, since you can increase the amount of light when the pendant is raised and reduce it when the pendant is lowered over the table to create an informal atmosphere for dinner parties.

Heating

If you have central heating, there will no doubt be a radiator in the dining room which you can turn on only when the room is being used to save on heating bills. Otherwise any form of space heating will be suitable, as long as it is situated far enough from the table to enable heat to be distributed evenly and to avoid one diner getting charred while the rest feel uncomfortably cool. Remember also to place your heater well clear of traffic paths.

Wall and floor coverings

Because a separate dining room is used only occasionally – and for relatively short periods – you can be adventurous here, perhaps using bright colours or dramatic patterns which would be inappropriate for areas of heavy use such as the living room. But don't be tempted to use a scheme which might make food look unappetizing, such as one incorporating bright purple and green.

The dining room does not require any special wall treatment; any covering is practical, so choose one which suits your taste and your budget. Unless, however, you do not feed children here – and your adult friends are extraordinarily tidy eaters – you should give rather more thought to your choice of floor covering. Try to find something which can be cleaned easily, but which has a fairly warm look and feel, such as wood, cork, vinyl or a dark-coloured short pile carpet. Carpet squares are an excellent choice, since you can replace one easily if it gets stained or damaged in any way.

Bear in mind the general warning about rugs, which applies as much to this room as to the living room. If you want to lay rugs on the floor, make sure they are secured in such a way that you will not trip on them or slide across the floor.

Top left Large and ornate pieces of Victorian furniture can still be found in antique and junk shops; some make ideal storage areas for bottles, dishes, glasses, linen and cutlery and provide a place to put additional lighting

Top Fit a rise and fall pendant over the dining room table so you can raise or lower it as necessary

Above Stylish bentwood chairs are perfect for the dining room and you can press them into service as additional seating in other parts of the home

Living room wall and floor coverings

Above Make a high room seem lower by painting the ceiling in a darker shade and extending this colour down to picture rail height
Top right Relieve plain walls by outlining skirting, cornice and other decorative features with a thin line in a contrasting colour
Centre right If you use a strong colour on your walls, keep the rest of the scheme simple by choosing fairly neutral colours

Opposite page
Top Cork tiles make a warm, attractive floor covering which will stand up to the kind of wear children may inflict. Choose ready-sealed tiles or seal them yourself after they have been laid
Below Make sure all scatter rugs laid on hard flooring are fastened down so they will not slip around and cause accidents

Previous page
Inexpensive hardwearing coir (coconut) matting comes in narrow or broadloom widths and is sometimes available with a latex backing

Your living room probably takes more wear and tear than any other room in the home, so never skimp on the basic coverings; any defects will soon become obvious and will lead to more expense if your furnishings need replacing prematurely.

Walls and ceilings

Most types of wall covering are suitable for the living area, as long as they will stand up to direct sunlight, the occasional knock and even concentrated heat if you have an open fire or spot heating system. Above all, whatever material you choose should retain its looks over a long period of time. The living room is generally the largest room in the home and therefore one of the most costly and time-consuming to redecorate, as well as causing major disruption to normal activities. Together walls and ceiling cover the greatest surface area and therefore tend to dominate.

Paint

Painting is the cheapest and easiest method of decorating the walls. Use a matt or silk paint and make sure your surface is clean, dry and free from loose plaster and cracks. There is no reason why the ceiling has to be white – try painting it the same colour as the rest of the room for a warm and co-ordinated effect. Again white is not always necessary for woodwork – a matching or contrasting colour might be more effective here.

It is not usually a good idea to paint or paper one wall in a drastically different way from the rest of the room, although at one time this was fashionable. This treatment tends to dominate everything else and throw the room out of balance; a subtle scheme, rather than a dramatic or very bright one, will be more successful in a frequently used room.

If your walls are slightly bumpy or have small cracks (which need not be filled), try using a textured paint; this is applied with a brush and will cover small imperfections, leaving an attractive surface which resembles rough plaster. The walls are prepared as for painting; so if you are covering bare plaster, you will have to prime the surface first. You can apply the textured covering straight onto ordinary paint and remove it, if necessary, with a proprietary stripper. Most brands of this covering come in a range of pastel colours; if you would like a deeper shade, brush a coat of ordinary emulsion paint in your chosen colour on top.

Wallpaper

A paper chosen for a room which will be used by adults only need not be particularly strong; but if there are young children around, it should be tough enough to take a few knocks, marks and scratches – and preferably vinyl-coated to enable any marks to be wiped off.

Wallpaper comes in a huge range of styles and colours, some with another material covering such as felt, hessian, foil, wool, grass or ordinary fabric. This type of specialized covering is, naturally, more expensive than paint or ordinary paper, so take into account the type and amount of wear it is likely to endure before making a final choice. One of the newest version of wallpaper is made from a polyethylene-based material which looks and feels like fabric. It is easier to hang than other coverings because you paste the wall, not the paper. When you want a change, or are moving house, it peels off easily and can be rehung elsewhere.

If your budget is limited, but you want a more decorative effect than plain paint can give, stick on a wallpaper frieze or cut-outs from a roll of paper whose design you like, but whose price prevents you from using it everywhere.

Other coverings

Ordinary fabric is sometimes used very effectively to cover the walls. Staple or glue it to a timber batten framework (and fix extra battens where you want to hang a picture or mirror), but remember it will have to be taken down and washed when it begins to look grubby.

Cork tiles have a warm look, improve heat and sound insulation and provide an informal and flexible pinboard for posters and children's drawings; but they are relatively expensive.

Cover one wall of a small room with a mirror to make it seem larger. If this wall is opposite a window, the mirror will increase the amount of light in the room as well.

For a rough and natural effect, leave brickwork exposed; where the walls have been plastered over, you will have to strip the plaster back to bare brick. If the brickwork is in good condition, cover it with a proprietary sealer to discourage dust and to prevent cracking or chipping. To improve the final finish, you may need to repoint the bricks before applying your protective covering. A slightly smoother finish will result if you paint over the bricks; but make sure they are absolutely clean and dry before you do this.

Timber cladding or panelling is another popular wall covering and one which is excellent on uneven walls; it will also help with heat and sound insu-

lation. Fix boards horizontally, vertically or diagonally, but make sure the wall underneath is completely free from damp before you start. Timber wall cladding is fairly simple to undertake.

Floors

Durability, comfort and resistance to dirt are the most important characteristics of living room flooring. This will be one of the areas most heavily used in the home and it is worth spending as much as you can afford to get the best covering.

Carpet

An 80 percent wool, 20 percent synthetic mix is an excellent choice here, especially if it has a dark colour or a subtle, dirt-masking pattern which will help the carpet keep its looks after many years of wear. Try to avoid a shaggy pile, which traps dirt and is difficult to clean, but make sure the pile is not too hard and scratchy so family members who like to lie about on the floor can do so in comfort. Rush matting has a rather rough surface, but is inexpensive so you can fit it wall-to-wall and add a large rug in the seating area. Cord carpet is a practical solution if your budget is tight; it wears well and resists stains. Here again, choose a darkish shade.

Carpet with an efficient underlay will give more sound and heat insulation than any other sort of floor covering; keep this in mind if your home is particularly noisy or cold. A small or unevenly shaped room will be improved by a fitted carpet, which tends to pull it together visually and make it look larger as well as disguising irregularities.

Carpet tiles give the same effect as a run of carpet or you can achieve a checkerboard effect if you arrange the tiles accordingly. Tiles have the advantage that you can rearrange them if some become worn or soiled – or replace individual ones.

Floorboards

If you are lucky enough to have floorboards in good condition, you may prefer to sand and seal them to provide a natural, warm looking floor covering. An assortment of rugs and small carpets can be set off against this type of surface, but the rest of the room should be kept fairly simple to avoid a cluttered effect. If you cannot restore the finish on the wood, remove all dirt and grease and cover it with an appropriate floor paint. Timber floors are sometimes draughty (the extent varies with the space between the boards) and will always be colder than a covered floor.

Other flooring

Cork flooring, usually chosen for a kitchen, bathroom or children's room, can be suitable for the living room, especially if young children are likely to be playing on the floor and therefore require a warm surface which will stand up to the damage they can inflict. Again, you might want to add some rugs for colour, but always make sure they are fastened down to prevent accidents.

Don't be afraid to consider other floorings which are normally used in specialized rooms; taking into consideration the needs of your family, your heating system, budget and personal taste, you may find ceramic or quarry tiles, or slate, stone, rubber or vinyl flooring perfectly practical. Although these may be hard, cold and noisy in the wrong setting, they may also help create precisely the right look and feel in your living room.

Colours and patterns

As with all major furnishings, such as large curtains and coverings for large pieces of upholstered furniture, try to keep any colour or pattern as simple and neutral as possible so you will not tire of it easily; this will enable you to make changes without having to replace costly items.

Windows

Living room windows tend to be large, so any treatment here not only affects the look of the room but often dominates it as well.

Blinds can be a practical choice for this room, especially when the window surround is particularly attractive or its shape interesting but difficult to curtain, such as a bay window.

If you choose to hang curtains allow plenty of fabric so they do not look skimpy; they should be lined, to improve their appearance and effectiveness, and given a fairly formal heading such as pencil or pinch pleats. Remember blinds and curtains give the most flexible covering of all.

Above left Ceramic floor tiles wear well but can be cold without underfloor heating
Below left Roller blinds make a practical window covering which you can decorate to blend with the rest of the scheme
Right Polished floorboards in good condition make an excellent background for a treasured rug
Below Fitted carpet makes a room look larger and helps to insulate against possible draughts and noise

Above left You cannot go far wrong using several shades of one colour as the basis for a scheme – look for its complement to use as an accent

Above Neighbours on the colour wheel – blue and green for example – have a naturally restful harmony which can be used effectively

Left An all-over treatment will make an awkwardly shaped room seem less so

Living room seating

Even before you start to equip your living room to cope with a number of different activities, you should make it an ideal place in which to relax. Seating is, therefore, one of the first things to consider when planning this area.

Seating requirements

It is wise not to set out on a spending spree before you have decided on your basic requirements. Points to bear in mind are the size of the adult members of the family and the way they like to sit for maximum comfort: do you have to accommodate a sprawler, for example, or someone who snuggles up with legs tucked underneath and arms resting on the back of the sofa? If so, look for something with a wide, deep seat and a low back. Anyone who sits fairly upright needs head and neck supported, so choose a seating range with firm, high backs. Tall people need a deep seat as well, so their knees do not come up to meet their chins when they sit down: short people have the opposite problem – if the chair is too deep, their legs will dangle short of the floor. Some people like to lean back to feel relaxed; others prefer a more upright posture. Low seating lends itself to modern furniture and tends to make small, low rooms look bigger; large traditional pieces are particularly suitable for the shape, size and design of older homes (although if you have a good eye for style and proportion, items from different periods can be mixed very successfully in either a modern or traditional setting).

Bear all these things in mind when you are deciding which combination of sofa and chairs will best suit your budget, your room and your family. If everyone has similar requirements, you might choose one or two large sofas. If, however, each member needs a different type of seating, one small sofa and several different chairs would be a better choice. There is no reason why all the furniture has to match exactly, as long as it has been chosen to look right and blend together. These pieces will, of course, cost quite a lot of money; there is a company that now provides some help in the form of a complete DIY kit for making up simply designed, feather-cushioned seating at about half the normal retail price.

Some young couples prefer a selection of huge floor cushions or 'bean bag' chairs (filled with polystyrene granules) to a more formal arrangement. Although this is certainly an economical solution to what can be an expensive problem, it is not always comfortable for more elderly people. If you are considering floor cushions as your only seating, make sure all the friends and relatives you will entertain are young enough and spry enough to enjoy this very casual style with you. If this is not the case, add some back cushions to the floor ones and put them all on a raised plinth, which could have shelves or cupboards fitted underneath for additional storage. One great advantage of separate cushion seating is it can be put anywhere and moved around easily.

Below Flexible unit seating lends itself to many different arrangements – and you can add to it when space and budget allow

Unit seating

Remember three people seldom fit comfortably on a three-seater sofa and a two-seater model will probably be used by only one person at a time. One way to overcome this problem is with unit seating, a fairly new and very useful development in the field of furniture. In its most basic form, it comes in straight and side (or corner) units and enables you to build up (gradually, if you are short of money) a sofa of any size by putting together straight units and adding a corner piece at each end; you can make a right-angled arrangement just as easily with a combination of these pieces.

The great advantage of this system is its flexibility; you can rearrange its components whenever you want a change or when a particular social situation requires a different seating plan. Most

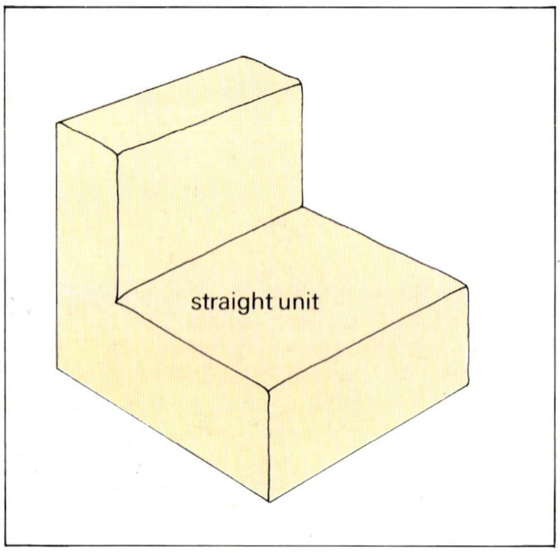

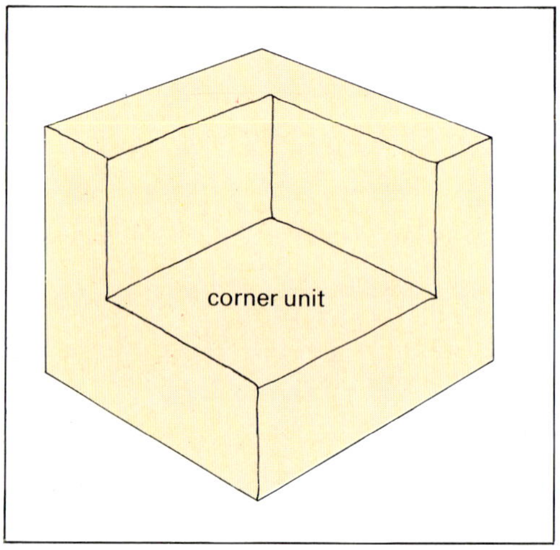

Top Unit seating which has been cut from blocks of solid foam is also available; this is less expensive than upholstered seating and wears well, so it is ideal when there are small children in the home
Left The basic components of unit seating and (**below**) various combinations which can be used

Opposite page Many people still prefer traditional seating, such as a chesterfield design (**top**); some newer models convert into a double bed (**bottom**)

Simple settee

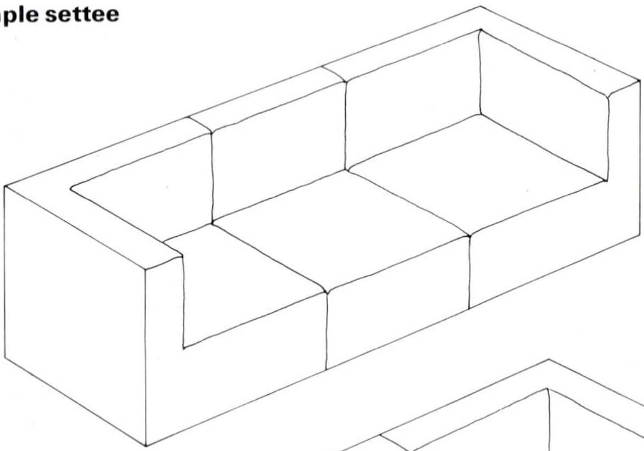

L-shaped unit without arms

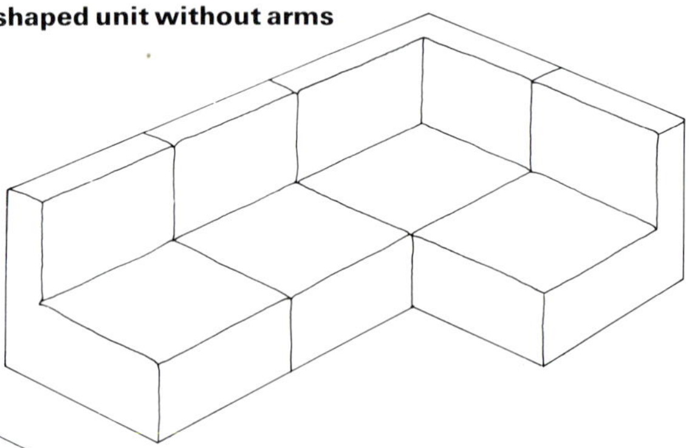

L-shaped unit with arms

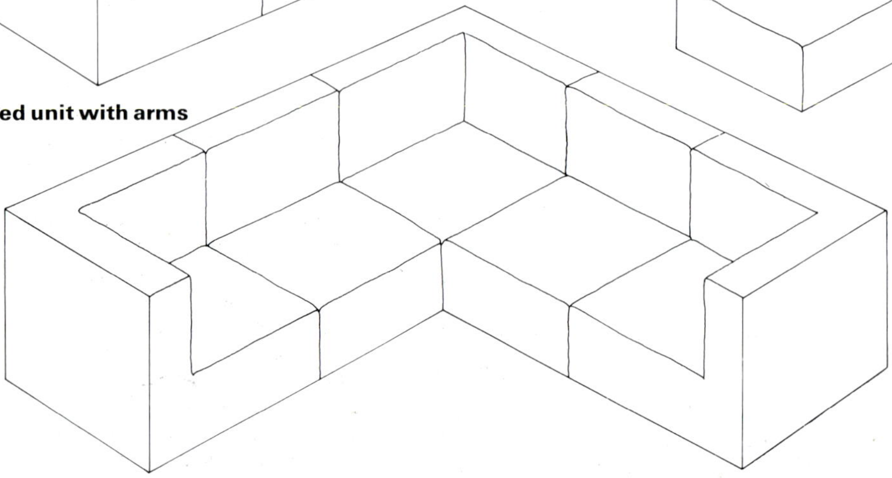

units come complete with castors so they are easy to move around and some ranges cater for those who like a totally co-ordinated look by providing separate but matching tables, pouffes and arm-chairs.

Space Be sure to leave enough space around your seating, whichever type you choose, so it can be used comfortably. Allow 600mm (or 2ft) between the back of a sofa or chair and a wall or table, and try to have the same amount of legroom in front; the minimum legroom is 450mm (or 1ft 6in).

Sofa beds

Although sofa beds are in principle excellent for accommodating occasional overnight visitors, they must be chosen with great care since some do not make either a comfortable sofa or a satisfactory bed. Before you make any such purchase, test it both as a sofa and as a bed to be sure neither you nor your guests will suffer unnecessarily. Check also that the process of conversion is a simple one; you will not want to follow complicated instructions or perform a minor joinery operation at the end of the evening.

One of the least complicated sofa beds is a single divan unit with an attractive cover and a few throw cushions. This arrangement should not, however, provide the main seating in the living room, because a mattress gets worn unevenly when people perch constantly along the side of it; one solution is to turn the mattress round periodically.

The use of any type of sofa bed will be much easier if you choose a duvet instead of the traditional sheet and blankets arrangement which takes much longer to set up.

Furniture covering

Upholstered seating has two main types of cover: loose and tight. Loose covers are, naturally, those which can be taken off for cleaning. If the fabric is washable, you can clean them yourself by soaking them in the bath with suitable soap or detergent. Put them back in place before they are completely dry, since the damp fabric will be easier to stretch into place and will dry smooth and without wrinkles – and with a tight fit.

Although loose covering is generally the more expensive type, it does allow you to keep two sets of covers so you can change the look of your furniture completely without having to buy new pieces. Some furniture is not suitable for covering in this way: straight simple shapes are best; so if your suite has lots of curves and embellishments, you will have to have it tight-covered.

Tight covers are attached to the frame of the piece of furniture with tiny tacks, which are normally hidden by braid or piping. Less expensive than loose covers, this type is particularly good for ornate pieces or those which are not completely covered with fabric, such as small wood chairs with upholstery on the seat, back and arms only.

Choice of fabric

Whichever type of covering you decide on, be sure to choose a suitable fabric. The most important

Right A single divan can be used during the day as general seating with the addition of an attractive cover and scatter cushions

Below Build your own feather-filled seating with a complete DIY kit; loose covers come ready-made

factor here is durability, so check the material you have in mind is designated for upholstery use. It would be a terrible waste to pay a great deal of money to have your sofa covered, only to find the fabric wears thin in a year or two. Tough cotton or linen is practical – or linen union, a mixture of cotton and linen. Some silks, wools and synthetics make good upholstery, as do heavy materials such as brocade. Fabrics with a slightly loose weave are not usually a sensible choice since they tend to stretch out of shape, especially when they are used for tight covers which expose any fabric to heavier wear than loose ones.

Colour and pattern

Large items of seating are a major investment and you will not want to think about changing them for a long time. Consider the design and colour of your fabric carefully: a plain, neutral colour or a simple, small pattern will blend in with different design schemes should you decide to change the look of the room before it is time to replace the furniture.

If there are children or animals in the household, select a fabric which will not show up spots and stains too easily. Darker colours and small patterns are ideal here, but avoid any regular design such as houndstooth check or tiny stripes which tend to highlight any dirty marks, however small they may be.

Top right Floor cushions provide inexpensive, flexible and comfortable seating
Right Leather wears better than most upholstery fabrics and adds a look of luxury
Below A matching suite is practical when everyone shares seating preferences

Top A large expanse of plain net curtains can make an effective window covering on its own if your room is not overlooked

Below Create a soft, restful atmosphere by using fabric on as many surfaces as possible – windows, walls, furniture, tables, cushions and lampshades

Lighting, heating and safety in the living room

The living room must accommodate two basic types of activity – work and relaxation; but no one can either work efficiently or relax completely when the room is not lit or heated effectively – or if it is a black spot area for accidents.

Lighting

Preferences and requirements in lighting are very much personal things and should be chosen to suit both you and your home; but it will be easier for you to get the kind of lighting you need and want if you follow a few basic guidelines.

Lighting has two functions: a practical one – to give sufficient illumination for the activities carried on under it, and an aesthetic one – to set a particular mood and highlight the room's most positive features. Because so many different and contrasting activities take place in this room, any fittings you choose should be as flexible as possible.

Making sure it is functional

If you are lucky enough to be able to decide where sockets should go, fit as many of them as you can to give maximum convenience and adaptability. You can, of course, fir new ones yourself without a

Below left These spotlights can be directed to illuminate specific areas of the room or turned towards the wall for a more subtle effect
Bottom left Fit concealed lighting in a display area to show a treasured collection to best advantage
Below Table lamps provide soft light in a seating area, but stronger illumination is needed for general use

great deal of difficulty.

Most older houses and flats have a central ceiling rose or point for a light fitting, but this type of lighting can make the room look dull and flat. Try fixing a track system instead with spotlights that can be directed at a work area or the wall or ceiling for a more subtle, atmospheric effect. Fit a cord deflector and extend the flex to move the light to a more useful position such as over a coffee or dining table; again you can add or move lights yourself, a technique which is also easily tackled by the DIY enthusiast.

You will need table or floor fittings near work or reading areas and close to awkward steps or traffic paths. Older people are often happier with a greater intensity of light than younger people, so keep this in mind if you have elderly relatives living with you or friends who pay regular visits.

Don't be afraid of using too much light because of running expenses – illumination needs very little power; less than three percent of the electricity used in the average home goes on lighting. To get full value for the money you pay, however, keep all fixtures free of dirt which builds up rapidly and cuts out a surprising amount of light; similarly white lamps will give more light than coloured ones of the same wattage. Dimmer switches will enable you to control brightness – from very high for working to very low for listening to music or watching television. If you do not have a room large enough to allow separate areas for these activities, this arrangement will extend the scope of your lighting effects quite drastically.

Avoid glare by covering the bulb of any lamp, especially a fluorescent fitting which can otherwise be very harsh. Fluorescent tubes are ideal for subtle lighting such as behind curtains, in recesses and for shelving units.

Using it for effect

The type of lighting you choose for your living room can change not only its mood, but also its apparent size and shape. A beam of light directed at the ceiling will make it seem higher, while low hanging lights or spots aimed down will give the impression of a lower ceiling. The deeper the colour you use to decorate your room, the more light you will need since dark walls will absorb a great deal of it and at the same time make the space seem smaller. Conversely a light coloured room will look larger and need less illumination to function properly since pale tones reflect light.

Spotlights are excellent for highlighting favourite pictures or objects on display; place treasures on a glass shelf and light them from underneath for a dramatic effect. Keep brilliant spots away from bumpy walls or at least refrain from lighting such an area from the side since this will cast shadows and show up every imperfection.

Choosing fittings

Never choose any light fitting as an additional piece of decorative furniture. This is a waste of money and rarely adds to the efficiency of the

Top As well as giving a cosy feeling to a room, an open fire fitted with a back boiler will also provide hot water
Left Warm air grilles, which are efficient and inconspicuous, are best installed while a house is under construction, so ducts can be built in

purpose-installed lighting; it can, in fact, detract considerably from the effects you have tried to create. Lighting should be chosen to suit the location and the purpose for which it is needed. Only when these criteria have been met should you begin to think of it as a decorative accessory.

Before you decide on any fitting or range of fittings, be sure you have investigated the market thoroughly. The selection has grown enormously in recent years, but most consumers are still conservative in their buying habits and almost invariably choose a central ceiling light plus one or two table or floor lights which match the rest of the furniture. You may not want to involve yourself in great expense or trouble, but newer designs such as uplighters, downlighters (often recessed in a false ceiling), spotlights and track systems work well with any style of decoration and will almost certainly improve the efficiency and flexibility of the lighting in your home.

Heating

More heat is generally needed in the living room than anywhere else in the home since people are likely to be relaxing or at least inactive here, whereas in other rooms such as the kitchen they will be more active; lower temperatures can, of course, be tolerated in the bedroom, where layers of bedclothes will protect against the cold.

Central heating If you are putting in central heating, decide first where you want to position large, permanent structures such as storage units so suitable walls can be kept free. If possible, plan your furniture arrangements so you can locate the radiators in convenient, safe and inconspicuous places. Those who find traditional radiators unattractive can cover their tops with a wide shelf or box them in with panels of a suitable open material such as cane, which will let out the maximum heat. Some people prefer the opposite approach and paint this type of appliance with a bright contrasting colour to make a feature of it. Skirting radiators or warm air grilles are ideal since they are inconspicuous and have very little effect on the grouping of furniture.

Don't forget most central heating systems have a very drying effect on the air and you may want to install a humidifier to make the air not only more comfortable to breathe, but also less harmful to furniture.

Open fires These offer a great deal of atmosphere as well as warmth to a room and some people have them in addition to central heating. It is possible to arrange such a fire with a back boiler which provides hot water for both washing and radiators; but if you are considering this type of arrangement, remember in the planning stages to allow a place for solid fuel to be stored near the fireplace so you will not have to keep running out to fetch more each time the fire burns down.

Solid fuel room heaters This type is enclosed by glass panel doors. You can buy them as self-contained fires or with back boilers, which will

Top Skirting radiators take up very little space and therefore allow your furniture arrangement to be more flexible

Left Woven cane panels with a timber surround make an attractive screen for bulky radiators, and let out the maximum heat – see Week 45 pages 886–889

supply hot water and any central heating requirements throughout the home.

Electricity and gas People without central heating have to choose some sort of spot or space heating. Electric fires are very convenient and efficient and are probably the best choice for emergency heating or in seldom used areas; but all types, even night storage heaters, are expensive to run as a permanent arrangement. Gas fires are slightly more complicated to install, but they are cheaper to operate and provide an efficient heat source. Again, some gas fires come with a back boiler for hot water and portable models with gas containers are also available.

Paraffin heaters These are probably the cheapest both to install and run but, like any form of heating, need care in handling. Now regulations are so strict, paraffin heaters are as safe as any other form of heating. They are designed so if you knock one over, it will go out automatically. Follow operating instructions precisely and don't adjust the heat control higher or lower than recommended by the manufacturer; if you are in doubt, consult your nearest service agent – a list of these is supplied with every new paraffin heater.

Saving heat

Once you have decided on a source of heat, you would be wise to do everything you can to keep the warmth you have paid for. Fifteen percent of all heat lost in the average home goes out through the window, so make sure yours are double-glazed or well draughtproofed. For even more effective insulation fit heavy curtains which are lined with Milium or interlined. Floors are another escape route for valuable heat, so cover them well. If you want a new timber floor, take the opportunity of first putting down underfloor insulation (in the case of a ground floor room) or a covering of plywood; carpets should be well fitted and should have an effective underlay.

Safety

If you decide on any structural work in your living room, be sure to keep safety factors in mind from the outset. If, for example, you want to remove a chimney-breast or all or part of a wall, consult an expert and check on the building regulations before attempting any work; otherwise a finished room could literally fall down around you.

Wiring Arrange the wiring of switches so one light at least can be controlled from the door; you should never have to stumble around in the dark looking for the switch. There should be enough sockets to avoid dangerously trailing flexes and you should never run them under a carpet or rug, since this will subject the flex to excessive wear and create a real hazard. Incidentally it will also in time damage the floor covering and the ridge it forms could be an extra hazard to people walking by. Consider having more than one telephone outlet to avoid long lengths of flex lying around.

Floors If you are planning to fit adjacent floor coverings which differ widely in height, such as ceramic tiles in the dining area and deep pile carpet around your seating, check whether you can either raise the lower level or recess the higher one into the floor slightly. It is this kind of neglected detail which could cause someone to fall.

Provide plenty of light sources, especially near any change in floor level where the type or colour

Top A gas fire is one of the most efficient and economical methods of domestic heating
Centre left Traditional stoves burn solid fuel and come in a wide range of styles
Centre right Most solid fuel heaters can be fitted with a back boiler
Left Modern paraffin heaters are not only very economical, but also safe to use since they incorporate a cut-out system
Above An electric fan heater is costly to run, but heats quickly and efficiently

Unsafe living room

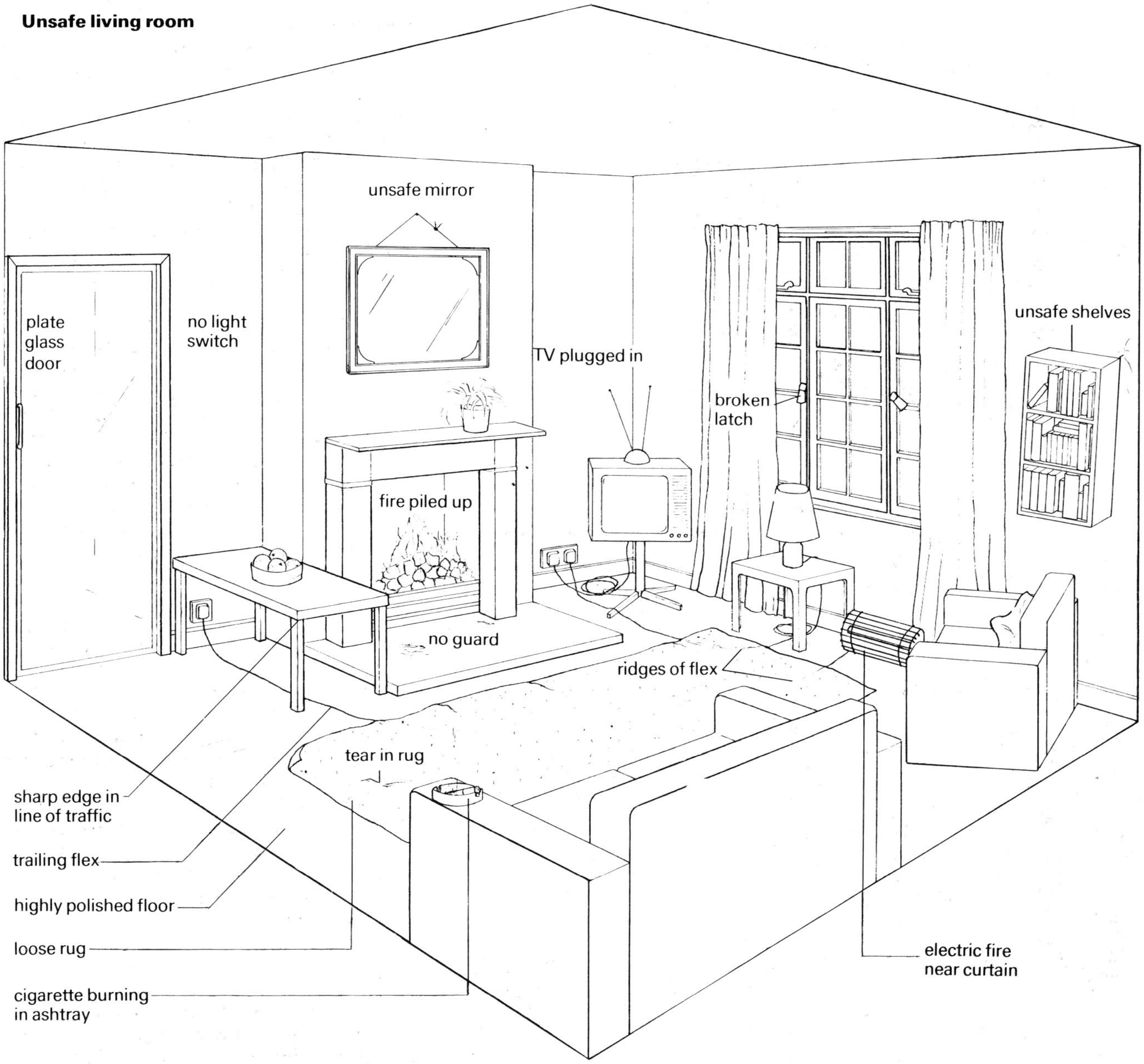

of the covering remains the same. Use a non-slip polish on shiny floors and fasten down all loose rugs with special backing or tape. Repair immediately any tears or worn spots in your floor coverings before they cause a nasty accident.

Doors Any large glass doors should be designed so you can see easily whether they are open or shut; horror stories of people walking through plate glass are not as rare as you might think.

Furniture When you come to arrange the furniture, consider traffic patterns carefully and avoid placing awkward or sharp-edged pieces near areas where people will be passing constantly.

Fires Open fires are an attractive living room feature, but there are a set of safety rules which must be observed. Always fit a large, secure guard, particularly if there are children in the home. Don't ever pile up a fire before you go out, even if only for a short time; and always make sure it is completely out before you go to bed last thing at night. Wear thick gloves when cleaning the grate to protect your hands from any sharp or hot objects buried under the ash.

If you have a portable heat source – a paraffin, gas or electric fire, for example – keep it well away from curtains or upholstery and, again, make sure it is turned off before you leave the room for any length of time. Try to avoid using this type altogether in a crowded room.

Hangings Fix all pictures and mirrors securely with the correct size and number of wall plugs and screws – this also applies, of course, to wall-hung storage units. If you use wire for hanging, make sure it is strong enough to hold the weight it supports.

Windows Those people with living rooms on an upper floor should make sure the windows have strong and secure catches. Children are often tempted to lean out for a better view and could fall.

Television Never watch television in a dark room since this is a great strain on the eyes; and try to make sure no source of light is reflected in the screen. Before you go to bed, check the set is switched off and unplugged and that all ashtrays are cold and emptied into a safe place such as a metal waste bin.

Above Because the members of your family spend so much time here, the living room should not only be planned for safety, but also checked regularly to make sure no potentially dangerous areas are developing

Above Bring the freshness of spring into your home by applying the special technique of stencilling to the walls. Stencilling, once a common practice in Britain and New England, has been neglected until recently; but its low cost and considerable charm have brought it back into fashion. Here a pattern of leaves has been used repeatedly to give the impression of a country porch

To achieve this effect, draw and cut out a pattern of leaves, tape it to the wall and spray paint evenly over it. Repeat over the wall until you have the design you want. Practise on a piece of paper to perfect the technique. Draw the picket fence in with a pencil and straight-edge and block it out with masking tape while you colour the leaves, then gloss-paint it in.

The Living Room: Top Designers' Tips

1. A small circular table, however old and beaten up, can become an **elegant asset** when covered with a circular cloth (cheap but pretty material will do), sweeping to the floor.

2. Bring down the height of an **over lofty room** by painting wide stripes or fixing a wallpaper border at picture rail level – or use coloured carpet tape to make the job easier.

3. Hang curtains clear of the windows to **reveal their shape** and bring as much light as possible into the room.

4. The **screen scene** is making a comeback – in all sorts of material, including rattan, perforated metal and fabric mounted on a wooden frame. They form an **excellent visual separation** between sitting and eating or sitting and working areas.

5. Use a mass of large plants as a **living screen** in a large room.

6. Cut down the (often ugly) legs on a 1930's dining table, strip it of varnish and cover it with matt polyurethane lacquer to make a really **large, low coffee table**.

7. Buy a junk shop load of tatty **Victorian bamboo furniture** – side tables, chests of drawers, mirrors, plant tables, chairs etc. – and unite the whole lot by painting it in one glossy colour. (Black looks stunning.)

8. If you want to **mix various patterns** in the room – on curtains, upholstery and walls for example – make sure they are linked by at least one predominant colour or the whole thing will become unspeakably discordant.

9. Use the widely available **decorative paper borders** to break up the bland wall surfaces of an over-large room into panels.

10. Don't be afraid of dark walls. Brown, deep red or forest green **give tremendous depth** to a room and make a splendid foil for a mass of pictures, books and other decorative objects.

11. Several manufacturers are at last making carpet in **small, neat modern designs**, so plain carpet is no longer a must.

12. Wood stain is available in pretty colours, so if you can't afford carpet, **have fun colouring your floor boards**.

THE CHILDREN'S ROOM

THERE ARE MANY SENSIBLE IDEAS IN THIS CHAPTER for the treatment of children's rooms: important information on the choice of lighting, heating, safety and wall and floor coverings is given in detail. But I think there is one overall concept that should be borne in mind before embarking on setting up a room for a child. This is that children, even the smallest, have strong likes and dislikes of their own. Therefore, it is quite wrong to imbue a room with too much of your own personality and taste, then plant the child (or children) in it. Far better, with due consideration given to the prime aspects of safety and comfort described later, to plan a room which is if anything, rather bland and anonymous, just waiting for its owner's personality to be developed in it.

Unless you are preparing a nursery for a new baby, or you have so much money that you can have a complete change of furniture every few years, do not make the mistake of buying special children's furniture. Apart from having an almost inevitably wee appearance, it will soon be outgrown, the child will resent it and you'll be lumbered with another round of buying. Instead, pick plain, sturdy furniture which is not too expensive and which the children can live with, refurbish, paint, stencil, varnish, stain, break down, join together or otherwise adapt as the fancy takes them. This will, over a long period, prove much more successful than carefully contrived pieces which allow no room for individual style and preferences and make too demanding a background for the owners' pictures, ornaments and general possessions. Let it be of reasonable quality though, since furniture which quickly becomes shabby and ramshackle can have the most demoralising affect.

Make sure there is, if anything, too much storage. Youngsters accumulate possessions at an even greater rate than their elders and feel miserable if they are continually being nagged to get rid of what to them are treasures, even if to you they look like junk. In addition, they have far less excuse for leaving their rooms in chaos and confusion if there are plenty of cupboards and drawers.

Just as you shouldn't inflict very personalised furniture on them, go easy on the colour too, certainly after they have reached the age when they have some taste of their own. With anonymous background colours, they are free to work out and execute the schemes they like. With a bit of help from their elders over the techniques required, they will then have a room which is genuinely reflective of their tastes, and therefore one which they will enjoy looking after.

As described later, tough wall and floor surfaces are essential – even teenagers are not particularly careful about the damage they might be inflicting with spikey boots and dirty hands. So in order not to have too much worry about the fabric of the house, put down heavy duty floor coverings and make sure at least some walls are lined with a material which takes drawing pins and sticky tape without too much distress.

If a child's room has been treated to reflect the occupant's ideas and interests rather than your own, it will be a delightful retreat which eases the strain on the public parts of the home and even one which your child will take care to keep reasonably tidy.

Planning children's rooms

Above any other consideration, children's rooms should be practical and flexible – practical because they will get much more damaging wear than any other room in the home, and flexible because children's needs change frequently between birth and the time they leave home.

Planning

As in all room planning, keep an open mind about which room will be used for what purpose. It may be slightly inconvenient to use a smaller bedroom for yourself, but there is a great deal to be gained by giving the master bedroom over to the children as a sleep/play area. Here they can spread out their toy soldiers or model railways and leave them ready for another day's play, instead of having to go through the frustration of dismantling their work before a meal or when company is expected. In addition, the whole family will benefit from a play area where children can knock about happily without having to worry about breaking ornaments or damaging furniture and floor coverings.

Most young children (and many older ones) do not mind sharing a room; but if they differ greatly in age, temperament or interests, life will probably be easier when they have their own. If there are not enough rooms to go round, you may be able to use partition walls or room dividers in the form of large pieces of furniture to make better use of space: just be certain each area has enough light and ventilation – separate entrances would be ideal although they are not absolutely necessary. Any structural changes must, of course, comply with Building Regulations.

Think of installing a wash-basin in the children's rooms; this will not only make it possible to wash and change small babies in their own room, but will also prove invaluable as the child grows up by relieving pressure on the family bathroom.

You may find it worthwhile installing an intercom here so you can keep in touch with a sleeping infant or a group of lively toddlers at play. These devices are not wildly expensive and can be put to use in another area such as a garage or workroom when the children grow up. If you are wiring children's rooms from scratch, install all socket outlets high on the wall, fit safety plugs to all flexes, and make sure each window, even on the ground floor, is fitted with childproof locks.

Decoration

Try to avoid wishy-washy nursery colours – children usually prefer bright colours which they see more clearly and find more stimulating. In addition, this type of colour suits children of either sex and will remain suitable as they grow older, so redecoration will not be governed by changing tastes. Choose all decorations and furnishings with the idea that they will be used later – and avoid a very babyish look; a tough five-year-old might object violently to carpeting covered with pictures

Below An ideal child's sleep/play area should be decorated in bright colours and contain plenty of storage space for toys, a working surface, a large play area and a good size blackboard and pinboard to discourage young artists from ruining the paintwork
Right Use peel-off transfers to turn the nursery walls into a large mural which will stimulate a baby's imagination
Below right Choose a neat, military type bed, space-saving storage furniture and practical parquet flooring to make your child's bedroom into a versatile work/play area as well

of fluffy bunnies or curtains which feature scenes from Mother Goose, although these might still be in good condition.

Equipment

A baby's needs are few – a cot or crib, a storage unit for clothes, accessories and stuffed toys and perhaps a high surface for nappy-changing if this is not done on the mother's lap. There should also be a comfortable adult-sized chair in the room. As the baby grows, you may find a playpen useful; look for something which folds flat when not in use so you can take it from one part of the home to another. If you have any knowledge of carpentry, you could make your own. You should also provide a large storage area for toys – something simple and low so young children will be able to get out and put away playthings by themselves.

A hinged safety gate in the doorway might be a good idea at this stage so the room can be turned into a giant playpen when there is no adult near to keep a watchful eye. As long as there are no dangerous heating or general electrical appliances around, a toddler can play happily here for long periods. You may be able to make one of these yourself, although there are plenty of adjustable ones on the market at a reasonable price. It is probably also a good idea to fix a large drawing surface such as a blackboard or piece of hardboard low on the wall so exuberant young artists will not ruin the paintwork.

The needs of older children are slightly more sophisticated. They will probably require a work surface fitted up with appropriate lighting and room for extra possessions such as school books and sports equipment. As they grow up, youngsters like to entertain and this could mean providing facilities for the odd overnight guest. Bunk or

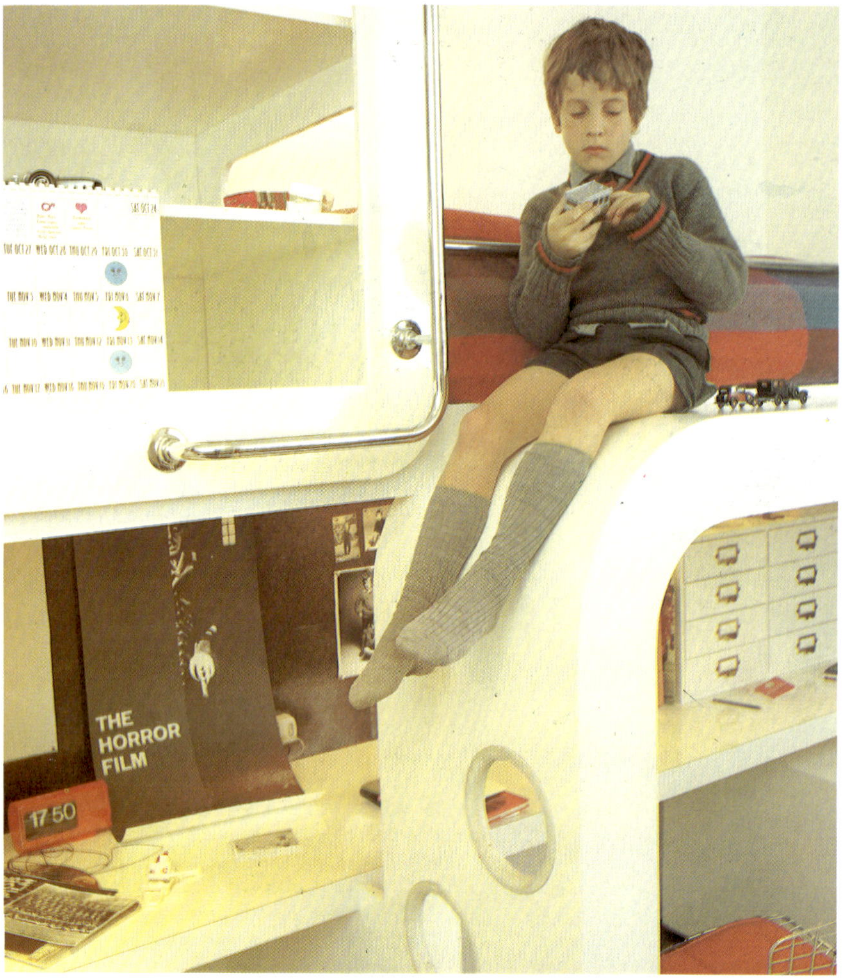

trundle beds could be the answer here, possibly arranged so the extra one can double up as a storage area when not in use. If space is very short, try turning the room into a bedsitter by putting the mattress up on a platform and using the space underneath as a work or storage area.

Teenagers like a lot of privacy and therefore need a room that is just as much a living area as a bedroom. Fit the bed with a plain cover and provide lots of cushions so it can be used for general seating when friends come round. Allow plenty of workspace and room for a record player, radio and all the paraphernalia involved with teenagers' hobbies and collections. A large pinboard will take posters and pictures of the current idol to prevent paint being pulled off the wall each time a new hero is adopted. Most adolescents would be grateful for an electric kettle, a few mugs and a small serving area to cater for guests.

Arrangement

Whatever the age of the children, the furniture and furnishings you choose must be arranged so they can be used comfortably and efficiently. Be sure to position cots and beds out of any draughts and well away from a party wall so there will be no unnecessary noise to disturb sleeping children. Furniture such as wardrobes, cupboards and chairs need just as much room here as in an adult's room, so measure carefully before you buy.

Remember the more attention you give to the children's rooms and the more workable and attractive they are, the more your children will enjoy being there instead of in your way and the more they will want to bring home friends instead of wandering off for long periods.

Platform beds with storage/work areas underneath work well for children of all ages
Above A slightly naval look has been achieved here by cutting out porthole-shaped steps, fitting a chrome handrail and decorating with lots of white paint
Right Teenagers will appreciate a fairly self-contained area with a sophisticated colour scheme, plenty of desk space and facilities for entertaining, such as these huge pencil-shaped cushions

Choosing cots and beds

Your children's growth as well as their comfort can be greatly affected by the beds you choose for them, so be sure to take plenty of time and trouble to select a design which is strong and suitable for their needs.

The needs of a baby are very simple – a small enclosed space is best since it provides a feeling of security and prevents the baby rolling about. It is not necessary to invest large sums of money at this stage – instead of going for a traditional wood or wicker crib, use a suitably shaped shopping basket, a carry cot or even an empty drawer, provided that it is well padded inside.

After three to six months your baby will have to sleep in something bigger anyway, so this is one area where you can cut costs without compromising the welfare of your child.

Cots

When it is time for the baby to sleep in something larger, you will have to invest in a good quality cot. Make sure the one you choose is strong and stands firmly on the floor. Check the bars to see if they are close enough so the baby's head will not slip through and get caught. The sides must be high enough – and preferably a type that can be dropped

Left Before you choose a cot, check it is completely safe. If your baby is very active or the room particularly draughty, fit a protective foam bumper at the top or at both ends
Below Choose bunk beds which can separate into singles if the need arises. Deep storage drawers are useful for clothes, bulky toys and sports equipment

Previous page A cot will continue to be functional as the child grows up if it converts into a junior size bed

Above When a child grows out of a cot, invest in a full single bed straightaway since junior size models have very limited use

down, which will make it easier for you to lift the baby in and out. Some versions are made to fold away completely so you can take them away with you when necessary or store them out of the way when they are not needed. There is a new stringent British Standard (1753) which applies to cots, so check the model in which you are interested conforms to it.

Many people inherit second-hand cots; as long as they meet these specifications, they will serve their purpose and save you money at the same time. One of the first things to find out about any used piece of children's furniture is the nature of the paint. Young babies in particular tend to gnaw at the bars of a cot; if they swallow any paint containing lead, they could be poisoned. Naturally, if you intend to paint such an article yourself, make sure the brand you choose is lead-free.

Parents of small babies may like to fit a bumper of foam or synthetic wadding to protect the child from draughts and any injuries which might be caused if the head bangs on the side of the cot. The bumper normally fits across the top and halfway along both sides of the cot; but if your baby is particularly active, you might consider fitting two – one at each end.

Infants respond very strongly to bright colours and moving shapes, so you might like to hang a string of small mobiles over the cot.

Some models of cot convert into a proper small size bed for when the child grows; these are an excellent buy since you can use them for a much longer period than an ordinary cot. If, however, yours does not do this, do not be tempted to buy a separate junior size bed since its life will be very limited. Instead, move the child into a full size bed right away; if you buy a good one, it could last until the child leaves home.

Beds

It might be a good idea to invest in bunk beds at this stage; even if you are not planning to have any more children, the extra bed will be very handy to put up overnight guests. Choose the type which separates into two single beds so they can be taken apart if the children get their own rooms later or when you want to put up a guest in another part of the home. Make sure the top bunk has a firmly fixed guard rail and a permanent ladder attached which does not wobble and will not come loose easily. In addition the slats should be even and smooth so they will not harm small bare feet.

If your child's bedroom is small, but has to be used as a play area as well, consider fitting a foldaway bed which leaves the entire floor area clear during the day. Choose a model which allows for the bedclothes to be kept on the bed, since stripping the linen each morning and putting it back on again every night will soon prove a frustrating and tiresome task.

Many beds come with storage space included in their design – either in the form of built-in drawers or purpose-made boxes which roll underneath; some have shelves at either end for books and small toys. A full size bed for an older child or teenager should be chosen with the knowledge that it will probably be used as a sofa when friends come to visit. Look for a high quality sprung mattress or one made from dense foam which may suffer less from the kind of damage inflicted when one side of the bed is sat on constantly. If you provide large floor cushions for seating and explain to your children the danger of perching constantly along the edge of a mattress, they may be more careful; but it would probably be a good idea to turn the mattress over periodically.

Lighting, heating and safety in children's rooms

Children have a way of doing everything they are not supposed to do – getting up in the night, running around half-dressed and examining minutely every appliance in sight. They have little appreciation of the dangers a dark, cold and potentially hazardous room might hold for them, so you must be extra careful when planning the lighting and heating in a child's room and check on all aspects of safety.

Lighting

Illumination in a child's room must be efficient and easy to operate – and at the same time out of reach of small hands. Wall or ceiling lights are a good choice here; spots are ideal since you can change their direction with each activity or whenever you rearrange the furniture. If you fix a dimmer attachment, you will be able to reduce any light to night-light dimness and increase it gradually to avoid startling a child should you have to enter the room in the middle of the night. Make sure there is a light switch near the door and that it is situated low enough for a child to reach. Avoid floor fittings which might come within a child's reach and choose table lamps only if you have fairly high surfaces on which to place them.

An older child will appreciate bedside and work-top lighting as well as general illumination; but wall, ceiling or clamp fittings would again be the best choice, if you want to prevent accidents. It is very important the lighting you choose for close work such as reading and studying is adequate, so young eyes will not be strained unduly.

Heating

Children, especially young babies, should be surrounded by constant and reliable warmth at a temperature range of 18–21°C (64–70°F); the safest and most efficient method of doing this is with a central heating system which ideally is thermostati-

Above Toddlers have a way of getting into everything; if there is an open fire in your home, be sure to fit a large and stable guard
Above right The light beside a child's bed should be steady and secure so it will not be knocked over easily. Although this one is in keeping with current film fantasies, it would not look out of place in other room settings
Right If space is at a premium or if your child is a particularly restless sleeper, choose a wall-fixed light, making sure it has a high enough wattage to avoid young eyes being strained

cally controlled. If possible, fit a thermostat in the child's room so its temperature can be controlled independently of the rest of the home. If this is not possible, arrange to have some additional form of heat to keep the child's room warm when the heating for the rest of the home is off or in need of repair. This extra heating and, indeed, any spot heating in this room should be fixed in some way – not free-standing; make sure there are no frayed flexes, loose connections or any kind of exposed element, even if it has a protective grille over it. Wall-mounted gas or electric heaters work well in this situation, as long as they have a fixed guard covering the entire unit and not just the heating element. Storage and oil-filled radiators are perfectly safe, as are ordinary wall-hung electric fires – if they are placed high on the wall, out of the reach of children. All appliances should be earthed with a three core flex.

Safety

The checklist below will help provide a guide to points to watch out for to avoid needless accidents; but make sure you examine the children's rooms in your own home and think carefully about any potentially dangerous areas which are particular to them.

- Make sure furnishings do not have sharp edges or corners which could harm a crawling baby or a stumbling toddler.
- If you want to protect the cot mattress from dampness, buy a purpose-made cover or fit a sheet

of thick, fairly stiff plastic; thin polythene can work loose and suffocate a baby if it gets too near the face.

- Never put a pillow in a cot, crib or pram – it could smother the baby.
- Avoid any kind of projection at eye level.
- If you choose a table lamp to put beside an older child's bed, make sure it has a heavy and stable base so it is difficult for a restless sleeper to overturn.
- Fit windows – even those on a ground floor – with childproof locks and consider putting in vertical bars to be absolutely safe. (Horizontal bars will only tempt children to climb up them.)
- Make sure all free-standing furniture is completely stable so, if children use it as a climbing frame, it will not topple over and fall on them.
- Check all furnishings for loose or removable pieces which are small enough for a young child to swallow.
- Check for toxic paint, which might harm youngsters who like to suck and chew everything in sight.
- Ensure all fabric toys, soft furnishings and nightwear are flameproof and flame-resistant.
- Never let a pet sleep with or near a young child.

Above Fit lockable gates at the top and bottom of stairs for maximum safety
Right Radiators are ideal for a child's room since they have no 'hot spots' which could prove dangerous

Wall and floor coverings for children's rooms

A couple of children are likely to cause more wear and tear on wall and floor coverings than a roomful of adults. From a practical point of view it is most important you choose these items for children's rooms with great care, bearing in mind they must be hard-wearing and easy to clean.

Walls

While the walls in the rest of your home are there to divide living areas and provide a pleasing background, it could be argued that the walls in children's rooms exist mainly as a surface for drawings, paintings and pasted-up pictures. They also serve as a natural buffer for toys and a fair target for any number of assorted missiles. It is therefore necessary to equip them to cope with this kind of assault.

Although your own tastes might be for pretty pastel colours and small patterns, remember your children will respond more readily to bright, clear colours and large, simple patterns.

If you plan to paint the room, choose something really tough such as vinyl silk for the walls and heavy duty gloss for the woodwork; alternatively strip down the woodwork and seal it so minor damage will be less noticeable. Any murals or designs you want to add should be executed with materials which will stand up to a similar type of punishment.

Wallpapers should be really durable – preferably vinyl coated – and stuck down with strong adhesive and great care so small fingers will not be able to pick away at the seams. The smallest tear could result in the loss of a huge chunk of paper and spoil the appearance of the room. When you buy the paper, it is a good idea to get an extra roll or two to cope with possible major disasters such as this; the pattern may be discontinued later or, even if it is still available, a different dye lot might be obvious beside your original paper. Textured papers show marks less than plain ones – and dark colours naturally stay clean-looking longer than pale ones.

You might like to cover a wall or part of a wall with fibreboard or cork tiles for pictures or drawings. If the wall separates the children's room from another bedroom or bathroom, this kind of surface will provide some sound insulation as well. Blackboard paint applied to the back of a door or to any other surface will make a working area for scribbling and doodling.

Floors

Here again you are faced with a surface which has to survive a range of functions. It will be at different times a play area, a rest area, a battlefield and a motorway, so you must always choose coverings

Top Well-sealed boards can make a practical floor covering for a child's room
Left Cork tiles are warm underfoot, extremely hardwearing and easy to clean

Above Fit sisal carpeting – a tough covering which will not show dirt easily. Cork pinboard has been fitted to prevent decorations damaging the walls and a unit system included for storage

Left Large squares of hardboard make a durable and inexpensive floor covering which you can paint up for an extra play surface

Below Carpet tiles offer scope for interesting floor patterns and have the advantage that any damaged ones can be replaced
Bottom left You can hang simple cotton curtains, which are easy to clean and give a cosy look to a child's room
Bottom right Roller blinds are efficient and smart-looking, but don't fit them in rooms where small children may use them as toys and break the spring mechanism

with these varying activities in mind.

Very hard floors such as those made from quarry, ceramic or brick tiles are not suitable. They are cold on small bare feet, dangerous in case of falls and damaging to toys accidentally dropped. Alternatively deep shag pile carpet will be impossible to keep clean and is impractical for children who like to play games with small toys – particularly those with wheels.

Cord or sisal carpet is quite suitable and carpet tiles would be an excellent choice since they are not only warm and comfortable but also simple to move around; with these you can equalize wear and they can be replaced easily when they are damaged. Timber flooring, cork and vinyl tiles and sheet vinyl are all practical since they are relatively warm underfoot as well as tough and easy to clean.

Even pieces of hardboard tacked down securely make an excellent base on which to paint designs, pictures or backgrounds for a model railway layout or games such as draughts. A few washable rugs (fastened down securely, of course) would add some warmth and colour to these types of harder floor coverings.

Windows

Window coverings in children's rooms should certainly be washable – or at least thoroughly wipeable – since they will be handled by grubby fingers and probably be subjected to minor disasters such as paint splashes. Cotton curtains in a bright colour would look cheerful and be fairly easy to look after; you can hang café curtains for a cottage effect or those made from a fabric which matches or co-ordinates with the wall covering or bedspread. All curtains should be lined – and interlined as well if possible – for maximum heat and noise insulation and to prevent early rising youngsters from stirring as soon as the sun comes up.

Blinds, if made from fabric, should have a thick backing for the same reasons. Roman, Venetian and vertical louvre types are suitable, but you may have trouble with roller blinds since a child who constantly pulls tightly on the cord and gets great pleasure from seeing the blind whizz up and down will almost certainly do permanent damage to the spring mechanism.

For a really hard-wearing covering – and one which will give maximum heat and noise insulation – fit secure and attractive timber shutters.

Above A young child often ends up with a very small room and it takes a lot of imagination and skill to stop such a tiny area looking like a boxful of bed.

Make the room look larger by treating all surface areas as if corners, joins and angles do not exist. Here the cleverly coloured floor covering not only provides a soft, grassy background for toy animals and a model railway, but it also appears to extend into the surrounding painted landscape. Try your hand at the basic forms such as mountains, lakes and sky; then add further details with stencilled figures or removable transfers.

Keep the bed low and unobtrusive, but be sure to build a small ventilated platform for it rather than place it straight on the floor where the mattress will become damp and eventually disintegrate. Bright rooms are bound to look bigger, so choose a window covering such as Venetian blinds which let in as much light as possible during the day and still keep out the sun's early morning rays

Storage and general furniture in children's rooms

A new baby has very few needs in terms of storage and play furniture – a place for clothes and toilet articles is all that is really necessary. As children grow, however, their furniture needs expand at an alarming rate, so make sure you keep this in mind when you first begin to plan the room.

If at all possible, try to avoid scaled-down pieces and those decorated especially for children; a tiny cane chair could be a charming addition to the nursery and will cost very little, but mini-wardrobes, very low tables and items adorned in an aggressively babyish way are likely to outlive their usefulness long before they need replacing.

Storage

Most pieces can be bought in an adult size straightaway. A full size wardrobe, for example, is fine for babies and older children as well as for adults: choose one with shelves or drawers as well as a hanging rail to take care of knitwear, shoes, nappies, underwear and similar items which are not normally hung up. Similarly, a full chest of drawers bought for a new baby could, if it is chosen wisely, last until the youngest member of the family has left home. A small bookcase can hold toys and games in the early years, before it takes up its regular function as storage for books. Buy or make a plain wood chest for bulkier playthings; it will later become an extra seating unit as well as a home for out-of-season clothing and equipment for sports and hobbies.

If you want to make these items an integral part of a children's room scheme, paint cartoon figures on them or apply removable transfers – anything which can be covered over or taken off when the child gets older. You must, of course, make sure the paint you use is free from lead or any other substance which could harm a young child who tends to suck or chew everything.

One of the most important aspects about storage in an older child's room is the amount provided. Children are not the tidiest of creatures, but there is a much greater chance of preventing their rooms from looking like a bomb site if there are plenty of handy places where finished-with toys can be thrown. A collection of large baskets or even brightly coloured plastic rubbish bins would be ideal, as long as they are easy for children to get at and move around. One company makes a storage/display system consisting of a large, slotted piece of metal into which you fit open-fronted plastic bins of various sizes and colours. This range is enormously flexible and could hold clothing in the top section

Far left Add interest to a piece of whitewood furniture by decorating it with paint or transfers
Above left Brightly coloured doors, cut in interesting shapes, make an ordinary run of fitted storage units into an unusual decorative feature
Left To make clutter less obvious, tuck away as many things as possible. Here books, toys, TV, blackboard and drawing board are hidden behind cupboard doors
Above and top right Some high chairs can be adapted to provide a table and chair
Centre right Choose a playpen which is light in weight with collapsible sides so you can move it from one part of the home to another
Right Simple bookcases are perfect for toy storage – especially if they have sliding doors to hide the mess

Below This roomy and attractive desk and chair are adjustable to suit all heights from child to adult
Bottom This bookcase arrangement includes a working surface which can be fixed at any height

out of the reach of tiny hands, as well as toys in the bottom part where children can find them easily.

Some sort of built-in storage system will take up less space than a collection of odd pieces. Again, choose the most flexible system you can find; hanging rails, shelves and baskets should all be adjustable to cope with the rapidly growing needs of a small child.

General furniture

While a new baby has no need of furniture, its mother will be very grateful for a comfortable chair which will give her correct support when she is feeding, changing or playing with the infant. Slightly older babies might need a play pen so they and their toys can be kept together and out of harm's way. Choose a model which is light in weight with collapsible sides so you can move it to another part of the home when necessary.

The items which children do need scaled down for them are tables and chairs; but with a little careful planning you can avoid wasting money on equipment which will be needed for only a short time. Small chairs, as we have mentioned, can often be picked up fairly cheaply, but it is a much better idea to choose a model which can be adjusted to several different heights so it grows with the child. Some high chairs convert to make lower level seating or combine chair and table, and these are worth investigating. Look also for an adjustable table; perhaps one with some provision for storing drawing and painting equipment underneath. A toddler might be happy working on a small coffee table which can later be pressed into service elsewhere in the home. If space is short, fix an adjustable wall shelving system and make the bottom shelf wider than the others so it provides a working surface which can be moved as the child develops.

Whether you are buying furniture for your child's room, or making it yourself, check to see the finish on each piece can be easily cleaned and is tough enough to withstand very hard wear.

The Children's Room: Top Designers' Tips

1. Invest in a **good quality full-sized single bed** for the nursery as soon as your baby is born. You can sleep there when he is ill or fretful, a baby sitter can do the same, and your child can take it over when he grows a little bigger.

2. Use brightly coloured **plastic rubbish bins** for toy storage. Alternatively, decorate metal ones with scenic or graphic designs painted on, sticky transfers or wallpaper cut-outs.

3. Choose **nursery sheeting** for curtains, lampshades, bedspreads, cushions and other soft furnishings – cheaper than fabric by the metre and available in delightful designs.

4. Whatever fabric you choose, buy enough to **make a matching sleeping bag** for young visitors – when it is not being used, roll it up and toss it on the bed as a lovely squishy bolster.

5. For babies and toddlers especially, make sure blinds or curtains **shut out the maximum amount of light** so you will not be disturbed at the crack of dawn, and afternoon naps will last as long as possible.

6. Use open shelves to **separate the two beds** in a shared room – the occupants will have some privacy and gain additional storage space.

7. Choose **bright and cheerful roller blinds** instead of doors to cover shelves; their colourful design might encourage little ones to tidy away their toys. Make sure the blinds are washable so small but grubby finger marks can be removed.

8. Fix up a piece of peg board or a metal grid to **support an ever changing display** of string bags filled with rocks, shells, cones and conkers as well as small toys and games.

9. Cover the door of each child's room with his initials in **huge letters** or a full name if it's a short one.

Appendix 1: Colour in the home

There are two basic ways in which you can make use of colour in your home: to alter the size and shape of a room visually and to affect the feelings and moods of the people in it.

Explaining the theory

All colours are made from one or more of the three pure or primary colours – red, yellow and blue: they can be used by themselves, mixed with one another or changed by the addition of black or white. These combinations can, of course, produce thousands of colour possibilities which must be studied and narrowed down before you find those which will make a comfortable environment for you and your family. This is made easier by the fact that the arrangement of colour has a natural order and sense which brings harmony with it. These theories, used as a guide, will bring you much better results than you would get from paying too much attention to fashions in interior design.

Different colours of equal purity (with the same amount of black or white added) are pleasing to look at and to live with – combinations of deep colours like brown, bottle green and maroon, for instance, or bright ones like clear red, blue, green and yellow. We all recognize this order and refer to it in terms such as 'pastel colours', 'autumn colours', 'spring colours', 'peasant colours' and 'bright colours'. There is a similar harmony between colours – and shades of colours – which are next to each other on the colour wheel: green and yellow, red and blue, blue and purple, for example. Monochromatic schemes (those made up from the same basic hue plus differing amounts of

Above The dramatic colour and contrast in this scheme are best suited to rooms which are not in constant use
Left Children love bright primary colours – use them on all surfaces of a play room to create a stimulating effect

Left Use soft colours like these to make a room seem light and spacious without being too harsh
Below Purple, the colour of privilege and rank, will give a formal air to your living room
Bottom Deep, rich colours are very restful to live with; if you find them too depressing, use touches of white to brighten things up

black and white) are also satisfying; a room done out totally in shades of green would be an example. Shades are hues (or colours) with black added and tints are hues with white added; tones are hues dulled by the addition of grey (black and white).
Contrast This sort of scheme is improved by the variation of texture – perhaps a combination of cork, glass, linen and shaggy carpet – and by the addition of small touches of a complementary colour (one which is approximately opposite on the colour wheel). A pink or peach-coloured room would be improved greatly by the addition of green for accent. Complementary colours like these are another good basis for a design scheme; apart from pink (a tint of red) and green, think of blue and yellow – or brown (a shade of orange) and blue. There are many variations on this idea, but you will achieve the best results if you stick to one or two dominant colours, leaving more exotic and varied schemes to the professional designer.

Start with a single colour which you feel drawn towards strongly, then look around for those which will go with it when you apply one of the guidelines given. Expand your feeling for colour by immersing yourself in it in the form of paint and wallpaper samples, coloured pencils, fabric swatches – anything which makes you more sensitive to different depths and shades. Look carefully at neutral colours such as black, beige, cream and white, since they often have overtones of a definite colour in them. Cream can be greeny, yellow or pinky and a pink-tinged version might spoil an otherwise carefully worked out blue scheme. Although white is often similarly tinted, a pure white will seem to take on other main colours in the room.

Bear in mind too colour values are changed by what is near to them. Thus red will look orangy next to yellow but purply next to blue. Likewise

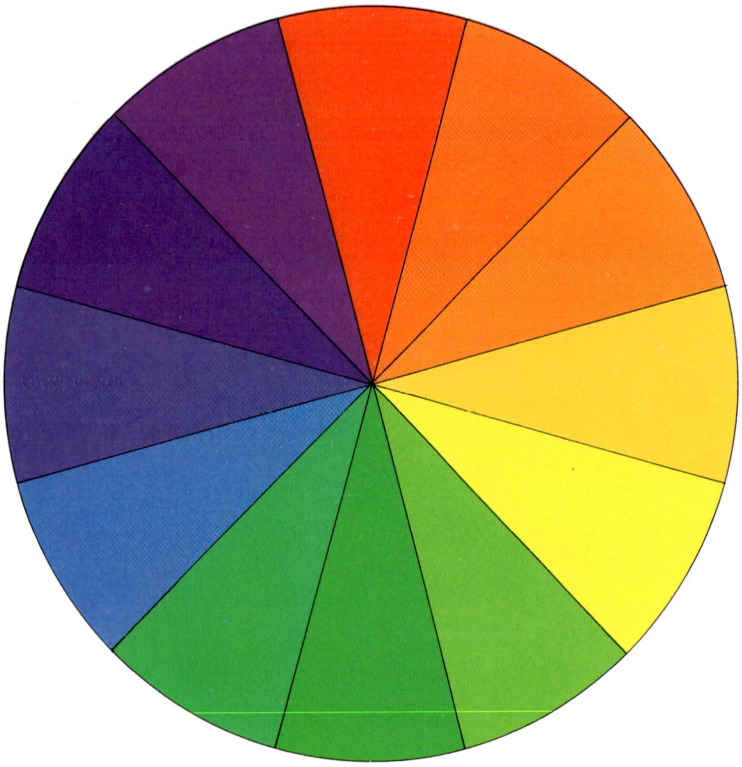

very bright colours may make pale, subtle ones look simply washed out.

Don't be intimidated into thinking everything must be matched precisely; any attempt to do this will be terribly restricting and the result may be tedious to live with. The natural harmonies we have mentioned will prove more satisfying than any obsessional matching.

If you are mixing colours yourself, be sure to go about it in the right way. For a pale version of a pale hue add white to it, rather than the reverse which will take up more time and paint. In the same way small amounts of black added to a hue will change it drastically, whereas large quantities of a colour must be added to black before it begins to show any change.

Altering the look of a room

Before you start thinking about individual rooms, consider how your home will look when it is completed and treat it as a whole when planning the interior decoration. If it is very small with pokey rooms, it will look larger and less bitty if you keep at least one design element (like carpet or walls) constant. The same principle can apply when you are dealing with a single room which has many cluttered features such as an odd shape, too many doors, projecting angles or a collection of pipes. Paint everything the same colour – even doors and their frames – to pull it all together.

There is no reason why a ceiling must always be painted white; you can give it the same treatment as the walls to make it seem higher as well as linking the various parts of the room and giving it a co-ordinated feeling. Likewise dark ceilings appear to be lower and light-coloured ones to recede; if you require either of these effects, use a lighter or a darker version of the hue used for the rest of the room.

Colour can also appear to change the size of any area; warm shades bring a room in and make it appear smaller and cosier, while pale, cool ones recede from the eye and make any room decorated in them appear larger.

The aspect of a given room – whether it faces north, south, east or west – should also affect the choice of colour used. Cool blues and greens may not work well in north-facing rooms where the light is cold all day; save these chilly hues for sunny south-facing areas and make use of warm bright colours such as yellow and pink to cheer up those parts of your home with a northern aspect. The light in east and west-facing rooms changes dramatically during the course of the day; when you are considering colours for rooms in these positions, be sure to view them in natural light at different times of the day as well as under artificial illumination.

Changing the way you feel

Those people who have a great deal of emotional, intellectual and cultural stimulation tend to feel more comfortable living with muted and neutral hues. In contrast primitive groups or those people with restricted education, opportunity or intelligence favour bright, pure colours. It follows we can relax more easily in a room decorated in soft, restful colours such as green, cream, brown and blue, while we work and play with more energy when surrounded by stimulating hues such as red, orange or yellow. The latter colours can be used freely in workshops, playrooms or home offices.

There are no hard and fast rules about which specific colours are most suitable in each room since, even using these general colour feelings as a guide, the subject is essentially a very personal one. In addition the same room in different households might cater for very different types of activity. For example a bedroom can be totally devoted to rest and grooming in one home, but adapted to suit many different hobbies and interests in another. Each colour does, however, have its own psychological meaning and effect on human beings, so keep this in mind when planning the colour schemes for the different areas in your home.

Red This is the colour most generally preferred, which is not surprising when you consider its psychological significance. Pure red suggests activity, power, conquest, force, immediacy, sexuality, anger ('seeing red') and competition; however people left for any length of time in a predominantly red room will feel disturbingly stimulated, uneasy and physically too warm. Their nervous systems will be affected so blood pressure and heartbeat increase and they begin to breathe more quickly. For this reason, a colour scheme consisting overpoweringly of bright red would not be appropriate in most domestic situations; it would prevent anyone exposed to it from feeling relaxed, peaceful and content. Alternatively the choice of red for a night club or a gambling casino would be an excellent one.

If you have fantasies of a totally red room, realize them in a bathroom, a utility room or any area where occupation is normally short-lived. Orange, a closely related colour, is even brighter and more stimulating than red; but similarly it tends to drive people away because it is so forceful. You can see the power of both these colours put to commercial use in packaging, road signs and other forms of graphic design.

Blue This has a psychological sensation associated with sweetness; notice how much packaging of sugar is done in blue. People forced to spend time in a totally blue room suffer from a drop in blood pressure, body temperature, pulse and breathing rate because this colour gives a feeling of quiet, calm, passivity, coolness, conformity and retreat – even, in certain cases, depression. This last association is given recognition in the expressions 'feeling blue' and 'having the blues'.

It might be a good idea therefore to avoid an overpoweringly blue scheme if you are prone to depressive illness of any kind. Purple, a slightly richer but similar colour, can prove overpowering in a small area but, due to its association with royalty, can add elegance to a large, formal area.

Yellow This is the most luminous colour and the one which most closely approximates to sunlight. It is associated with hope, generous nature, happy feelings and a general sensation of ease and good nature. A completely yellow room, however, would be impossible for anyone to be in for any length of time; it will produce a blinded insane feeling and cause erratic pulse and breathing rates. Tone its brightness down a little for use in interior design or add it generously as an accent colour only.

Green This is often used in the packaging of soap and shampoo because its psychological sensation is one of astringency and freshness. It has feelings of jealousy ('green with jealousy'), inexperience with a willingness to learn (someone starting a new job may be referred to as 'still green'), defence, self-preservation, protection and security (hence the tradition of 'hunting green'). Above all this is the colour of nature, man's natural environment and as such is an extremely soothing colour to live with; in general it is an excellent – perhaps the best – choice for interior decorating. People left in an all-green room suffer no physical symptoms whatsoever, only a quite natural eagerness to escape from the effects of any single colour used so intensely.

Top Yellow has exactly the right kind of stimulating properties for a kitchen or work area

Above Large areas of blue can work well in an area of concentrated activity if you choose a pure clear shade and team it with an active colour such as red

Left For a warm, restful feeling, soft peach or pink works very well with various shades of neutral beige and brown

Appendix 2: Where to go for free help and advice

Manufacturers will normally send brochures about their products and offer technical advice. Your local Citizens' Advice Bureau or Consumer Advice Centre can help you find suppliers and services. Some Home Interest magazines run free information and advice services for their readers. The 'Yellow Pages' remain an incomparable source of information. The organisations below are all willing to help members of the public.

British Ceramic Tile Council
Federation House, Station Road, Stoke-on-Trent ST4 2RU. Tel 0872 45147.
An association of tile manufacturers who will send technical information on tile laying, but no brochures.

Builders Merchants Federation
15 Soho Square, London W1V 5FB. Tel 01-439 1753.
They can supply a list of over 500 Approved Display Centres, where advice is available and materials can be bought. The list's information on specialists in kitchens, bathrooms and interior decoration can save time.

Building Centre
26 Store Street, London WC1E 7BT. Tel 01-637 8361.
The public is welcome to visit this permanent exhibition of building and home improvement products and use the excellent products information service. The centre is open all day Monday-Friday plus Saturday 10am–1pm. There are specialist advisers on gas, electricity, solid fuel, solar energy, timber, bricks and energy saving. The centre houses the Building Bookshop, with its fine stock of books aimed at the non-specialist. Consultations with independent professional designers can be arranged. Outside London there are Building Centres at:
Colston Avenue, The Centre, Bristol BS1 4TW; 15–16 Trumpington Street, Cambridge CB2 1QD; Green Lane, Durham DH1 3JY; 3/4 Claremont Terrace, Glasgow G3 7PF; 113–115 Portland Street, Manchester M1 6FB; Grosvenor House, 18–20 Cumberland Place, Southampton SO1 2BD.

Crafts Council
12 Waterloo Place, London SW1Y 4AU. Tel 01-930 4811.
Visitors can consult the extensive colour slide library illustrating the work of more than 350 active craftspeople from all over the country. Exhibitions are held in the new gallery space. Books and magazines are sold in the bookstall. Closed Monday.

Design Council
28 Haymarket, London SW1Y 4SU. Tel 01-839 8000.
The Council encourages good British design. The public can consult the Design Centre Selection, a photographic file of over 7000 Council-approved British goods. A copy of the Selection is on view at the Scottish Design Centre, 72 Vincent Street, Glasgow G2 5TN (Tel 041-221 6121). In Cardiff the Council runs a small shop and exhibition area. The London centre contains a useful bookshop specialising in design-related topics.

Fire
Contact your local fire prevention officer at the fire station for free advice and leaflets on safety in the home.

Glass and Glazing Federation
6 Mount Row, London W1Y 6DY. Tel 01-409 0545.
Free leaflets are available on double glazing and condensation, together with a list of member firms in any area, with details of any specialist services they offer.

Heating and Ventilating Contractors Association
34 Palace Court, London W2 4JG. Tel 01-229 5543.
The Home Heating Enquiry Line provides elementary advice on central heating systems and the names of two local member firms who can install central heating. The Association guarantees members' work. In Scotland telephone 031-225 8212. In Northern Ireland telephone Belfast 742930.

Interior Decorators and Designers Association
24 Ormond Road, Richmond, Surrey TW10 6TH. Tel 01-948 4151.
The membership list names over 100 members, mainly in London and the south east, and describes each one's particular interests. The Association cannot advise on materials and suppliers.

International Wool Secretariat
Wool House, 6 Carlton Gardens, London SW1Y 5AE. Tel 01-930 7300.
Send a large stamped self-addressed envelope for the free booklet 'Wool Interiors', which lists professional interior design specialists area by area. Services range from blind-making to lighting design and decoration.

Lighting Industry Federation
Swan House, 207 Balham High Road, London SW17 7BQ. Tel 01-675 5432.
They will direct members of the public to the right lighting manufacturers and suppliers to deal with a lighting problem.

National Bedding Federation
251 Brompton Road, London SW3 2EZ. Tel 01-589 4888.
A range of free leaflets covers choice and care of beds. They can supply names and addresses of suppliers or particular types of bed.

Plastic Bath Manufacturers' Association
Fleming House, Renfrew Street, Glasgow G3 6TG. Tel 041-332 0826.
A free leaflet answers most standard questions. Written enquiries will be answered.

Police
Every local police force has a crime prevention officer who will visit your home and advise on securing it against burglars. The service is free.

Royal Association for Disability and Rehabilitation (RADAR)
25 Mortimer Street, London W1N 8AB. Tel 01-637 5400.
RADAR is the central source of information on design for the disabled. Staff can always refer you to somebody who can help. Free general leaflets on design principles are available.

Royal Institute of British Architects
66 Portland Place, London W1N 4AD. Tel 01-580 5533.
The Clients' Advisory Service will explain the architect's services and supply names of local architects likely to be interested in your problem. Free leaflets are available. the public can use the bookshop and library, open Monday–Friday and Saturday morning. Clients' Advisory Services also operate in Birmingham (021-233 2321) and Knutsford, Chesire (0565 52927).

Royal Institute of Chartered Surveyors
Information Centre, 12 Great George Street, London SW1P 3AD. Tel 01-222 7000.
When you are planning structural changes in your home, write or telephone for free leaflets explaining the role of the surveyor. The Referral Service will supply the names of suitable surveyors in your locality.

Royal Society for the Prevention of Accidents
Cannon House, The Priory Queensway, Birmingham B4 6BS. Tel 021-233 2461.
Advice on preserving your life and home. Enquirers are encouraged to write in with their problem rather than telephone. A charge has to be made for booklets.

Solid Fuel Advisory Service
Seventy local offices cover the country. Look in the telephone directory to locate your nearest one. Free advice is available on fuels, equipment, central heating, together with a list of approved installers.

Index

Numbers in *italics* refer to illustrations